When Women Come First

When Women Come First

Gender and Class in Transnational Migration

Sheba Mariam George

UNIVERSITY OF CALIFORNIA PRESS
Berkeley / Los Angeles / London

University of California Press
Berkeley and Los Angeles, California

University of California Press, Ltd.
London, England

Library of Congress Cataloging-in-Publication Data

George, Sheba Mariam, 1966–.
When women come first : gender and class in transnational migration / Sheba Mariam George.
p. cm.
Includes bibliographical references and index.
ISBN 978-0-520-24319-4 (pbk. : alk. paper)
1. Women, East Indian — United States — Social conditions. 2. Women immigrants — United States — Social conditions. 3. Women, East Indian — Employment — United States. 4. Women immigrants — Employment — Social aspects — United States. 5. Nurses — United States — Social conditions. 6. East Indians — United States — Social conditions. 7. Sex role — United States. 8. Man-woman relationships — United States. 9. Man-woman relationships — India. 10. Transnationalism. I. Title.

E184.E2G46 2005
305.48'891411073 — dc22 2004020977

Manufactured in the United States of America

14 13 12 11 10 09 08 07
11 10 9 8 7 6 5 4 3 2

Printed on Ecobook 50 containing a minimum 50% post-consumer waste, processed chlorine free. The balance contains virgin pulp, including 25% Forest Stewardship Council Certified for no old-growth tree cutting, processed either TCF or ECF. The sheet is acid-free and meets the minimum requirements of ANSI/NISO Z39.48–1992 (R 1997) (Permanence of Paper).

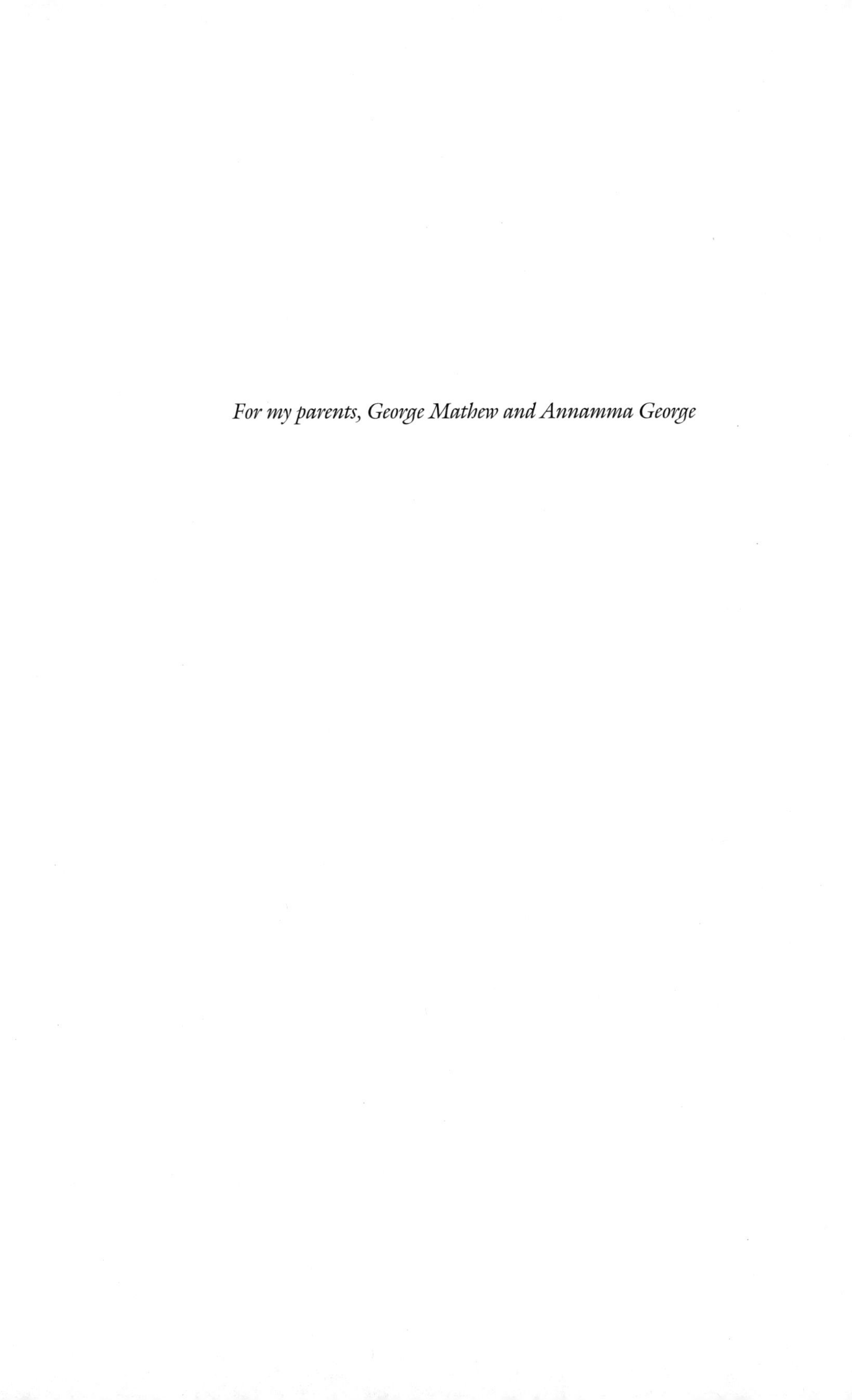

For my parents, George Mathew and Annamma George

Contents

Illustrations and Tables

Figures

Tables

Foreword

Immigration is the great American drama, assimilation and upward mobility its great dream. But you won't find these dreams in Sheba George's moving tale of emigration from Kerala, India, to the United States. Hers is a narrative of continuing connection back to communities of origin — visitations on the occasion of birth, marriage, or death; the exchange of kith and kin (parents, children, and spouses); the flow of material aid and gifts; visual memories in photographs and homemade videos; and frequent phone calls and, increasingly, electronic mail, not to mention the old-fashioned letter. (Kerala, after all, has the highest literacy rate in India.) Sheba George focuses on the families, divided and unified in the process of transplantation, and how they create a Kerala of their own in Central City that is still tightly bound to the Kerala of India. Her ethnographic eye dwells on the different spheres of life in the United States — work, home, and community — on their interrelations and their internal composition, rather than on their degree of absorption into the wider United States.

To conduct ethnographic research is to continually revisit the people one is studying. But as Sheba George does so, she also nostalgically revisits her own childhood. When Sheba was ten, her mother departed for the United States to ply her nursing skills, leaving Sheba and her two younger brothers in the gentle care of their father. Two years later they would be reunited with their mother in a new land. *When Women Come First* uncovers the sociological meaning of this journey.

Sheba spent a year and a half in Central City interviewing, observing, and participating in the community created by an unusual migration stream, one originated by nurses from Kerala. What happens, Sheba George asks, when women come first and the men follow later, when women are the main breadwinners and men are secondary earners? How resilient is the traditional hierarchy in the family in the face of challenges created by female-led immigration? The answer is by no means singular, depending as it does on the age and number of children, the shift work of the nurses, and the presence of supportive kin from or in Kerala. Women are as likely to voluntarily compensate for their men's loss of esteem by ceding them authority in matters of finance, for example, as they are to flaunt their command of the purse strings. And men are as likely to accept a redivision of domestic labor and child care as they are to insist on conventional patterns. More often than not, more egalitarian households result.

If relations are renegotiated in the family, male leadership is reasserted in the community, in the Indian Orthodox Syrian Christian Church, which brings Keralites together from far and wide. The men organize food and festivities, and the women are passive onlookers, prodded into subordination by other members of the congregation. The church is perhaps sowing the seeds of its own demise, however, given how out of touch it is with the gender expectations of the next generation, now being brought up in American schools. Thus, Father John, the priest at St. George's, knew what he was doing in welcoming the sociologist into his parish. He sought to broaden the vision of the church elders by involving Sheba in Sunday school teaching and in caroling, the latter being an activity monopolized by men. Sheba's compact with the priest led to a transgressive ethnography that, for all the discomfort it brought, served her well by revealing the strongly held norms that bound the older parishioners together.

Even as they try to create a space of domination and leadership, "nurse-husbands," as they are pejoratively called, are stigmatized by the middle-class men who came to the United States under their own steam, with their own social and cultural capital. The "nurse-husbands," these middle-class men scoff, are living off the earnings of "dirty nurses." Tragically, the defense of their dignity through the assertion of traditional norms within the church is thus turned against the husbands of nurses, who are humbled and hobbled by the stigma against nursing. In India, nursing is "polluted" work because it involves the touching of random bodies, a practice traditionally shunned by Hindus. It is more easily taken up by Christians, who have effectively taken advantage of the global demand for their profession, only to experience, in turn, the resentment aimed at the female parvenu.

The community of Keralites in Central City is tightly bound, materially and spiritually, to the world of Kerala. To understand the former required returning to the latter and examining the changing world of India and its floating stigma. Sheba George retraced the path of migration, but in reverse. She sought out the kin of her informants in Central City, as well as the community's connections to the Syrian Christian Church, which is the most powerful source of norms at play in the immigrant community. But here she confronted the limits of multisited global ethnography, because the connections led her all over Kerala — to no single community, and to no single set of norms. She found Kerala to be much more diverse than the sheltered, reconstituted community of Central City that it sustained. So, she asks finally, can the Keralite community in Central City, and those all over the United States, sustain themselves from one generation to the next despite their inner tensions and contradictions, despite the temptation of assimilation? Are we really living in a new era of globalization wherein diasporas can be sustained from one generation to the next? And how will American society greet the children of these immigrants? Will it be possible for a transnational Keralite community to be part of the plural world of the United States?

We live in a world that has loosened the bonds of patriarchy. Women now are as likely as men to migrate. We must adjust our theories accordingly. When women take off from Kerala or the Philippines, from Russia or Guatemala, do they come as single workers who will later be reunited with their country of origin, or do they come as members of families to settle in their country of adoption? In the one case, we find the creation of the transnational family, and in the other we find the migration of families or even whole communities. Sheba George casts light in both directions, demonstrating the significance of women coming first but never losing sight of the men they left behind, or the men who then follow.

Michael Burawoy

Acknowledgments

It has been noted that most occasions, even birthday parties, begin with prayer and thanksgiving among Indian Christians from the state of Kerala. So it is fitting that I begin this study of Keralite Christian immigrants by acknowledging my gratitude to God, who guided me through a maze of uncertainties to complete this book. I am also thankful that I have been given this wonderful opportunity to study and write about a topic very close to my heart.

I could not have written this book without the willing participation of the men and women at St. George's Orthodox Church and their families in Kerala, who generously shared their lives and their precious time with me. I am especially grateful to the priest at St. George's for the abundant hospitality he showed me. His sponsorship was critical to the success of my research. Furthermore, various people in Kerala—nurses, nursing school deans, church leaders, and seminary professors—took the time to talk with me and teach me a great deal from their experiences. Although I do not name them individually for various reasons, including confidentiality, I am ever grateful to all of them for their indispensable help.

Similarly, while there are many who taught me much along the way, I acknowledge in particular two teachers who were instrumental in shaping my thinking about this book. The first is Michael Burawoy, without whom this book would not have been possible. As chair of my dissertation committee, Michael was there at the inception of this project and enthusiastically helped plant seeds and watered the dream that resulted in this publication. He was an ever-present sounding board and provided a critical but encouraging ear to the most underdeveloped ideas. My work has benefited greatly from his consistent and engaged interest and generous involvement. The second is R. Stephen Warner, who has believed in the value of my research from the start. He has extended both academic support and personal friendship in several key ways, helping bring this project to fruition. His thoughtful insights and careful readings from beginning to end have been extremely important in shaping the direction of this book.

I was fortunate to receive a great deal of institutional support that provided necessary intellectual and financial assistance throughout my research and writing. I began this endeavor as a predissertation fellow of the New Ethnic Immigrant Congregation Project (NEICP) directed by R. Stephen Warner of the University of Illinois and funded by the Lilly Endowment, Inc., and the Pew Charitable Funds. I am grateful to Steve for seeing the potential in a quickly put-together proposal and to his codirector, Judith Wittner, and the other NEICP fellows for all their encouragement.

Along the way, I was supported with fellowships from the American Institute for Indian Studies for conducting research in Kerala and from the Louisville Institute in Kentucky, the Sloan Berkeley Center for Work and Family, and the University of California in the early writing stages of the project. The final process of revising and writing was facilitated by a residential scholarship in the Department of Sociology at Pomona College in Claremont, California; a National Institute of Mental Health postdoctoral fellowship at the University of California, Los Angeles; and support from the Charles R. Drew University of Medicine and Science in Los Angeles. I am especially grateful to Ricky Bluthenthal for his timely help and to Richard S. Baker at the Research Center for Minority Institutions at Charles Drew for his unquestioning support and belief in a project that was quite outside his disciplinary boundaries.

Several people in the broader academic community, particularly at Berkeley, helped me in the development of my research and writing. I am thankful to them even though I did not always heed their suggestions. Evelyn Nakano Glenn and Raka Ray, as members of my dissertation committee, provided essential constructive criticism. I was the recipient of many intellectual generosities from all the participants at the Berkeley Center for Work and Family, particularly Arlie Hochschild, Barrie Thorne, Anita Garey, Julio Cammarota, and Scott North. While the process of writing is long and often lonely, I have been fortunate to have the support of colleagues who have made the journey much more collective and collaborative. Maria Cecilia Dos Santos, Naheed Islam, Elizabeth Rudd, and Millie Thayer gave me helpful feedback in the early conceptualization and writing stages. More recently, Naheed Islam and Elizabeth Rudd painstakingly read and commented on my manuscript, improving it greatly. With the encouragement of the Global Ethnographers — Joseph Blum, Zsuzsa Gille, Teresa Gowen, Lynne Haney, Maren Klawiter, Steven H. Lopez, Seán Ó Riain, and Millie Thayer — I expanded my project to include transnational connections to Kerala. Troy Duster, Michael Omi, David Minkus, and the Institute for the Study of Social Change have supported me in several ways by their sheer presence. I am grateful to Kamau Birago for always looking out for me. Leslie Salzinger and Louise Lamphere, at Berkeley, were very helpful in the early conceptualization of this project. Russell Jeung, Carolyn Chen, and Jane Iwamura provided intellectual and spiritual companionship in thinking about Asian American religion, among other topics. I owe special thanks to Jonathan VanAntwerpen, who helped me get back on track with his thoughtful feedback and tons of encouragement.

I am grateful to several individuals who were instrumental in helping me complete this project. Leyla Bijan, Vrinda Koovakadu, and Shermin Zarabi transcribed and helped code interviews. In Kerala, Santhosh Varghese not only helped with transcription but also accompanied me on several research trips around Kerala, where it was difficult for a woman to travel without a male escort. My cousins Manasseh Zechariah and Jasleen Kohli, during their graduate student days at University of California, Irvine, and University of California, Riverside, took time out of their busy schedules on many occasions to search out the books that I needed from their respective libraries. Susan Koshy, Karen Cheng, and Peter Hammond all gave of their time and energy to read and comment on the entire manuscript. I am particularly grateful to Naomi Schneider and her staff at University of California Press for believing in this project and remaining calm and cool despite the delays. I especially thank my reviewers, who gave me thoughtful comments that helped improve the book.

Last but not least, my family played an integral part in helping me complete this project. I thank my brothers, Mathew George and Jacob George, and my sisters-in-law, Soli George and Sajini George, for all the ways they loved me and kept me grounded as I moved between Berkeley, Central City, and India. My aunt Rachel Zachariah not only helped me in a professional capacity by sending me information on nursing matters, but she has always been a role model to me in balancing family and academic commitments.

I am thankful for all the help I have received from my husband, Kirk Edwards. He has been a constant source of encouragement and tireless support, reading and editing sections, solving word-processing problems, and helping me to finally complete this book. He is an inspiration, and I am grateful for his partnership.

Both my children were born after I began working on this manuscript. My daughter, Roshni, and my son, Vinay, were deprived of time with their mother without having been given a choice. I am especially grateful to Vinay, who had exquisite timing coming into this world: he was born the day after I sent off a revised copy of my manuscript to the board of the press for final approval. I was doubly overjoyed when the book was approved for publication a few weeks after he was born.

I dedicate this book to my parents for their pioneering spirit and their courage to leave behind the comfortable and the familiar to emigrate to the United States. I appreciate the magnitude of their decision much more now that I have a family with small children of my own. But most of all, I am grateful for their unconditional love, which gave me a bedrock on which to build my life.

MAP 1. The state of Kerala within India.

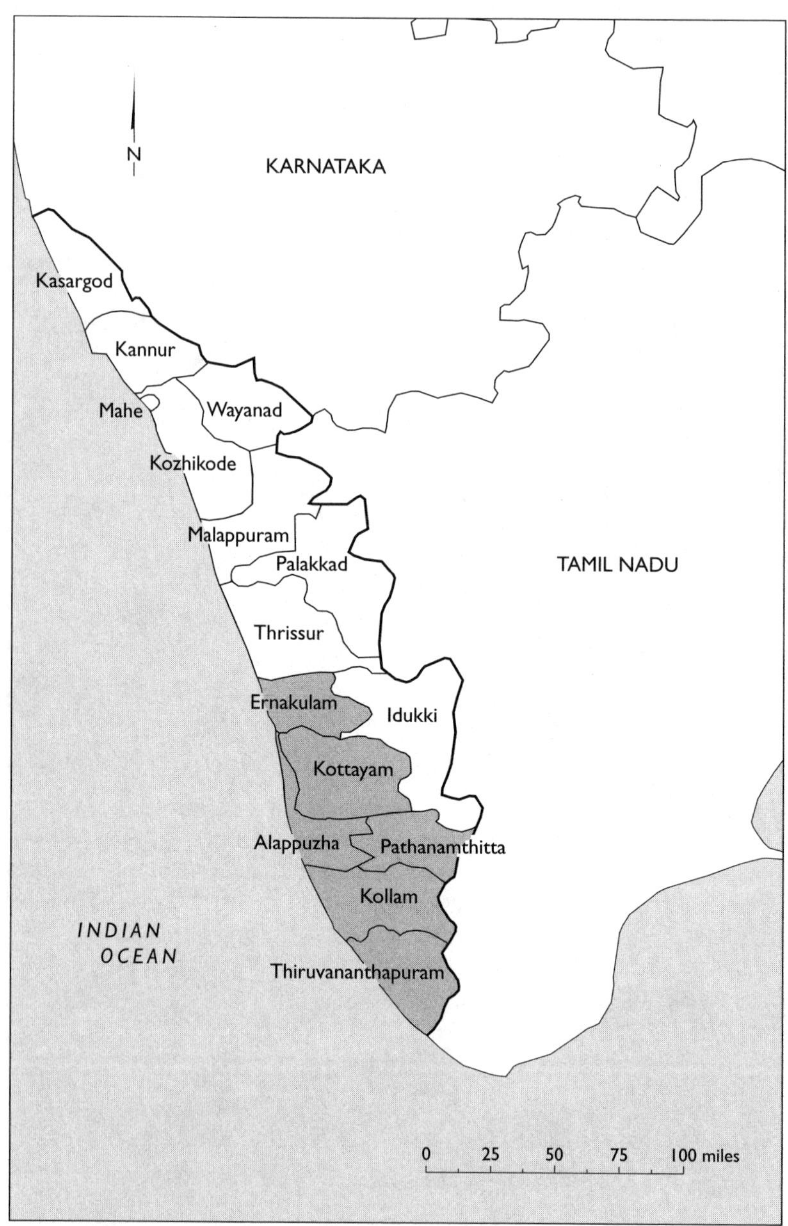

MAP 2. The districts that make up the state of Kerala. The shaded districts are those where I conducted interviews with family members of the individuals I interviewed in Central City, and with church officials and focus groups composed of nurses.

Introduction

I remember pressing my face against the warm glass of the airport window as I watched the plane whisk my mother away. My father and two brothers stood with me at the airport in Bangalore, India. My mother was off to the United States to work as a nurse. I was ten at the time and my brothers were both younger than I was. As the *chechi*, or big sister, I tried to be brave. But I felt my heart breaking, and I remember that I could not stop crying. I cried so much that I fell sick with a fever for several days after my mother left.

We did not see my mother again until two years later, when we too emigrated to the United States. In the time spent away from us, my mother stayed with her sister and then a friend (both nursing professionals) as she prepared for, and passed, the licensing examination to practice nursing in the United States. She was then able to work as a registered nurse and save the money needed to bring us over.

As an adult, I have had the unusual opportunity of revisiting this significant childhood experience of immigration. In writing this book, I have begun to understand my family's experiences within a larger historical and sociological context of displacement and change. From a distance afforded by time, and with a set of sociological lenses, I have been able to interpret my family's postimmigration experiences as an attempt to find balance again at both the family and the community level. On the face of it, this story is no different from the typical immigration saga: It is about a group of people who leave home to seek better opportunities. In the process, their lives are irreversibly changed in unexpected ways.

However, a closer look reveals how a reversal in the usual gender order of immigration results in a unique immigration experience.

As immigration stories are commonly imagined, the primary male immigrant arrives first, to be followed by the wife and children after he is settled. Atypically, in this story we encounter an immigration wave made up of women who came first and then sponsored their families. In fact, many women, like my mother, left their village homes in the state of Kerala and migrated to the larger cities of India to study nursing. From there, in a step-migration process, they emigrated to different parts of the world, relying on mostly female networks. In this book, I study one immigrant community in the United States made up mostly of nurses. I ask the question of what happens to gender relations when women come first and are the primary breadwinners.

As my family began to settle down in the United States, we went through the typical challenges faced by immigrants adapting to a new society. While we children were not so aware of it at the time, it was particularly difficult for my father, armed with skills and work experience that did not easily translate, to find employment in a U.S. economy facing recession. My father, who had been a white-collar worker in a British company in India, found that his credentials and work experience were not recognized in the United States. I remember my father's presence around the house as he looked for work while my mother worked double shifts to meet our expenses. Finally, after many months, my father found a clerical job for which he was overqualified.

My family's experience was not unusual relative to the other immigrant families we knew. However, historically in the United States, it is unusual for women to be the first immigrants and primary breadwinners for the family. In most immigrant communities, when women have worked outside the home, typically they have had access only to secondary and tertiary labor market jobs such as service and domestic work. But immigrant nurses like my mother are skilled professionals who enter a labor market experiencing a consistent shortage in nursing staff, and who therefore have more of a say in setting the terms of their employment. Meanwhile, their husbands are unable to find jobs comparable to the ones they held before immigration. Consequently, this affects gender relations in the family. That women typically earn more than the men who initially depend on them raises difficult questions, particularly for the men. These issues, which run the gamut from definitions of masculinity and femininity to basic self-worth, affect both men and women individually, as well as the dynamics of the family. A second broad question I explore in this book is how men and women deal with such changes in the delicate balance of gender relations after immigration.

Without relatives or friends nearby, my family found community and support in the immigrant Indian Christian church. The church service—which took place in rented halls in the early years—met both a religious and a social need for us. People drove many miles to attend the three-hour-long Sunday morning service and the potluck lunches that usually followed. There were frequent parties and regular prayer meetings in the homes of church members. I, as well as my contemporaries, found it difficult to distinguish between the parties and the prayer meetings. Every event began with lengthy Orthodox prayers—which were required to properly respect the priest's presence—and ended with food. Our social lives revolved around the church as church members became our extended family and community in the United States. The unusual dynamics in my own home made me aware of the tensions surrounding gender relations in the community.

I did not understand this at the time, but my parents were atypical in their gendered behavior. My father had always involved himself in child rearing and enjoyed taking an active role in our affairs even when nannies and others cared for us at home in India. By nature, he was—and indeed still is—extremely nurturing, and we three children gravitated toward him. My father was also a very creative person who enjoyed cooking and inventing his own concoctions in the kitchen. Consequently, even while we were in India, my father was not a stranger to the kitchen or to child-care. My mother often stayed in the background but participated in our care in a different way. Especially in the two years when our mother lived apart from us in the United States, our father became our sole parental caretaker.

After my family was reunited, my parents continued to behave as they always had. Without the help they had had in India, my parents both took part in the household and child-care tasks. However, I noticed many an occasion where other men in the community would tease my father for his ability to cook, and he would laugh it off. There were times when my mother made a point of cooking when we were expecting company, so that my father would not be teased. Even as a child, I sensed the underlying tension concerning this subject.

I remember thinking that my father's contributions to the household were unique, but since then I have found that it is not uncommon for men to take the lead in cooking and child care in the Keralite immigrant community. What was unique about my father was that, despite social sanctions, he did not adhere to the prescribed gender norms and was open about his role in household affairs and child care. I realize now that I noticed the shift in gender relations after immigration only because my parents were atypical in their behavior relative to the rest of the community. The social pressure that made them hide this difference allowed me to notice it.

This social pressure manifested itself not only in gender relations in our home but also in the explosive politics of the immigrant church. While I did not understand this at the time, the heated debates in the meetings of the church's general body that sometimes led to physical fights and the threat of schism in the congregation were often artifacts of the radical postimmigration changes in gender relations and the marginalizing experiences faced by first-generation men. The women were mostly silent spectators in this arena.

In this book, I also examine immigrant gender relations in three spheres — work, home, and community — and the interrelationships between these spheres. How do changes in the lives of men and women and in the work sphere affect the domestic and communal balance of gender relations? At the community level, how do men and women work out these tensions? It is not unreasonable to expect that changes in gender relations in one sphere often affect gender relations in other spheres. But this cannot be taken for granted. Economic gains in the work sphere do not automatically result in gains in other spheres for women, as was evident in my church and community. As I discovered through my research, gender and class relations are at stake at the community level as played out in the ideological constructions of nursing and in the divisive politics of the immigrant church.

Despite having grown up in this community, I was truly surprised by a particular finding during what became a pivotal moment in my research. At an informal tea party with a group of immigrant nurses, I heard a chance comment by one of the women about how she was considered just a "dirty" nurse in her home state of Kerala (see chapter 5). Having grown up with a mother who was a nurse, and in the company of other nurses, I had never heard such a sentiment expressed. Pursuing the meaning of this statement led me to trace its roots to Kerala.

Of course this was not the first time I was going back to Kerala. My own family had strong ties to Kerala. After our arrival in the United States, we had eagerly planned our return visits, buying many gifts to take back to my grandparents and extended family. My parents had wrung their hands with worry as they helplessly heard about the troubles of old age from their parents during their frequent phone calls home. Then there were the inevitable trips back for funerals, marriages, and other occasions, and the collective watching of videotapes of these events by everyone who could not be there. My parents also sponsored several relatives who came to the United States, including two aunts and an uncle and their families, who stayed with us for periods of time.

In this era of greater ease in global communications and travel, my family was not unique in this immigrant community for having many transnational ties to India. Particularly in the domestic and communal spheres, both the immigrant community and the sending community exhibit a mutual dependence, resulting in a flow of people and resources in both directions. Consequently, in this book I consider the question of how these ties affect the community, particularly with regard to gender and class relations. How is the sending community's stigmatization of nurses, who are considered "dirty" — a description attached, in Kerala, to lower-class and sexually deviant women — reproduced in the U.S. immigrant community despite the nurses' relative success?

Research Sites and Methods

This project is the result of three years of formal ethnographic research (1994–97) that I initially conducted for my dissertation in a metropolitan area of the United States — in a city that I call Central City — and in Kerala, India. I spent eighteen months between 1994 and 1995 in Central City, where I began fieldwork at the immigrant Indian Orthodox Syrian Christian parish of St. George's Orthodox Church.

Using the church as a base, I conducted interviews with twenty-nine couples, interviewing men and women separately, employing a convenience sampling method. I also interviewed several priests, bishops, and other church leaders, either when they visited St. George's or when I met with them at national church conferences. I also volunteered as a patient visitor on a regular basis in a nursing home in Central City that employed a large number of Keralite nurses. I then conducted ethnography in Kerala for six months in 1997. There I carried out fieldwork in an Orthodox church, interviewed family members of those I had interviewed in Central City, and conducted focus group interviews with nurses.

When referring to the subjects of this study and their locations, I use pseudonyms, with some exceptions. Before interviewing them, I always reassured the members of St. George's that I would not reveal their names or any other directly identifiable information they shared with me. While some said they did not care if they were identified by name, the majority seemed more comfortable not being identified. Consequently, it was important to disguise the name and location of the immigrant congregation as well, given the smallness of the community and my desire to protect the identities of those who generously shared their opinions. Where I have identified the actual names of bishops (Bishops Thomas Mar Makarios, Mathew Mar Barnabas, and Yuhannon Mar Milithios) and the retired dean of a well-known nursing school (Aleyamma Kuruvilla of the Christian Medical College in Vellore), it is because they are public figures who in newspaper articles and other research projects have spoken out on the topics discussed here (for example, see Williams 1996; and Abraham 1996). Revealing their real names is not a breach of confidentiality.

Whereas I began my research with the goal of focusing on nurses and their families at St. George's, I soon found another category of immigrants who did not come to the United States on the basis of nursing. This group, which I identify as "traditional householders," was made up of men who arrived on educational or work visas and then went back to marry women who, typically, were not nurses. Also in this group were couples who had arrived together and couples who had immigrated independently and married after immigration. Another significant difference about this group is that the men were not downwardly mobile after immigration. Rather, they tended to have professional jobs in the United States, being better educated than the men who came as dependents of their wives. Nearly a quarter of my sample (eight couples) were traditional householders.

Since most of the Keralite nurses in the United States are Syrian Christians, it is important to take a brief look at the history of Syrian Christianity in India. Syrian Christians from Kerala, the state at the southernmost tip of India, claim descent from the early converts of the apostle Thomas, who, tradition has it, was martyred in southern India in A.D. 72. These Christians of Kerala are called Syrian not because they have Syrian ancestry but because they use Syrian liturgy. The influence of Syrian missionaries starting in the seventh century led to the establishment of the church under the patriarch of Antioch, and a liturgy that still retains some Syriac.

Over the centuries, the Syrian Christians became divided among themselves into different denominations. There are Catholics and Eastern Orthodox, as well as Protestants of every stripe, who claim Syrian Christian ancestry. The Orthodox Syrian Christian Church of India is one such denomination in this Syrian Christian tradition. It broke off ties with Antioch in 1912 and is currently led by a patriarch from Kerala.[1]

With the first wave of Keralite immigrants in the late 1960s, there was an increasing need for religious institutions in the United States. Many of these pioneer immigrants became actively involved in renting churches or community halls and organizing makeshift congregations.[2] Faced with the shortage of clergy, they paid for priests from other congregations in sometimes distant areas in the United States to come once a month—often on Saturdays—to conduct the service.

When the number of congregations increased in the United States, the mother church in India formed a North American diocese and assigned a bishop to oversee the new diocese on behalf of the patriarch in Kerala. St. George's is an immigrant offspring of this Indian Orthodox Church and is one of fifty-nine congregations in the United States and Canada (appendix 3).

A Reluctant Participant in Central City

Entrée into St. George's was not difficult for me since I was raised in the Indian Orthodox Christian tradition. I introduced myself as a visiting student researcher, aiming to have an inconspicuous level of participation in the church. Having come to observe gender relations in the church, I wanted to remain on the sidelines and listen. Since I did not know any of the church members personally, I thought I could conduct my research on the "unobtrusive observer" end of the participant-observer spectrum. I was willing to let the field speak to me, but I was less willing to speak back and enter into a conversation.

However, I was pulled into the limelight by the new priest, who insisted on recruiting me to work with the junior high and high school age members of the church. The priest had inherited a congregation emerging from a recent and terribly divisive split in its membership. In his attempt to increase general enthusiasm, he thought that new ideas—specifically mine—would help inspire the participation of high school and junior high members. Consequently, I reluctantly became involved in teaching Sunday school.

I began by going to church early on Sundays to lead the Sunday school classes in song and to teach the ninth grade class. As Christmas approached, I was asked to coordinate the Sunday school Christmas program. I wrote and directed the Christmas play that year, which meant long practice sessions on Saturdays at the homes of the young actors. These occasions gave me the opportunity to get to know several of the parents, who were the first married couples in the church that I approached for interviews, ultimately resulting in a convenience sampling method of interview subject selection.

Because I was interviewing men and women separately, it was often difficult to find a five- to six-hour period where both husband and wife were home. As a result, I stayed overnight in the homes of several parishioners, interviewing the husband in the evening, sharing a family meal and prayer time, and then interviewing the wife in the morning, or vice versa. In some cases, I had to go back more than once, either because the husband or wife could not make the interview or someone had more to say and we had run out of time.

My participant observation in the church and community influenced the content and the tenor of the interviews, and the experience of interviewing in turn affected how I understood what I saw in my fieldwork. Conducting ethnography and becoming a participant of sorts allowed me to recognize important issues and ask questions in a way that would have been difficult with other modes of research. Working with the young people allowed me to have a general sense of legitimacy in the church and a familiarity with their parents that was necessary for the deeply personal interviews I later conducted.

My involvement in the Christmas program led to weekly planning and practice sessions after church on Sundays. It soon became a habit for me to have a late lunch with the priest after the practice session. This weekly custom allowed me to meet and interview several priests and bishops who visited the priest at St. George's. While receiving the culinary generosity of the latter, I was allowed to listen in and sometimes participate in several conversations among the all-male leadership of the church.

One rule of research that I gleaned from this experience was that involvement begets even more involvement. I was soon asked to organize the young people for a Christmas caroling venture, which, at St. George's, was an exclusively adult male activity. While I was close to the mostly female teenagers who wanted to go caroling, and I wanted to help the priest, I did not want to be in the midst of controversy. As a young, unmarried woman, I found that my presence among the men generated expressions of resistance that threw cultural and religious assumptions into relief. If I had taken the safe way out by remaining an observer, I would not have seen the significance of caroling — it had been redefined as an adult male domain forged in reactive compensation for their loss of status at home and at work.[3]

Despite my reluctance in the beginning, I came to see the priest's initial invitation to help with the youth program as a blessing in disguise. First of all, working with the young people allowed me to get to know their parents. Second, I felt that contributing my time and energy to the youth program was one way to reciprocate for the valuable time that church members were giving me. In retrospect, I realized that many of these very busy men and women might have not given me their precious time and entrée into their lives if they had not come to know and trust me through my work in the church. Finally, taking leadership in the caroling turned out to be a uniquely revealing experience that helped me understand the importance of church participation for the immigrant men.

Transgressive Ethnography in Kerala

Similarly, going to Kerala was not my idea and not one I welcomed. After eighteen months of being out in the field, I thought I had done enough research and was ready to come back and write my dissertation. My dissertation advisor, Michael Burawoy, in his own convincingly insistent manner, told me that I was not ready. After perusing my field notes and visiting me in Central City, he recognized the importance of a research venture to Kerala before I did.

The research in Central City had allowed me to observe the complex interaction between different spheres that resulted in male assertion of privilege in the congregations. But without going to Kerala, I would not have understood the importance of transnational connections and the role they played in Central City. Only in Kerala did I perceive the nature and importance of family ties and the role of the church as a transnational institution. The biggest puzzle was the stigmatization of nurses in Central City. Given the positive evaluation of nurses in the United States, the persistence of the stigma attached to them in the immigrant community could be explained only after analyzing the transnational connections that sustained the stigma.

To explore this transnational re-creation of norms, I studied the dense flows of meaning, people, and commodities between the two locales. I rejoined the flow myself, traveling to Kerala for six months to seek out the kin of the Central City couples and see what immigration looked like from the perspective of the sending community. It was when I spoke to the Keralite family members of the traditional householders — the category of community members who did not immigrate on the basis of nursing — that I became aware of the level of stigma that still was attached to nurses. The recent economic mobility of the families of nurses who went abroad did not always translate into upward movement for them, especially on the social ladder. The relatives of the traditional householders I interviewed in Central City, a part of Kerala's nonmigrant elite who acted as the gatekeepers of old wealth and status, were candid about their reservations about nurses. In conversations with them and church officials, I saw how the old gender- and class-based stigmas were still in place under the thin layer of societal approbation for nurses with green cards.

While in Kerala, I also submerged myself in a church to compare it with St. George's in Central City. Among this new congregation, I learned that the church is a transnational institution that serves as a space in which immigrants make status claims in their Keralite communities of origin. In having conversations with Keralite church members, and by attending Sunday services and group meetings in the church, I became aware of the strength and nature of the immigrant presence in the Keralite church. My interviews with clerical leaders of the church in Kerala also gave me insight into the great challenge that this transnational administration has become for the church.

Finally, from individual and focus group interviews with nurses, nursing administrators, and teachers, I learned how their labor was stigmatized, indeed more stigmatized as their wages became more prized. By recreating this global field for myself, I saw how norms were reproduced in Kerala and from there transmitted and appropriated in the community around St George's. My own presence, participation, and transgressions in Kerala brought me further insight into the unstated presumptions at both ends of the migration stream.

While traveling in an auto-rickshaw with my aunt, I asked the driver to stop at a particular place. He did not seem to hear me, so I tapped him on the shoulder to get his attention. My aunt was aghast: "He could get the wrong idea about you," she exclaimed. I had broken one of the cardinal rules of male-female interaction — I had touched a male stranger. From this and other such incidents, I began to understand better why immigrant nurses in Central City harbored the view that they were regarded as "dirty" women. I reflected on those young aspiring nurses who, twenty to thirty years before, had left behind a Kerala that probably had stricter prohibitions against the interaction of the sexes. These same women who were not allowed to enter the living room when male visitors came to their homes had to touch, clean, and nurture hundreds of male strangers as part of their professional duty.

My aunt's reaction in 1997 to my touching the driver gave me insight into the almost tangible gender boundaries among the Keralite immigrants of Central City. Although my study relies heavily on interviews, it was only through the transgressive ethnography of breaking rules and through getting my own hands "dirty" in the fields of Kerala that I understood the views expressed by people at both ends of this transnational migration.

Autobiographical Proximity and Its Consequences

I remember that, even as I began to conceptualize my research agenda for this project, I was both compelled by and concerned about pursuing a topic so close to home. As an insider, I had some distinct advantages and limitations in doing this research project.[4] Because my autobiographical proximity to this project has been the source of countless anxieties for me, I wish to enumerate some of the key issues with which I struggled.

FLUIDITY OF IDENTITY

As I mentioned already, entrée into research sites was relatively easy, but it also created tensions. I often found myself straddling or caught between competing identities. At St. George's I was both researcher and congregationalist, and yet at the same time I was neither adult nor child (adulthood is attained by entering marriage; however, in my late twenties I was too old to be a child). Nor was I a first-generation immigrant or member of the second generation. I am a 1.5er, having immigrated as a twelve-year-old. First-generation immigrants are adults, and the second generation is typically made up of those born in the new country. But 1.5ers tend to be those who immigrate at a young age and whose bilingual and bicultural capacities allow them to function in both cultures. In Kerala I was no less a hybrid. I spoke Malayalam fluently, I looked like a Malayalee, and I dressed like other young women, but I could never completely hide my difference. My cousin said it was the way I carried myself and made eye contact. Still, my in-betweenness and my liminality, which I usually considered an autobiographical headache, gave me the room to maneuver among different identities and see the field from different points of view. I could associate with both the adults and the teenagers, with men and women, nurses and nonnurses, without being locked into any one group.

But it was not all easy going. The fluidity of identity made it a constant challenge to position myself. I was asked to follow scripts no one else could follow. On several occasions my presence, my clothing, and my body became the objects of sanctions, which allowed me to see firsthand the control exerted over women's bodies. Because I was seen as a member of the community, I was required to behave according to traditional gender norms.

At a national conference of the American diocese Father Mathew, the priest from St. George's, pulled me aside to tell me that two other priests at the conference had complained to him about my attire. On the opening night of the conference, Father Mathew had asked me to introduce one of the speakers. The whole affair had appeared to be quite informal and, since we were in the middle of a hot summer, I wore a pair of blue denim shorts that went down to my knees and a T-shirt with a loose, long-sleeve, unbuttoned shirt over it. I was surprised to learn that anybody had found anything wrong with my outfit. Father Mathew told me that the two priests had found my attire inappropriate because there were bishops present. The problem was not the informality of the clothing but rather that the shorts revealed my legs below the knees. Even though several of the high school boys and girls were wearing shorts, I was selected for reprimand because I was older and seen as a leader among the young people.

Later that same day, my attire inspired discussion at a meeting for the women's group, where the focus was on the needs of the second-generation women and single first-generation women. One of the bishops and one of the priests attended this meeting. The wife of one of the priests who had complained about my attire raised the issue of suitable clothing for young women. She complained that pants (and by the same logic, shorts even more so) were not fitting in religious settings. The bishop enthusiastically agreed and said, "They all say that we are conservative. Mothers should be responsible for training their children in these matters." The priest complained that he had asked one girl in his congregation not to wear pants and she had asked him, "Why not?" This was said as if it was obvious why girls should not be wearing pants and that the question showed her impertinence. The bishop commented that it is all right for girls up to the age of twelve to wear pants. It was clear that my apparel the night before was probably the stimulus for this discussion. While I was not comfortable with having my own body made the object of gender-patrolling forces, this incident allowed me to see how gender rules are enforced over generations.

Having to maneuver between the identities of researcher and community member was a foreseeable challenge that I had expected to encounter in the field. What I had not expected was that this challenge would continue after I left Central City and Kerala, when I had to wrestle with the data and present my findings to an academic audience for whom I had to translate a different worldview.

As I began to transcribe, and sometimes translate and analyze, my interviews, the first issue I tried to understand was women's lack of participation in the church. I saw how men had expanded their participation by redefining existing positions to make them exclusively male and by creating new positions for themselves. In my interviews, I heard one explanation for the men's increased participation — an explanation championed by traditional householders as a means to differentiate themselves and mark their own premigration status — that the "nurse-husbands" who had lost status at home were trying to recover it in church. As I struggled with the data, I unconsciously adopted the hegemonic, shaming term *nurse-husbands* used by the traditional householders and the upper-class bishops and even replicated by some of the husbands of nurses.

While intellectually I had seen use of the term *nurse-husbands* as a declassing move on the part of the Keralite upper classes, I had difficulty applying this insight because I had trouble seeing who was doing the declassing. Only after I analyzed my interviews and wrote chapter 3 did I see that the traditional householders were indeed a reality in my sample set, that they had names and faces and a coherent and congealing ideology that they expressed in their interviews. Only then could I see how it was in their interest to emasculate and declass the husbands of nurses and downgrade nurses as deviants. It was then that I could stop using the very terms they used and to see the powerful ways that stigma works on those who are stigmatized.

The explanation given by the traditional householders concerning men's increased participation in the church was a narrow one that stereotyped the households of nurses. Once I realized my mistake, I could see that the majority of the immigrant men who increased their participation in the church were responding to a loss of status not only at home but also at work and — as marginalized minority men — in the wider society. Their participation was also a generous response to the need among immigrants for a vibrant central community space such as the church to meet social, economic, religious, and cultural needs. Furthermore, by their remarks, the traditional male householders, who were also marginalized in the wider American society, were complaining about a loss of status positions that in Kerala had been traditionally and unquestionably theirs.

A QUESTION OF AUDIENCE

It is unsurprising that my position as a member of the larger Keralite Christian immigrant community and my own family's experiences helped shape my research experiences and my final analyses. But what was somewhat unexpected was how being an insider continued to affect me as I began to share my work with the academic community. From objectifying the subjects of my study as data to explaining the differences of cultural beliefs and the underlying logic of different worldviews, I found myself involved in a self-alienating process of clarifications and justifications.

When speaking about Keralite Christians, I found it necessary to say "these men" or "these women" to create the distance that seems necessary in all such research. I suppose that all ethnographers who have spent months and years getting to know their subjects intimately must represent them similarly. In some ways, I did not really have to try. It was one of the consequences of doing the research. I had to separate my family and myself from the research to function on a daily basis. However, this separation was more difficult to maintain when I shared my work with an academic audience. Because I was also a part of the phenomenon I was studying, I felt alienated from myself when I had to objectify the familiar aspects of my life for an audience who came with their own conventional expectations of the nature of gender relations in an Indian community.

Sometimes, it was hard to think about and discuss complex and sensitive issues openly with those who did not have the prerequisite understanding of cultural differences. The dominant caricature of patriarchal South Asian culture is that the men are oppressive cavemen and the women are surely being beaten up and abused in their homes. For example, in a discussion about my research, a well-meaning scholar asked me why I had not found any domestic abuse in the community. Perhaps noting the surprise on my face, the questioner explained, "Everyone knows that domestic abuse is very common in South Asian communities—all the feminists say so." The assumption that patriarchy with a capital *P* is the essential nature of all South Asian communities leads not only to the expectation that there is rampant domestic abuse in such communities but also to the assumption that all women naturally flee such oppressive conditions if given the chance.[5]

Relatedly, several people asked me why immigrant single women went back to Kerala to the constraints of arranged marriages rather than marry Americans of their own choosing. Why would they not find someone here — presumably a more egalitarian relationship that is the antithesis of a patriarchal Indian arranged marriage? For most American academics, when discussing Indian immigrants the reference point is the cosmopolitan academic or professional who hails from a typically upper-class background and is relatively more at ease with American dating habits. Consequently, it is understandable that my academic public would conjecture that immigrant nurses would be comfortable with cross-cultural mate selection options.

To answer my audience's questions required various conversations. First, I would start with the Indian nurses' cultural lack of comfort with both their American setting and the dating habits of Americans, which would prevent the nurses from pursuing such options even had they encountered any propositions. Second, I would address the cultural differences that allowed Indian women to welcome guidance from their families and accept arranged marriage as their preferred way to find a partner. Despite the negative possibilities of an arranged marriage, many men and women follow the wishes of their families. Third, I would explain that the individual nurses who migrate often carry the hopes of an entire family and are beholden to help them. Marrying outside their community might not only bring shame to their families but also present an obstacle to carrying out their obligations to them.

While writing about my findings, I was conscious of my different audiences. I knew I could be reinforcing existing stereotypes about South Asian patriarchy among my wider academic audiences. I was afraid that ultimately I would contribute to an objectification of Keralite Christian social relations that limited their complexity to nurse-husbands and silent women caught in oppressive patriarchal institutions such as arranged marriage or the church. I fear it may be all too easy for readers of this book to go hunting for a Keralite Christian immigrant church and find the emasculated husbands of nurses exercising their patriarchal power. I understand that this is part of the danger of writing ethnography, because the particular phenomenon that one analyzes may become *the* representative and identifying characteristic of the group. I hope I have painted a more comprehensive picture encompassing the complex, multivalent reality of life for this immigrant group.

Another audience I have kept in mind while writing is the Keralite immigrant community. It is a common trope in ethnographic writing to reflect on the reception of scholarship in the community studied. Unlike the majority of scholars who engage in such reflection from the safer spaces of academia, I am still a part of this community, being a member of the Orthodox Church and an active participant. I struggled with how much I should reveal of what I saw. I was aware that community members could view my project as dirty laundry that should not be aired in the sight of outsiders.

I know that gender relations are not at the top of this community's list of urgent issues. However, I chose to focus on this topic because I believe that the particular characteristics of this immigration pattern highlight the everyday struggles around gender and class that are not unique to this community or to immigrants. Rather, in our rapidly changing world, where two-job families have become the overwhelming norm, most couples in industrialized societies struggle with the domestic division of labor. The resulting tugs-of-war over the definition of normative masculinities and femininities resonate not only at the familial level but also within communities and societies at large. Gender, race, and class tensions intersect on the grounds of these everyday battles. For example, one type of division of domestic labor can become the hallmark of a particular masculinity or femininity and tinged with racial or class overtones. While I understand why community members may not want these issues discussed, I hope I have risen to the challenge of portraying what is universally human about the conflicts that my subjects faced and the creative solutions to which they resorted.

Despite all the difficulties discussed above, I consider it a privilege to have undertaken this project. While being an insider presented several challenges, I was able to sustain my interest in this project over a long period of time only because these issues were important to me. As a result, I have learned a lot about doing ethnography and about my own identity.

A Road Map

This study examines an unusual immigration pattern of primary female immigration and its implications for gender relations in the three spheres of work, home, and community, as well as the role of transnational connections in the reproduction and transformation of gender relations in the immigrant community.

In chapter 1, I situate the questions that guide this study within several bodies of literature, from the feminist-inspired gender and immigration literature, to the literature on religion and immigration, to that on transnationalism. Furthermore, I outline a broader theoretical framework that informs my understanding of the interrelationship of gender relations in the spheres of work, home, and community.

Next, in chapter 2, I focus on the genesis of the female-led nurses' migration from Kerala. I trace the journeys of Keralite nurses who gained employment in different parts of India and then sought lucrative opportunities all over the world, including in the United States. I then examine the work experiences of nurses who confronted the racialized hierarchy of the American ward floor and yet developed a new sense of professional pride, a pride not possible in Kerala. I contrast the rising social status and economic power of the nurses with the experiences of their husbands, who lost status both at work and at home when they joined their wives in the Unites States.

The downward mobility of the men raises questions about what happens in the domestic sphere and how men deal with their loss of status. In chapter 3, I reveal the consequences of immigrant men's declining social status, and of their dependence on their wives' jobs, for gender relations in the home. Using in-depth interviews with twenty-nine couples, I identify four types of immigrant households: traditional households, where the women do the housework and child care and the men are in charge of the financial decision making; forced-participation households, where the men are forced to share the child care; partnership households, where all aspects of domestic labor are shared; and female-led households, where the women shoulder almost all the labor in the household, including the financial decision making (see appendix 1 for the list of participants in the in-depth interviews, by household type).

In chapter 4, I demonstrate the necessity of examining spheres beyond work and home in order to understand the effect of migration on gender relations. I analyze the complicated relationships between men's status in the immigrant church and their status in the wider U.S. society. I show that men who lost status in the workforce and at home as a result of immigration began to expand and elaborate their roles in the church and even push women out of activities traditionally open to them in Kerala. However, even as these men created a necessary space of belonging for the immigrant community, they also relied on male privilege, with the support of the church hierarchy, to compensate for loss of status suffered in the process of migration and settlement. Yet ultimately, the husbands of nurses became connected to the stigma attached to nurses that was reproduced through another set of transnational connections with Kerala. But why were these seemingly successful immigrant families, who appeared to have achieved the American dream, still plagued by social stigmas that originated thousands of miles away?

Chapter 5 takes a close look at the nature of transnational connections between the immigrant community in Central City and Kerala and at the complex influence of these connections upon gender relations in the immigrant community. In this chapter, I argue that, while transnational connections are a valuable resource for the economic and social reproduction of the immigrant community, they also help reproduce established gender- and class-based power relations. Immigrants' identities remain oriented to Kerala as a result of concrete practices largely organized through relationships with family members left behind in Kerala, practices such as finding marriage partners and help with raising children. These practices foster the reproduction in the United States of family forms and gender roles rooted in Kerala. The cultural construction of nurses as dirty, or lower class, from Kerala is reproduced in the United States through many different channels, including the media, film, and the transnational marriage market. Transnational connections in the church at both the individual and the institutional levels help reproduce Keralite gender norms in the immigrant community. However, I show that Keralite gender ideals and practices are selectively adopted in response to the specific conditions of an immigrant community based upon female-led migration.

Finally, in chapter 6, I revisit the questions and themes raised in earlier chapters and address some of the broader implications for the study of migration, gender, and transnationalism that emerge from this project.

CHAPTER 1

Contradictions of Gender When Women Immigrate First

Historically, most of the academic research on global workers in the United States has focused on the ideal type of the male sojourning laborer, such as the Chinese railroad worker in California and the Mexican bracero in the Southwest, who arrived as primary emigrants to the United States. An exception to this ideal type was the Irish migration in the latter part of the nineteenth century. The scarcity of opportunities for women to find employment and marriage at home after the great famine in Ireland, coupled with the availability of service jobs and help from kin networks in the United States, led to the migration of a greater number of Irish women than men (Diner 1983; Jackson 1984). Currently it is less rare to see the primary migration of female workers (Hondagneu-Sotelo 1994; Repak 1995; Williams 1996; Espiritu 1997, 1999; Parrenas 1998). I study one such case of a female-led emigration of nurses from India.

The shortage of nurses in the United States in the 1960s resulted in heavy recruitment of nurses from Asian countries, including nurses from the state of Kerala, India. The Keralite community in the United States is unique among Indian immigrant communities in the prominent role that women have played in the migration process. This cohort of female immigrants became the uncontested breadwinners, and men became downwardly mobile, both economically and socially. This was the opposite of the situation in the sending country, where female nurses tended to be in a lower wage bracket or, at best, earned salaries equivalent to those of their husbands.

At a general sociological level, my project was motivated by the question of what happens to gendered practices and discourses in the process of immigration when women become economically dominant as the primary breadwinners. How do these immigrants experience the change as they negotiate, challenge, and transform conventional gender practices and discourses? More specifically, do the respective changes in their economic and social conditions result in a reaction from either the women or the men? If so, where and how? Do women leverage their improved economic status and bargain for greater gains in the home and communal spheres? And do men try to compensate for their downward mobility in the work sphere by asserting themselves in other spheres? What is the role of the wider U.S. society in the unfolding of immigrant gender relations? And what is the effect of the long arm of the sending community in Kerala?

This instance offers a test case for the durability of patriarchy. By *patriarchy,* I mean the various discourses and practices that allow men to set the terms and limits for women in different arenas of society. However, men have varying degrees of power to do so, and women are able to resist to varying degrees. Despite female employment outside the home in India, most families had adequate support systems in the form of relatives and servants to maintain a lifestyle that kept domestic patriarchy in place. That is, few of the men did household chores, child care, or other labor of the sort that makes up the second shift for many women working outside the home. Furthermore, while in India, most of the men had societal support and the economic basis to maintain their position as the breadwinning head of household even though their wives contributed to the families' livelihood.

With immigration, there was a break from the status quo as men suddenly found themselves dependent on women for social and economic resources and lacking auxiliary help from relatives and servants with the household labor. What happens to the taken-for-granted model of patriarchal gender relations under these conditions? In other words, how resilient is patriarchy when its material basis is eroded? This case provides an experimental situation in which to look at what resources men can draw on when they lose the material and symbolic resources taken for granted in India. How effective are the cultural and political resources in the host society and immigrant community in mitigating their losses?

Historically, sociologists of immigration have not been in a position to answer such questions, because they have not considered the experiences of women or the effect of their presence on gender relations (Nakano Glenn 1986; Seller 1981; Brettell and Simon 1986; Pedraza-Bailey

1991). In the sociological literature, the typical immigrant was the male sojourning laborer who tended to come alone. Even when families immigrated, they depended on having the male head of household find work. However, Katharine Donato tells us that 55 percent of the immigrants to the United States from 1930 to 1979 were women, and that they outnumbered men by over a million (1992). Yet women's labor historically has been ignored in most scholarship on this subject.

When sociologists and immigration scholars began to pay attention to the experience of women in the 1970s and 1980s, there was a significant shift in the trend, resulting in a substantial body of work on women and migration. In fact, there has been enough scholarship produced to inspire several review articles, anthologies, and at least three journal issues dedicated to the literature on gender and immigration (Phizacklea 1983; Morokvasic 1984; Brettell and Simon 1986; Pedraza-Bailey 1991; Tienda and Booth 1991; Gabaccia 1992; Pessar 1999; Hondagneu-Sotelo 1999; Kelson and DeLaet 1999).

While this scholarship covered significant new ground, there are some distinct shortcomings. First, it almost exclusively examines migration streams in which women are secondary migrants. Part of the reason for this trend is that women historically have followed men in the immigration process. As already mentioned, there is the notable exception of Irish female immigration.[1] In the last two decades, it has become less rare to see women immigrate before the men. Terry Repak's study of the primary immigration of Central American women whom Washington diplomats recruit for domestic work remains one of the few exceptions, and it gives full treatment to this distinct migration pattern (Repak 1995). And in Repak's study, despite the Central American women's primary immigration for prearranged employment opportunities, it was the men who were more successful in the U.S. labor market because of the broader range of options available to them. With this research, I plan to focus on Keralite nurse migration to understand how primary female migration and the nurses' breadwinner status affect the family.

Second, existing scholarship focuses on working-class immigrant women, most of whom have entered the tertiary labor market as low-waged and undocumented workers or as workers in family enterprises. There is empirical evidence that over 28 percent of the women who migrated under occupational preference categories in the 1970s entered to pursue highly skilled occupations, taking jobs as nurses, managers, teachers, and administrators (Houstoun, Kramer, and Barrett 1984: 944). Several scholars have pointed to the absence of studies on professional immigrant women who have some economic power and status in the host society (Mejia et al. 1979; Pedraza-Bailey 1990, 1991; Espiritu 1997; Kelson and DeLaet 1999). The sociologist Pierrette Hondagneu-Sotelo, in her 1999 introduction to a journal issue devoted to gender and migration, underscores the issue when she notes a lacuna in the literature regarding work on professional immigrants. With this study, I hope to begin to address this gap.

Third, when women are the focus, scholars lose sight of immigrant men as agentic beings who are also coping with change and often a loss in status. Most studies of immigration and gender relations take for granted that immigrant men are independent of the women. The gains and losses of women after immigration are calibrated against the standard of a relatively more independent and economically powerful immigrant male. In my study, Keralite men are initially completely dependent on the women's income even if eventually they contribute a secondary or equal income.

The literature on gender and immigration is ill equipped to explain how men who depend on women in the process of migration cope with their losses and, in turn, how this might affect gender relations. This absence of information is surprising, given that several scholars have found that, by most indicators of socioeconomic status, immigrant men appear to lose status relative to their premigration standing and relative to their spouses (Espiritu 1997; Grasmuck and Pessar 1991; Kibria 1993; Lamphere et al. 1993; Pedraza-Bailey 1991; Hondagneu-Sotelo 1994). Do men try to regain their status in some way? What are the spaces where they might do so?

The root of this problem may be found in the common mistake of equating gender only with women. Rather, it is a set of social meanings given to sexual difference.[2] Gender not only affects individual opportunities but also organizes the social relations of both men and women. Consequently, when studies that claim to examine gender and immigration do not include the experiences of men, they are forfeiting a relational and dynamic understanding of gender. To answer the question of what happens when women lead the migration and become primary breadwinners, I examine the interactions of both men and women as they immigrate, settle, and develop transnational ties.

In order to look at women's roles in the migration process, their professional status, and men's experiences, it is necessary to enlist an understanding of gender relations that goes beyond the individual's experience. To appreciate how immigrant women and men negotiate and balance their new circumstances requires a comprehensive framework that allows us to study gender relations in the different spheres of home, work, and community.

Gendered Spheres and Their Interaction

For this project I use R. W. Connell's framework of gender relations as specified in *Gender and Power.* Like Connell, I see gender relations as being organized by gender structures. By structures, Connell means constraints on practice that typically operate through social institutions. As Connell puts it, "The crucial point is that practice . . . is always responding to a situation. Practice is the transformation of that situation in a particular direction. To describe structure is to describe what it is in the situation that constrains the play of practice" (1987: 97).

In this book, I look at two structures of relationships between men and women that Connell identifies — namely, the gender structures of labor and power — to see how they shape gender relations in the lives of the immigrants I study. The term *gender structure of labor* refers to the sexual division of labor, which affects not only the allocation of work but also its organization and design. By *gender structure of power,* Connell refers to authority, coercion, and control, which are achieved by different tactics, ranging from brute force to the assertion of hegemony.[3]

These gender structures are present in particular institutions and also function to order society as a whole. The inventory of gender structures in a particular institution — such as the home or church — is what Connell refers to as a gender regime. The structural inventory, or the gender regime, of an institution accounts for the structures of gender — such as labor or power — that constrain the play of practices in a given institution and result in a given sexual politics.

For Connell, the relationship between gender regimes is an important part of understanding the gender order of a given society. He identifies three potential types of relationships between gender regimes where the gender structures in a particular institution may affect the gender relations in another institution. First, the relationship could be an additive or complementary one, where the gender relations in one institution function to support the gender relations of the neighboring regime. Here the gender structures of two institutions can dovetail, pointing to a meeting of different strategies used by actors in these institutions. Second, the relationship could be conflictive: gender relations in one institution could contradict those of another, indicating a lack of harmony between strategies. Finally, the gender relations of two institutions could function in a parallel manner as part of a common strategy (1987: 134–36).

While Connell asserts that the relationship between gender regimes in different spheres can be complementary, conflictive, or parallel, he does not explain how these relations emerge and are reproduced. In his view, gender structures and practices appear to be autonomous and dynamic responses to particular situations, but his argument lacks the underlying logic showing how the interactions between regimes can be conflictive or complementary. Consequently, the relationship between gendered regimes (or gendered spheres, as I call them) seems unelaborated in his framework. In this project, I aim to theorize the importance of the gendered spheres of home, work, and community and the mutual interactions between them.

A systematic analysis of the three spheres of work, home, and community requires the examination of three sets of possible interactions. These include interactions between work and home, between work and church, and between home and church. Rather than deal with all three possibilities equally, I prioritize the work sphere to look at how gender relations in this sphere affect gender relations in the other spheres. There are two reasons for this. Historically, changes in gender relations happen first in the work sphere as women immigrate and find jobs before men. Moreover, changes in the work sphere have the greatest effect, as they set limits on and shape what happens in the other spheres.

Does women's shift to primary status in the work sphere after immigration result in parallel shifts for women in the domestic and communal spheres? Or does this lead to conflict because the men attempt to reinforce their patriarchal rights in the home or community? Or is there a conflict-avoiding complementary strategy, where men are compensated for the loss of status in the work sphere by a gain in status in other spheres? While Connell recognizes the importance of the different spheres, he does not tell us how gender relations are transferred between spheres.

Connell also fails to look at the larger context in which these spheres operate. To his credit, he does recognize that the relationships between gender regimes contribute to the gender order at a societal level. However, his framework does not address the different ways in which these spheres may operate at the city, country, and global levels. Furthermore, it is important to look at relationships in their historical specificity. When looking at immigrant gender relations in an era of globalization, it is necessary to look at how transnational connections to the sending community affect the unfolding postimmigration gender relations. Are some spheres more transnationally connected than other spheres? What are the institutional and individual avenues by which transnational ties shape gender relations in the immigrant community? I introduce such contextual analysis to broaden Connell's framework.

In the rest of this chapter, I raise a number of questions that I explore in the book. I begin by examining the effect of work on the domestic sphere. That is, what are the consequences of primary female migration for gender relations in the household when there is a major gendered shift in labor-market status after immigration? Second, what is the effect of work on the community sphere? In my research, I limit the communal sphere to the immigrant religious congregation. For Keralite immigrants, the religious congregation proves to be the most important space for community.[4] As the changes in the work sphere reverberate in the immigrant religious congregation, what effect do these changes have on gender relations?

And finally, the particular configuration of gender relations in the community point to transnational ties to Kerala, raising questions about what role, if any, they play in the unfolding postimmigration gender relations. In addition to illuminating the processes and consequences of immigration, my research sheds light on the social processes that underlie the reproduction and transformation of gender relations in general.

The Effect of Work on the Household

Most scholars of immigration and gender have focused on the household as a key site where gender relations are most transformed by the effect of immigration. Scholarship on the domestic sphere has looked at women's gains and losses in the household after immigration and has viewed the entry into the wage labor market as the catalyst for these changes. The focus of the literature has been on how women's entry into wage labor affects their level of oppression in the family. Early feminist literature saw the family as a sexist institution oppressive to women. Emancipation was gauged by the amount of freedom that a woman's wages provided her to escape the patriarchal structures of the traditional family.

Scholarship on gender and immigration shows that immigrant women who enter the wage labor market in the United States, even as secondary breadwinners, gain personal autonomy and independence. Yet immigrant women continue to stay within the oppressive structure of patriarchal families. Given the greater autonomy experienced after immigration, do they take advantage of their new power and at least challenge the patriarchal arrangements in the household? The literature is divided in its treatment of this issue. While some scholars contend that the household is a bastion of resistance,[5] others hold that it can simultaneously function as a locus of negotiation.

THE HOUSEHOLD AS A BASTION OF RESISTANCE

Scholars who looked at the social location of immigrant women achieved a broader understanding by focusing on the experiences resulting from class and racial marginality and xenophobia. These contrasting feminist theories come from the experiences of ethnic minority and working-class women (Fernandez-Kelly and Garcia 1991; Nakano Glenn 1986, 1992; Kibria 1993; Pessar 1995). These theorists found that in the United States the family is a bastion of resistance against racism, which is systematically directed against poor women of color. Mirjana Morokvasic (1984) extends the argument to all immigrants. She points out that the oppression experienced by foreigners makes the home the one secure place in a xenophobic society, and women will put up with gender subordination in the home to maintain it as a safe place.

Consequently, it became evident that the family structure, even when it was patriarchal, was a necessary support, especially for poor, working-class immigrant women and racial minorities. Among the working class, unstable low-paying jobs and secondary positions in the labor market promote female dependency within the family, perpetuating gender hierarchy in the home (Nakano Glenn 1986). Morokvasic (1984) argues that work is not always satisfying for working-class women, who might see household tasks as giving them more personal satisfaction. Consequently, they are less likely to question their subordinate roles in the household.

Along with the racism and lack of satisfaction that often make work unstable and unfulfilling for immigrant women, an ideology of advancement also motivates them to stay within the conjugal unit and even to stop working as a sign of middle-class attainment (Fernandez-Kelly and Garcia 1991; Pessar 1995). Employment for many immigrant women becomes an extension of their obligations as wives and mothers, resulting in the maintenance of patriarchy in the household despite their working outside the home (Pedraza-Bailey 1991; Segura 1991; Pessar 1995; Hurh and Kim 1990). In fact, Patricia Pessar (1984) found that employment allowed immigrant women to redefine these roles in a more satisfying manner. This is evident in the case of Nazlia Kibria's study of Vietnamese immigrant women who strategically chose to work in the informal economic sector—which gave them less economic stability and power in the home—in response to the male loss of status, as a way of softening the blow of this loss on their husbands. Their main intention was to keep the family together, since this also gave them authority over the second generation (Kibria 1993).

Because these scholars focus on women whose labor-market experiences are unstable if not unfulfilling, the household is logically the sphere that the women protect, even at the cost of maintaining patriarchal gender relations. What happens when the women in question are professionals courted by the labor market? Are these women likely to overturn customary gender relations, especially when the men in their lives are dependent on the women in the immigration process and downwardly mobile in the labor market after immigration? This approach sheds light on how the household acts as a bastion of resistance against the societal inequalities of racial, class, and xenophobic discrimination outside the household. However, it pays little attention to what is going on within the household. Does female entry into the labor market after immigration result in a renegotiation of gender relations that lessens the inequality between male and female members within the household?

THE HOUSEHOLD AS A LOCUS OF NEGOTIATION

While the household can be a symbol of security, it also can be divided along gender and generational lines, so that the interests of individuals are not always the same (Hondagneu-Sotelo 1994; Kibria 1993; Grasmuck and Pessar 1991). Consequently the household can be a bastion of resistance against racism and, simultaneously, a location of negotiation.

In this scholarship, the struggle in the household is characterized as centering on men's role in the household division of labor and women's role in decision making. Some theorists argue that work affects gender relations in the home: the smaller the wage gap between partners, the more willing men are to participate in domestic work, and the more authority and status women have (Pessar 1995; Lamphere et al. 1993).

Scholars such as Hondagneu-Sotelo (1994) take issue with such a position, describing it as too economistic. Other scholars point to a variety of factors to explain the uneven consequences of higher earnings for immigrant women relative to their husbands, countering any simplistic expectation that the higher a woman's wage earnings, the greater her authority and status in the family (Espiritu 1999; Menjivar 1999a). They identify several factors emanating from the social context of work and community that contribute to an active negotiation of gender relations in the household.

For example, in her work on Mexican immigrants, Hondagneu-Sotelo (1994) finds that the division of labor in the immigrant household and family decision making processes is more egalitarian after immigration, and women experience greater spatial mobility in the settlement communities. But, she argues, the new economic arrangements are insufficient to explain the transformation of gender relations. A broader explanation would have to take into account the social context of the changing community of incorporation and network assistance. For example, the Mexican women who emigrated and found employment with the help of assistance networks composed of natal families were likely to experience greater independence after migration as opposed to those dependent on their husbands.

Cecilia Menjivar (1999a) argues that cultural ideals held at the point of origin affect the negotiation of gender relations after immigration. Among the Guatemalans she studied, women's higher earnings threatened Ladino men (those of mixed European and indigenous ancestry) after immigration, but indigenous men welcomed it because theirs was a more egalitarian culture from the start.

Menjivar also finds that the social context of work after migration affects how gender relations are reconstructed. Women who work as domestics are exposed to the more egalitarian division of labor in American households, which prompts them to lobby for change in their own. Similarly, Espiritu (1997) finds that, because Asian American nurses often work among coethnics, they gain from the social support systems — both emotional and material support — to challenge male dominance. Latino men who work with other Latino men in segregated work environments find social support for maintaining their old ways (Menjivar 1999a).

Espiritu (1999) points out that women's professional status, easily transferable skills, and demanding job schedules are variables that affect the renegotiation of gender relations. In the case of Filipina nurses, their demanding schedules help explain men's greater participation in housework. Nonprofessional women are more dependent on their families and do not have greater bargaining power.

Kurien (1998) notes that relative spatial isolation from one's ethnic peers tends to solidify conjugal bonds. Without servants or relatives to help, middle-class husbands with professional working wives do more housework. In the same vein, Espiritu (1997) writes that professional couples are more interdependent and equal in their relationships, because they are forced to depend on each other in the immigrant setting.

So far, I have highlighted two ways in which the literature addresses the effects of immigration and work on the domestic sphere. In the first approach, the household's function as a site of resistance against discrimination by the host society supersedes its function as a site of the struggle for equality that comes with women entering the labor market. In the second approach, the household is simultaneously a bastion of resistance against external discrimination and a site of internal negotiation where several factors from outside the home shape the bargaining process within. In this latter approach, the social contexts of the changing immigrant community as well as the social context of work affect gender relations in the household. Here, the particular characteristics of work and community condition the resulting gender relations in the household.

For Keralite Christians, the primary defining factor emanating from the work sphere that shapes gender relations in the home is the immediacy of the female nurses' work constraints. From finding temporary work, to preparing for and passing the nursing board examinations, to finding employment that includes shift work, Indian nurses have to navigate difficult terrain to work as registered nurses and support their families. The nurses' work requirements set limits on their families' economic and geographic stability.

Immigrant men's ability to obtain work and the type of work they obtain are also aspects of the work sphere that affect gender relations in the domestic sphere. When men are able to find jobs that allow them to become breadwinners, women work less outside the home and carry the greater load of labor in the domestic sphere. The household has to adjust to these work-related constraints, which affect where and how the family lives and how they divide household labor — namely, housework, child care, and financial decision making. Different forms of cultural and social capital intervene in this adjustment process.

Cultural capital refers to resources within the cultural tool kit that individuals and groups utilize to shape the raw materials of their lives.[6] Many of the immigrant men and women I interviewed relied on cultural notions of the male headship of the household or religious beliefs about the importance of wives obeying husbands to justify the particular gender relations in their households. Others challenged these beliefs with alternate cultural beliefs of egalitarianism in the marital relationship or a nonauthoritarian approach to disciplining children, which they ascribed to the influences of the American host society. These alternate beliefs were critical in the negotiation process in several households and resulted in different patterns of adjustment with respect to gender relations.

Immigrants also mobilized their social capital in different ways. Social capital arises from resources available to an individual or group as a result of their connection to a durable network of institutionalized relationships.[7] Some immigrants relied on parents and siblings — either in Kerala or the United States — for help with child care. Others left their children in boarding schools in Kerala with the help of relatives who would oversee their education. Some women were able to sponsor the immigration of their entire family, creating a base of strength for themselves. Others relied on nursing networks of fictive kinships, in which friendships from nursing school became family-like bonds as friends helped with immigration and settlement.

While their use of these social and cultural resources within the constraints of work resulted in varying patterns of adjustment in the household, there was a universal outcome in gender relations for all households. There was a reactive reconfiguration of gender relations in the domestic sphere in response to the demands of the work sphere, resulting in a refashioning of conventional patriarchy. That is, the effect of the work sphere on the domestic sphere imposed some necessary changes on all households, so that all the immigrant men had to assume some domestic duties that their fathers would not have dreamed of taking on.

Even as the changes in the work sphere after immigration significantly alter gender relations in the domestic sphere, they also have an effect on the communal life of immigrants. Just as the gendered adjustments in the domestic sphere are made in response to the immediacy of work constraints, the gender relations in the communal sphere are also shaped — but in a very different manner — by the work sphere.

The Effect of Work on the Community

There is a long tradition in sociology of studying immigrants and their adaptation to the American society. Whereas earlier studies done by the Chicago school in the 1920s and 1930s were ethnographies of families or entire communities, scholars of immigration in the 1970s and 1980s have focused on the individual as the unit of analysis to gather demographic and economic data (Simon 1992). Perhaps as a result of this trend, the literature on gender and immigration has paid little attention to immigrant communities.

While most of the current literature on immigration and its effect on gender relations focuses on the private sphere of household relations, references to the public sphere seem to concern only those sites where immigrants interact with the wider host society, such as the labor market. The public spaces in which immigrants congregate, such as ethnic organizations and churches, tend to be seen as part of the private. Thus Pedraza-Bailey suggests that more research should be done on the "private world of immigrant women and their community" (1991: 318).

Commenting on the dearth of scholarship on gender relations in the immigrant community, the historian Donna Gabaccia highlights an analytical problem posed for the gender and immigration literature that depends on a distinction between public and domestic spheres. Gabaccia asks, "Where exactly does the ethnic or church-centered immigrant community fit into this analytical scheme? Were such communities informal extensions of the domestic world, thus ones in which women could easily move and mingle with men? . . . Or were immigrant communities instead the first in a series of public spaces from which immigrant women were largely excluded?" (1992: xxi).

The sociologist Pierrette Hondagneu-Sotelo (1994) conceives of community in the former sense when she argues for the importance of the social context of the community in the reconstruction of gender relations in settlement. She holds that, when the community of incorporation before 1965 was mainly one of men, the bachelor-style living forced men to do domestic work, which made them more amenable to helping their spouses when they joined them in the United States. Consequently, such men do housework without portraying any sense of emasculation.

Perhaps Hondagneu-Sotelo fails to look at the public spaces of the community, where there may be successful efforts to reconstruct patriarchy in the face of forced egalitarian gender relations in the marital relationship and household division of labor. The same Mexican immigrant men who do the housework without a sense of emasculation in the home may not be as willing to own up to this in front of their friends. Furthermore, there may be mechanisms within the institutions of the community and immigrant arenas where gender relations are reconstructed, compensating for the loss of usual patriarchal practices in other spheres of immigrant life.

Although Hondagneu-Sotelo does refer to public and private life, by *public life* she means the socioeconomic status of immigrants in the wider society, and she categorizes as private all aspects of immigrant life. Consequently, she finds that, whereas women have greater spatial mobility within the public realm and greater decision making power in the private realm, men lose out in both arenas. What is missing in her analysis is a conceptualization of exclusively immigrant public spaces that are ethnically singular, where immigrants gather and where social relations, such as gender, are both reinforced and transformed.

Hence, although I do not wish to detract from the major contributions Hondagneu-Sotelo makes, I believe she nonetheless falls into what Yen Espiritu argues is an all too common problem with scholarship on immigration. Focusing particularly on Asian American studies, Espiritu notes that, "reflecting sociologists' concerns with economic issues and the structures of immigrant opportunity in the United States, most studies of post-1965 Asian Americans have focused on Asian American relations with and adaptation to the larger society rather than on relations among group members" (1997). By not examining those exclusively immigrant public spaces, Hondagneu-Sotelo misses a crucial arena where gender and class hierarchies may be contested as well as affirmed. The immigrant congregation is an important public sphere of this kind.

The immigrant congregation serves as the religious, social, and cultural center and has traditionally functioned as a safe haven for immigrants in the United States. As Raymond Williams explains, "In the United States, religion is the social category with clearest meaning and acceptance in the host society, so the emphasis on religious affiliation and identity is one of the strategies that allows the immigrant to maintain self-identity while simultaneously acquiring community acceptance" (1988: 29).

Some of the sociological literature points to the unique nature of U.S. religious congregational space that affords gendered leverage and increased participation for immigrant women. For the sociologist Stephen Warner, one of the unique attributes of organized religion in the United States is that religious institutions play an important role in the empowerment of marginalized groups such as women. He argues, "If the religious community simply mirrors the local patriarchy (or the local gerontocracy), women (or young people) will have reason to escape it" (1993: 1072). Because they afford extrafamilial organizational leverage, Warner argues, religious organizations in the United States allow women to play one patriarchal institution against another through the formation of women's organizations. In her study of women in the black Sanctified Churches, Cheryl Gilkes (1985) provides evidence that such organizational space exists in American religion. Like the Indian immigrant women, many black women she wrote about are breadwinners for the family and able to harness their substantial organizational and financial capacities in the formation and running of women's departments in the church.

Furthermore, in the case of immigrant congregations, there is some evidence that women participate more fully in churches in the United States than in their native countries. For example, Yvonne Haddad and Adair Lummis (1987) argue that the Islamic centers in the United States play an important role in the social integration of women, whose lives may be isolated and lonely without the social events at the mosque. Won Moo Hurh and Kwang Kim (1990) note that greater numbers of Koreans have become churchgoers in the United States, and that Korean women's mental health is significantly associated with church involvement. Similarly, Pyong Gap Min (1992) states that many Korean immigrant women who cannot continue their preimmigration occupation of teaching in the United States find it meaningful to teach Korean language classes in immigrant congregations.

The existing literature leads one to hypothesize, like Warner, that "typically, women assume a more prominent role in the congregation in the U.S. than they did in the country of origin" (1992: 5). One would expect participation of immigrant Keralite Christian women in the religious sphere to be even more accentuated because of their greater economic and social status relative to the men. Yet in immigrant congregations in the United States, the gendered nature of the immigration contributes to making the congregation an almost exclusively male-dominated sphere.

In summary, while the literature on gender and immigration has not recognized the importance of exclusive immigrant public spheres where important renegotiations of social relations take place, some scholarship on immigrant religion recognizes congregations as spaces where social relations such as gender are challenged and transformed. This scholarship would lead us to expect that the immigrant congregational terrain is one where women make advances. However, this literature does not consider the effect of the work sphere on the communal sphere, or the interaction between spheres, on enfolding gender relations in the congregation, and these factors have a determining effect on gender relations in the immigrant congregation.

The immigrant congregation provides space for the recouping of losses suffered by men in the migration process, particularly in the work sphere.[8] Work constraints, which also have an important effect on the domestic sphere, play a part in the shaping the communal sphere but with different effects. Whereas gender relations are necessarily refashioned in the domestic sphere, the communal sphere of the immigrant congregation allows for reinforcement of conventional patriarchal gender relations, creating a complementary balance of sorts through the interaction of the spheres.

As noted earlier, female nurses are able to find jobs relatively easily, while most of the men have trouble finding employment in the United States, leading to multifaceted consequences for the men. At home, and at the work place when they do find work, they have difficulty maintaining a central part of their identity as providers for the household. Furthermore, they have little access to civic participation in the wider host society. It is under these circumstances that the immigrant men turn to the congregational space.

For a number of reasons, the religious congregation is a particularly apt place for male participation and the recovery of status. First of all, church leadership positions are inherently associated with high status since, in Kerala, only economically well-off men from well-known families have access to these positions. Second, the religious congregation tends to be an overwhelmingly male space: ritual and administrative duties lie exclusively in the purview of men. Finally, because the immigrant congregation is a space where members attempt to re-create Kerala—the imaginary homeland—men may appeal to conventional gender ideologies and practices that originate in Kerala. Consequently, in the immigrant congregation a man's status as head of household and prominent leader in the community becomes reinforced.

For the female immigrant nurses, the effect of the work sphere on the communal sphere decreases their already limited participation in the immigrant congregation, for both practical and ideological reasons. Shift work and irregular schedules make it difficult for nurses to commit to any extracurricular activities. Because nurses have little time to participate extensively or consistently in church affairs, by default the church becomes an exclusively male-run space.

Furthermore, the nurses also refrain from challenging the status quo because of Kerala-based negative gender and class stigmas attached to nursing that are present in the immigrant congregation. The gender stigma against nurses stems from a relative loss of patriarchal control over the mobility and sexuality of young women. In the beginning, the working requirements of nursing, which put the women in direct contact with men who are not kin, gave rise to allegations of sexual immorality against nurses as a group. Moreover, the nurses were also identified as low-status workers from poor families, which constituted a class stigma against nursing. Because nursing involved cleaning sick and diseased bodies, it was seen as dirty work. Consequently, the low status of nursing led to a common stereotype that nurses came from families who had no other recourse but to send their daughters away to make money.

Because nursing became a marker of deviant femininity, it was considered even more important for immigrant nurses to stay within gendered boundaries, guarding their carefully forged respectability in the public forum of the U.S. immigrant congregation. None of the nurses in my study wanted to confirm the negative image of nurses as overly independent and bossy women who challenged their husbands' authority, especially in public arenas such as the congregation.

Whereas both practical and ideological constraints emerging from the work sphere limited women's participation, immigrant men were able to mobilize social and cultural capital to extend their participation in the communal sphere. Relying on male privilege and supported by the church hierarchy, they created a necessary space of belonging almost exclusively run by men, which served to compensate for the losses suffered in the work and domestic spheres after immigration.

Yet, ironically, even while asserting their male privilege in the congregation, the husbands of nurses became stigmatized as emasculated and lower-class men for their connection to nurses. The stigmatization of nurses in the immigrant community does not make sense, given the positive evaluations of nurses in the United States. To understand the persistence of this stigma, we must look at the transnational connections between the Keralite sending community and the immigrants in the United States that reinvigorate the old oppressive gender- and class-based stigma attached to nursing.

Transnational Connections

Overall, attempts to theorize the effect of immigration on gender relations do not give enough attention to the important ways in which the ongoing connections to the native country shape the discourses and practices of immigrants in the United States. To be sure, there is an emerging field of transnational studies, which looks at the processes by which post–World War II immigrants maintain linkages and identities that cut across national boundaries and that bring two societies into a single social field (Appadurai 1990; Kearney 1991; Clifford 1992; Rouse 1992; Glick-Schiller et al. 1992, 1995). In these studies, global capital is seen as a menace that can permeate the diversity of cultural and political systems, and resistance is centered in local informal economies. Transmigrant streams in particular are included among the resistant practices that can circumvent the imposing power of the global forces by creating new spaces for the creation of liberatory practices (Smith and Guarnizo 1998).

This literature, however, fails to look at how transnational connections may also reproduce and strengthen existing hierarchies of power. As the anthropologist Sarah Mahler puts it, "Much of the literature to date on transnationalism from below paints it as empowering, democratic, and liberating, particularly in light of other global trends toward the concentration of wealth and power. This subaltern image needs to be tested consistently" (1998: 92). One of my main objectives here is to examine the question of whether transnational connections reaffirm or erode gender and class hierarchies among Keralite Christian immigrants.

Along with the celebratory assumption regarding transnationalism goes the notion that transnational migrants are deterritorialized, unbounded social actors functioning in a space between nation-states, an imaginary third space (Bhabha 1990; Basch et al. 1994; Soja 1996). In *Transnationalism from Below,* Michael P. Smith and Luis Guarnizo are critical of both the deeply embedded celebratory impulse and the characterization of transnational migrants as rootless people, a term "implying their total disconnection from local constraints and social moorings" (1998: 12). My intent here is to show how transnational connections in the spheres of work, home, and community tie migrants to a particular sending community, with its attendant set of shared beliefs and practices.

I argue that the three spheres are part of a transnational social field that stretches to Kerala. Consequently, to explain the meaning of home for immigrants, the literature must expand and discuss the sending community in the conceptualization of home. For these immigrants, the domestic sphere reaches beyond the nuclear family to include extended-family members in Kerala who were pivotal in supporting their migration, and who depend on the migrants for their livelihood. In order to understand the work experiences of nurses in the United States, we must not only deal with the meanings of nursing work as perceived in Kerala but also understand how those meanings are actively reconstructed in the immigrant community via transnational connections. To fully comprehend the participation of men in the immigrant congregation, we must not only grasp the inherent importance of church leadership roles in Kerala but also understand how the church as a transnational organization creates opportunities for the new migrant elite to claim status. Thus, research on these immigrant spheres would be incomplete without attention to the Kerala end of this transnational community of meaning.

Luin Goldring makes a similar argument in her study of Mexican immigrants in the United States. Goldring sees migrants as being embedded in transnational social communities, or "communities of meaning in which status claims are interpreted based on shared histories and understandings of practices, rituals, goods and other status markers" (1998: 167). She further argues that one reason migrants maintain transnational ties is to have a context where they can make status claims and have them validated. The sending community provides this special context because those left behind are able to understand and interpret the migrants' status claims more effectively than those in the host society, since they share "mutually intelligible meanings" (1998: 173). For instance, the immigrant's choice of a particular style of vehicle or of certain other goods may not mean anything to the American neighbor, but the sending community can validate ownership of such goods as a measure of progress relative to a premigration past.

In making these status claims, Goldring asserts, migrants may end up "reorienting regimes of stratification" such that "individuals and families may change their own status, alter definitions of how status is achieved, and perhaps help shift the position of the community" (1998: 167). In one of her examples, Mexican immigrants in the United States, who are leaders of hometown clubs and other such associations, have opportunities to meet and negotiate with high-level politicians from Mexico, who come to the United States for the express purpose of soliciting funding for projects. Goldring characterizes these immigrant leaders as "people who would have had little or no pull in Mexico" but who "now have an alternative source of social capital and power as representatives of transmigrant organizations," which they leverage for social mobility (1998: 173).

My own findings show that Keralite immigrants seek to validate their status claims in similar ways. First, they look for status in the immigrant congregation, which operates under the meaning system of the sending community. Second, they make status claims in their Keralite communities of origin at the individual and family levels and through the transnational organization of the church. And in making these claims, immigrants, especially men, who may have had "little or no pull" in Kerala have the opportunity to reorient the existing regime of stratification through church leadership positions and proximate contact with the church hierarchy. Individuals with green cards have an alternate source of social capital and therefore greater appeal in the transnational marriage market.

While making status claims provides the migrants with a distinct liberatory possibility to alter the existing pecking order and introduce new elements of status, there are limits to this potentiality. First, those on the top of the existing stratification system who function as gatekeepers present obstacles to the migrants' attempts to claim status. Second, even when migrants are able to partially reorient the system of stratification, as in the case of the men in church leadership, they may be simultaneously reproducing other dominant power relations.

The reemergence of the stigma associated with nursing in the immigrant community is a clear indication that established power structures do not easily allow for the validation of new status claims. Nursing is used as a marker of premigration status to hamper the efforts of not only the nurses but also their families to make status claims in the transnational social space. For example, in the transnational marriage market, otherwise appealing candidates can be considered unacceptable for the sole reason that one parent is a nurse. The gatekeepers of old wealth and status in Kerala — the nonmigrant elite — struggle to keep nurses and their families from joining them on the status ladder.

Even when migrants such as the immigrant church leaders are marginally successful in making new room for themselves on the ladder, they may be reaffirming established gender relations that are oppressive to immigrant women. My research shows that the transnational organization of the church allows men, at both an individual and an institutional level, to make status claims through financial donations and leadership in the immigrant church. And while the church hierarchy allows some space for the reconfiguring of status relations for men, it helps reproduce patriarchal gender relations by allowing only a selective transnational transfer of ideas, keeping out those who might challenge established gender relations and male headship of the household.

Despite marked progress in their economic standing, the fact that migrants cannot always successfully make status claims points to the importance of studying intervening factors such as class and gender. In a review article on theoretical and empirical contributions to transnationalism, Mahler (1999) points out that both gender and class are addressed rarely, if not sidelined, in current scholarship. Among the Keralite immigrants I studied, gender- and class-based stigmas against nursing were resurrected and sustained through transnational connections in order to thwart claims to social status by the nurses and their families.

By bringing gender and class to the forefront, I wish to show the multidimensional character of transnational connections. First, these connections provide invaluable assistance for immigrants and their children in their struggle for economic and social survival in a host society that is at best indifferent, if not hostile. Second, transnational connections are a source of resistance that helps reconfigure established status hierarchies and makes room for limited social mobility. And yet, these connections can also help reproduce oppressive relations of power.

CHAPTER 2

Work

Nursing, Women's Networks, and Men "Tied to a Stake"

It is difficult to get exact numbers on Keralite Christians in the United States, given that the Immigration and Naturalization Service does not break down immigration by region of origin, religion, or profession. While no accurate figures exist on the population of Indian nurses in the United States or of Keralite immigrants, a directory on Keralites in the United States indicates that 85 percent of these immigrants are Christians, whereas Christians make up only one-fifth of Kerala's population. Scholars attribute the disproportionate presence of Christians among the Keralites in the United States to the nursing professionals who tend to be from the Christian community (Williams 1988, 1996). A survey conducted in the Keralite Christian community in Dallas found that 49 percent of adults surveyed reported nursing as their occupation (Thomas 1978: 30–31). The overwhelming presence of nurses in the community points to a distinct pattern of immigration.[1]

As mentioned in chapter 1, women's migration and entry into the labor market has relatively recently become a topic of interest for scholars of migration and immigration. While scholars agree that gender relations change after migration, they disagree widely on the nature of the changes. Their discussions, which focus primarily on the question of whether women gain or lose autonomy, are predicated on an autonomous, bounded notion of the individual. In one scenario, the female immigrant is seen as strategizing to increase her autonomy when faced with the conflicting agendas of the household or the pressures of the workplace. In another scenario, her autonomy is limited by a false consciousness that fails to reject the patriarchal structures of control. In yet another, her liberty to pursue her own ends is affected by her minority position in a hostile host society and her consequent need to make the household a bastion of resistance against racial oppression. In all these scenarios, autonomy is an unexamined concept measured by how much the woman is able to pursue her own individual goals unhampered by her relationships to others.

In order to understand how women (and men) from non-Western cultures assess their own loss or gain of autonomy, we must first recognize that their notion of personhood may be very different from notions of personhood found in Western cultures. Keralite Christian immigrant men and women perceive the self as connective — less bounded and always in relationship with others. Following the anthropologist Suad Joseph, I use the term *connectivity* to mean "psychodynamic processes by which one person comes to see himself/herself as part of another. Boundaries between people are relatively fluid so that each needs the other to complete the sense of selfhood" (1993: 55).[2] In societies such as that of Kerala, where the group — especially the family — is valued over the individual, the connective selfhood is valorized and upheld.

I use *connective autonomy* to characterize the changes that take place in the lives of the Keralite Christian immigrant nurses. Whereas entry into paid labor and emigration increase their mobility and independence — both financially and socially — they experience this autonomy only within a set of relationships and obligations. As Joseph puts it, "Connectivity entails cultural constructs and structural relations in which persons invite, require and initiate involvement with others in shaping the self" (1993: 56). While the nurses operate within these structural relations, they are also negotiating and challenging the status quo and, indeed, democratizing the patriarchal norms of their cultural milieus.

Their husbands, on the other hand, lose status and experience downward mobility in the immigration experience, both in patriarchal status and connectivity. They are dependent on their wives in the immigration process and in settlement. Many of them feel isolated without the support of family, friends, and a wider net of social relationships.

To better understand the significance of nursing in this story, I begin by looking at the sending community and negotiations over the new earning power of nurses. Second, I examine the immigration process — the aspects of demand and supply that draw these women into the nursing profession, as well as the importance of networks in helping them develop connective autonomy. Third, I turn to the experiences of nurses in the

United States—the challenges of getting licensed and negotiating the racialized environment of the workplace, as well as the positive change in professional self-esteem. Finally, I look at the experiences of the nurses' husbands as they immigrate, settle, and enter the U.S. labor market.

The Sending Community and Nursing

In 1914, the first Indian nurses were recruited by the British colonial forces under the guidance of Florence Nightingale and eventually were organized into the Indian Military Nursing Service. According to the sociologist Ranjana Ragavachari, the nurses were recruited mostly from Indian Christian communities in the state of Kerala or from Anglo-Indian communities. These communities were relatively more open to allowing women to work outside the home, even in a low-status profession such as nursing. Ragavachari attributes the low status of the profession to "existing cultural norms deeply rooted in Hindu philosophy" that defined nursing as polluting (1990: 15).

The relative openness of the Christian communities to nursing had much to do with the active role that English missionaries and mission hospitals took in representing nursing as noble Christian service. Given that Nightingale's model of nursing was explicitly religious in nature, it seems probable that Christian nurses were more easily trained and therefore perhaps more aggressively recruited by the British colonial powers.[3]

Despite the religious packaging of the profession highlighting its noble aspects, nursing was seen as a low-status trade rather than as an education. In the early years, nursing schools, eager for students, were known to accept those who had failed to complete high school. After three and a half years of simultaneously taking classes and working in hospitals affiliated to the nursing schools, the nurses received diplomas rather than degrees.

Within the Christian community in Kerala, mostly young women from the less well-off families responded to the recruitment efforts of the nursing schools. Many nursing schools provided free education and a monthly stipend to the students they recruited, in return for a period of bonded service by the nursing graduate. A number of women I interviewed remarked that they really had wanted to go to medical school, but that their families had not been able to afford the expense.

As nursing opened up a window of opportunity for young women to contribute to the family income, there was a concurrent change in their status both in the family and in the wider Keralite society. These young women were transformed from burdens and liabilities into financial assets within the family. But because of nursing's negative status in Kerala, and its gender and class stigmas, society was not without ambivalence about this transformation. Moreover, the greater autonomy of nurses was offset by their culturally prescribed dependence both within the family and in their gender and class positions in society.

FROM BURDENS TO ASSETS

The story of the Keralite nurses and their immigration is connected to another story about the transformation of women's worth in Kerala. The discourse around the female child in Kerala was, and to a great extent still is, one that designates her as a liability. In a society where arranged marriage is still the norm, daughters are often seen as burdens because the family is obliged to provide a dowry, or *streedhanam,* for the marriage of a daughter, whereas they receive a *streedhanam* upon the marriage of a son.[4] The anthropologist Susan Visvanathan argues that, whereas the *streedhanam* was ideally a premortem inheritance, it has become a means of contracting marriages into desirable families, with different rates for each economic class. In addition to the economic status of the families, the educational and employment qualifications of the bride and groom, as well as the woman's complexion, are important factors in the negotiation. Visvanathan explains, "It *[streedhanam]* expresses the fundamental severing of economic ties for a woman from her natal home, and her incorporation into the conjugal household" (1989: 1341). As one of my female respondents put it, investing money in a girl's welfare and education was seen as "watering the fruit trees in your neighbor's garden."

The more daughters there were in the family, the greater the burden, since it meant that parents not only had to pay dowry for each daughter but also had to give appropriate gifts when their daughters came back home to give birth to their grandchildren. One woman I interviewed, Mrs. Varghese, described the nature of the "burden" for her parents when she said, "I am one of nine children and one of five daughters. As we started getting older, my father and mother had the burden of getting us married. Our dowry system is very hard, because you have to give to all the daughters for marriage. I noticed when each of my older sisters got married, and each time they had children, they would come to our house for the delivery and my parents would have to give a lot of money. You have to do everything according to the custom. And it was really very difficult for my father to do it." In the face of such difficulty, Mrs.

Varghese explained, she chose to become a nurse because "that is the only thing you didn't have to pay for."

Often it became a family project to scrape up enough money to send the aspiring nurse to begin her training.[5] In my interviews with the immigrant nurses, many recounted that a father or a brother had made the initial long train journey with them to register them at nursing school. As a result of such family participation in the establishment of a daughter's career, the typical family eagerly awaited completion of her training, her subsequent employment, and her eventual contribution to the family income.

In interviews, some women told me they had postponed marriage to first finish building their natal family house or help siblings complete their education. For example, Mrs. Patrose described the collective effort in her family: "My parents did not have a good house back in Kerala, and I wanted to build a good house for them. That is why I wanted to work in the military for sometime more. My brother also was employed at that time. He too wanted to help for the same cause. My parents never asked me for anything. But I wanted to help my parents before I got married." Mrs. Varghese explained her own reasons for putting off marriage: "I thought, you know, when I get married, I will be in trouble. Sometimes you don't know what kind of person you marry? Sometimes, according to our culture, they don't want to help the wife's side. I am not talking about everybody. I didn't know what kind of person I might get, and then I wouldn't be able to do my wish. When I was single, I could do whatever I wanted with the money I made."

Whereas most of the women talked about going into nursing to ease the burden on their families, some who were considered less of a burden to their families talked about choosing nursing for other reasons. One woman told me that she was inspired by the story of Florence Nightingale and had decided in second grade to become a nurse, much to her family's dismay. More frequently, I heard women talk about going into nursing because they wanted to travel. Younger women were inspired by seeing older nurses coming back from the urban areas of North India with new fashions and gifts for family members. As Mrs. Patrose explained, "When I was small I liked to see people coming from outside the country with lots of money and gifts for other people. That was in my mind, and I always wanted to go." One woman identified another influence for her travel dreams: "There were a lot of magazines, and there were a lot of stories written about them [nurses] . . . like [in] the *Malayala Manorama* [a popular weekly magazine]. They are like ideal things, not really practical things. They come back rich, and they will bring all this stuff?" But for most of these women, the focus was less on going away than on returning to Kerala with gifts and money for their families.[6]

Whether they took up nursing to ease the financial difficulties of their families or to fulfill their own dreams, these nurses challenged the traditional characterization of women as burdens. In most cases, they became assets to their families because they used their newfound autonomy to act in collective ways toward collective ends. The financial and social autonomy they gained did not lead to an individualized notion of the self, because the very definition of the self is embedded in a set of obligations and duties to others.

However, there is tension between the autonomy these women gained and the cultural prescription of dependence for women, first on their parents and then on their husbands. When parents or husbands sought control over the new earning power of the nurses, these relationships became sites of potential conflict. For the Christian community in Kerala, young women making a living outside the home was an unprecedented social phenomenon. All the mothers of the fifty-eight immigrant men and women whom I interviewed, with the exception of one, did not work outside the home.[7] For the families of the nurses, the experience of a wage-earning woman was brand new. At both the individual and social levels, this new female earning power was undefined and unnegotiated.

Control over this new power was the cause of conflict between some parents and their nurse daughters. As Mrs. Thomas explained to me, her family did not want her to marry because they assumed that her contribution to the family would be cut off when she entered the husband's family.[8] She complained that they wanted to extract as much money as they could from her, and that they are angry with her to this day despite the fact that she has sponsored all her siblings in their emigration to the United States after her marriage.

In some cases, this new earning power led to spousal conflict, as with Mrs. John, who tearfully told me about her husband's betrayal of a pact she had made with him before their marriage. Because she was the eldest child of her family, one of her main intentions in becoming a nurse was to help her family. She claims that she had told her husband before marriage that she intended to continue helping them. She found that her husband did not keep his word, and this became one of the causes for their severe marital problems. That she had to negotiate this points to cultural expectations that a married woman belongs to her husband's family, and that her natal family no longer has any rights over her. Mrs. John was aware of this expectation, but she felt that the tradition might apply only to women not working outside the home. She bitterly observed that her husband might have agreed to her request before marriage only because he wanted to come to the United States, and she was his ticket.

Conflicts such as these, between parents and daughters and husbands and wives, became the basis for the societal evaluation of nurses as too independent. While the young women and their families negotiated the implications of this new earning power, the cultural reverberations of these negotiations earmarked the nursing professionals as lower-class deviants with respect to the customary gender and class norms in Keralite society.

GENDER- AND CLASS-BASED STIGMAS

Besides their increased financial power, young women experienced other changes upon entering the nursing profession. They had greater social independence in their lives and more control over their mobility and sexuality. Yet these changes too were cause for social stigma. Being away from home and having to make choices for themselves made nurses relatively more independent. Whether or not they abided by family dictates, their increased independence and earning capacity gave them new means to negotiate control over their incomes and their lives. For example, some women talked about their antipathy toward the dowry system. Mrs. Kurien put it rather emphatically:

> I think that dowry is unnecessary. If a person is working and earning money, why should you have to give more money? I am dead against it, but who am I? I am just one person against all these other people. . . . Yeah. It is different if you are going to marry a person and stay in their home and eat their food everyday, and you have no income and you are not working. That is different. Then you give them a share of whatever it is that your parents have given you. But if a woman is working, and she is going to earn all her life, why should you give a dowry to them? I don't agree with that.

As a result of her stance, Mrs. Kurien told me, approximately ten of the marriage proposals she received did not work out for her.

The greater independence in nurses' thinking was matched by a parallel increase in their freedom of movement. Enrollment in a nursing program required that many of the aspiring nurses leave Kerala and study and work in cities far away from home. Consequently, there was a relative loss of patriarchal control over their mobility and sexuality. Whereas a young unmarried woman was expected to live under the control of her father and older brothers, and a married woman under the control of her husband and his family, the nurses had clearly traversed these social conventions.

That nurses were breaking social norms became apparent when they came home to Kerala for vacations. Mrs. Samuel narrated an incident that illustrates the collision of her two worlds:

> When I went to Kerala on vacation, I would go to my parents' house. If I wanted to go to my sister's house or somewhere and it was dark, I would think that it was okay to walk there. One day my father said to me, "This time, at this time you are going there! No! You can go there tomorrow." I said, "No, it is okay. It is only eight o'clock. We [she and her sister] can walk there. It is not that far. How do you think I am working there in Bombay? I am doing night duty. Every night I am walking, crossing the street, and going and doing night duty. So, you didn't know that, did you?" Like that I told my father.

The greater freedom of thought and movement associated with nurses led to questions about their moral status. Mrs. Mathew, a more recent nursing graduate, told me why she did not want to go for nursing training outside of Kerala: "Also a lot of times that feeling about nursing was towards the people that left Kerala and went for their training outside of Kerala. Like even now, you hear of stories of girls who went off to do nursing training in other states, and they are never heard of again. So my parents would not have wanted to send me outside of Kerala."

As noted earlier, nurses were also suspect because their work involved constant and close contact with unfamiliar male patients and doctors. Traditionally, in Kerala it was not appropriate for young women to even speak in the presence of males who were not relatives. For instance, as Mrs. Philip explained, "I could speak to my mother and even my brothers, but not when other men were around. I was not even allowed to go in the front room when other men were around, like my brother's friends." Working in direct contact with men who were not kin gave rise to allegations of sexual immorality against nurses as a group, because, as Mrs. Kurien explained to me, people "all thought we were prostitutes. They think that once you go outside the house, you are doing all kinds of things that you are not supposed to. Maybe some of the people who went for nursing did go in other ways. But everybody put you down, and they looked down on you as if to say, 'Oh, you're only a nurse.'" When asked whether anyone said anything directly to her or her family, she replied, "Not directly, but there is always this talk, 'Oh, she is a nurse.' That means that she is nothing." And in some cases, the nurses who opted for late marriage in order to help their families were especially vulnerable to suspicions about their sexual purity.[9]

Nurses were also identified as being low-status workers from poor families, constituting a class stigma against nursing. Because nursing involved cleaning sick and diseased bodies, it was seen as dirty work. Mrs. Jacob, who went into nursing against her family's will, described why nursing was not acceptable to her family: "In those days nurses were looked down upon, especially the nurse who went to Bombay for school. They were the ones who were doing menial work." When asked what was menial about the work, she replied, "Probably the daily activities and care for other people — cleaning them, bathing them, and things like that. At home you have servants to do things like that, and in nursing school you are doing the same thing your servants do for you. . . . My father was somewhat of a prominent person, and he was a Panchayat member [local political position of high status]. So it had more to do with his dignity, that one of his daughter went for nursing and did not go to college." Thus, nurses who left Kerala were seen as doing menial work, equivalent to that of servants, because, in Kerala, family members customarily took care of the immediate bodily needs of patients. In the large cities of northern India, patients depended more on nurses for such aid.

Furthermore, the three years of schooling required for nursing was not seen as an education, especially in Kerala. Mrs. Peter explained that, before she began her training, she too had not been cognizant of the education involved in nursing: "The general public did not know about nursing, the kind of work a nurse is doing. They thought that nurses do not learn anything medically. Before I went for nursing, that was also the understanding I had. I did not know that a nurse had to study all kinds of medical sciences. I thought the nurses only give shots. It was only after joining that I learned that a nurse had to learn a lot about taking care of patients."

Consequently, the low status of nursing led to the common belief that nurses came from families in dire straits who sent their daughters away to earn money for the family. Conversely, aspiring nurses whose families were not under economic duress met with resistance, as was the case for Mrs. Philip:

> Well, in those days, nursing was associated with the option for the poor, who would send their eldest girl to help save the rest of the family. But I was not in that category, so the family said no way. . . . Then a friend of mine decided to go to nursing school. She was really secretive about it. . . . I found out that this friend got the address for the nursing school from the local doctor, so I ran to him and

said that I was interested in going to nursing school. He insisted that I not go, pointing out that my friend was the eldest child of many, and how she was doing this to save the family.

In the archetypal figure of the eldest daughter who became a nurse and put off marriage to "save her family," the class- and gender-based stigmas against nursing combined, showing that gender and class are inseparable. On one hand, when nurses attempted to achieve class mobility by putting off marriage to contribute to the family, they were seen as morally loose women. On the other hand, the greater independence gained by nurses had a declassing effect because their deviation from gender norms was attributed to their class origins.

And again, the self-sacrificing eldest daughter who became a nurse symbolized the tensions between autonomy and dependency for women in Kerala. The new earning power that she brought to the table was a disruptive force that challenged social norms of female dependence. Parents, siblings, husbands, and the nurses themselves have had to figure out what this means in the context of existing sets of ties and obligations.

The entry of women into nursing broadened their basis for negotiation within the patriarchal system in place. However, when nurses have challenged social and familial norms of patriarchy, they have not done so in a language of rights based on an autonomous bounded self. As young women working far away from home, they stood outside the norm of controlled female mobility in order to help their families. When they challenged the patriarchal authority of their husbands, it was because of obligations to their natal families. Immigration offered opportunities for even greater autonomy for nurses, who carried with them obligations to their families in Kerala.

The Immigration Process: Demand, Supply, and Networks

The history of nursing in India, especially for Keralite Christians, allowed the development of an orientation toward migration as a survival strategy. Often nursing schools were located in the large metropolitan areas of India. Typically, Keralite nursing graduates established themselves in the same area after graduation in order to complete their bonded-service commitments.[10] Many women have reported a further incentive to stay in the large Indian cities: the opportunity to sponsor siblings and other extended-family members seeking better educational and employment opportunities outside Kerala. Saskia Sassen-Koob (1984) notes that the large-scale incorporation of women into a labor market may disrupt unwaged-work structures in a community, minimizing the possibility of workers returning to their communities of origins and, consequently, creating a pool of workers willing to migrate.

The incorporation of Keralite Christian women into the Indian labor force and the resulting pool of migrant workers became a source of supply to meet the emerging demand for nurses in the global market. As families began to depend on the incomes of their pioneering daughters, many Keralite nurses accepted the more lucrative nursing opportunities found in other countries. And just as these nurses had been the first in the family to leave Kerala and had facilitated the migration of family members, once settled in the United States they continued to sponsor family members.

The supportive role of the family during migration is anomalous relative to other female migration patterns. Scholars of migration typically find that patriarchal family systems accept and support male migration but usually act as an obstacle to the migration of women with or without men (Hondagneu-Sotelo 1992, 1994; Massey et al. 1994; Kanaiaupuni 2000). In fact, Hondagneu-Sotelo found that the single Mexican women who migrated to the United States came from "weakly bonded families that provided little economic support and lacked patriarchal rules of authority" (1994: 87). What is interestingly different about the nurses in my study is the overwhelming support they got from a patriarchal family system (and from families who were strongly bonded) to migrate alone. Perhaps this shows that patriarchal family systems can be flexible in the face of economic need.

Nurses had little control over the sale of their labor, since they depended on national and international demand and supply. Nevertheless, they exercised connective autonomy, determining where and how they immigrated within the context of a new set of relationships formed through nursing networks. Consequently, Keralite nurses were part of the transnational nursing labor force that met the demand in the United States.

DEMANDS OF A RACIALIZED LABOR MARKET

In the United States, a number of factors contributed to the demand for nurses. The post–World War II expansion of Medicare and Medicaid programs created a greater need for health care professionals. Economic growth in the 1950s and 1960s allowed more employers to offer medical insurance to their workers. However, the supply of nursing personnel did not keep up with the expansion of demand for health care, leading to cyclical patterns of nursing shortage.

One of the main reasons for the shortage was the decline in the traditional labor pool of U.S.–born women in the nursing profession. Attractive alternate career choices for women opened up in that period. Furthermore, sex-based occupational discrimination, along with poor working conditions for nurses, resulted in not only the shortage of new nurses but also a high exit rate for those already in the profession (Jackson et al. 1989).

More important, as Paul Ong and Tania Azores explain, "the endemic and recurring shortage of nurses" in the United States "is tied to wages that have remained below market level because hospitals, which employ 70% of nurses, have colluded to set rates" (1994: 167). Since the economic crisis of the late 1970s, hospitals have been under tremendous pressure to cut costs by such means as keeping nurses' wages low. As a result, nurses typically reach their peak salaries in the first five or six years of practice. Using data from the American Nurses Association, Ong and Azores calculated that, between 1976 and 1986, real wages for nurses rose by only 2 percent.

Such low wages, along with negative work conditions, have led to severe shortages of nurses. For example, the vacancy rates for registered nurses in hospitals doubled during 1985–86, according to a study done by the American Hospitals Association (Curran et al. 1987). Staffing problems are especially difficult for inner-city hospitals, which are often under extreme budgetary pressures. In addition, they must pay higher wages to attract nurses to work under relatively more difficult conditions than in suburban or rural hospitals.

The liberalization of immigration, specifically in the form of the Immigration and Nationality Act of 1965, was an attempt to respond to such labor shortages in the United States. The third preference category in this act allowed for the entry of skilled professionals needed in the United States. Because this act also increased immigration quotas for formerly restricted areas, it helped induce immigration of Indian nurses, among other Asian nurses. By the late 1970s, immigration of Indian nurses to the United States was exceeded only by that of Filipina nurses and was closely followed by Korean nurses. From 1975 to 1979, while 11.9 percent of the nurses admitted to the United States as permanent residents were from India, 11.2 percent were from Korea, and 27.6 percent were from the Philippines (Ishi 1987: 288).

Although foreign nurses make up only a small percentage of the nursing workforce (4 percent in 1984), they are a critical source of labor, particularly for inner-city hospitals that have difficulty attracting and retaining nurses. In a guide to managing the nursing shortage, Barbara Shockley (1989) justifies foreign nurse recruitment by arguing that hospitals are able to offset the cost of foreign nurse recruitment in thirteen weeks versus the cost of temporary staffing and payment for double shifts.[11] It is the inner-city hospitals that have actively conducted recruiting campaigns in countries such as India, leading to what some have characterized as a "brain drain" (Yamanaka and McClelland 1994: 86) and what others cite as a "skill drain" (Mejia et al. 1979). Consequently, foreign nurses are most likely to be concentrated in the critical care units (high stress areas) of urban hospitals, where native nurses are less likely to work.

The United States has not been the only destination for nurses emigrating from India. In the OPEC countries, expanding oil economies in the mid-1960s led to a greater need for foreign labor, especially in the service sector, health sector, and other professional sectors. Again, Indian nurses were part of the immigrant workforce that was recruited by a number of Middle Eastern countries. In fact, among the women I interviewed, several had worked in countries such as Kuwait, Saudi Arabia, and the United Arab Emirates. Others had spent years working in African countries such as Zambia and Nigeria before coming to the United States as part of a global step-migration process.[12] Consequently, besides supplying the labor demand in India, Keralite nurses have been an important part of the labor pool supplying the global demand for health professionals.[13] To understand why the nurses left Kerala and India, it is important to examine the economic and social conditions that led to the development of a transnational labor force.

SUPPLY OF A TRANSNATIONAL LABOR FORCE

Even while the state of Kerala has been the focus of international attention for its success in achieving social well-being in areas such as education and health, it also has had a poor record in industrial and agricultural productivity.[14] Between 1970 and 1986, Kerala's per capita income increased by only 4 percent as compared to the rest of India's, which rose by 26 percent. Unemployment has been high in the state. Comparisons of survey results over nearly a decade show that unemployment rates have been twice as high for women as for men (see table 1).

TABLE 1. Changes in the Incidence of Unemployment in Kerala *(Unemployed as a Percentage of the Total Labor Force)*

Year	Male	Female	Total
1977–78	14.0	30.6	19.9
1983	10.8	18.4	13.1
1987–88	12.8	26.3	17.1

SOURCE: Gulati 1996: 39.

The severe unemployment in the state has been an incentive for young people, especially women, to seek both educational and employment opportunities elsewhere. Consequently, urban areas in India have attracted young people like the nurses who sought employment in hospitals outside of Kerala after completing their education. For many nurses, the next step has been emigration to different parts of the world.

Mrs. Eapen, who attended nursing school in North India in the early 1970s, described the process to me. After three years of nursing school, graduates were obligated to contribute one year of bonded service to the hospital. While completing their terms of service, she and her classmates—some thirty-odd women—traveled to nearby cities like Delhi to get a head start on their professional lives. They registered with employment agencies, secured interviews at hospitals, and filed for visas at the American embassy.

Mrs. Eapen recalled that, soon after she got her first job, the director of nursing at the hospital jokingly asked her if she had her passport ready, referring to the extremely high turnover rates for nurses in metropolitan hospitals. As Mrs. Eapen put it, "These people thought that we were just there to use the hospital like a motel, because they knew that all of us, especially the Keralite nurses, were only going to be there for a short time. And as for my batch, nobody is left there. Everybody's gone."

For the nurses I interviewed, the question was not whether they were going to emigrate, but where. The United States and countries in the Middle East were top recruiters, but nurses were emigrating to African and European countries as well. A number of factors influenced the choice of destination. For instance, some nurses mentioned that it was much easier to emigrate to Arab countries because the process did not include sponsorship or tests. Typically, recruiters from countries like Kuwait or Saudi Arabia would hold interviews in India and pay all travel expenses for those selected to work. In fact, nurses working in a number of the Middle

Eastern countries did not have to pay their own living expenses and vacation travel expenses, making these jobs extremely appealing.[15]

Many nurses used the strategy of step migration, as did Mrs. Samuel, who told me that she first migrated to Zambia and later ended up in the United States. Her friend, who had migrated to Zambia as a nurse, had sent her many letters encouraging her to come as well. In Mrs. Samuel's words: "The ticket was free. I didn't have to pay for anything. Everything was free, so I went there. . . . Then everybody started coming to America. As their three-and-half-year contract finished, they started coming here one by one. So I started this way too."

Today, Kerala still contributes nurses to a transnational labor pool, as I discovered during my trip there in 1997. In the focus group interviews I conducted with nurses, as well as in interviews with nursing school deans and retired nurses, I learned that the profession continues to offer a survival strategy for many Keralite women. As Mrs. Mathew, a nursing school superintendent in Kerala, put it, "There are about twenty-five nursing schools just in this area [she is referring to Kottayam, a small town in central Kerala]. They get certificates from one of these schools, get a passport, and go abroad. So once these girls study and go abroad, the whole house is saved."

However, even as more nursing schools sprout up around Kerala, with increasing student bodies, the profession itself is in great disarray. To meet the demand for nurses, many schools offer various short-term auxiliary health-worker courses, whose graduates often get away with using the title of nurse, discrediting the profession. Mrs. Mathew explained the cause for the disarray: "Nowadays nursing education just happens on paper — in theory. Nursing has become a business. . . . If they build a hospital, its main source of income is the nursing school they attach to it."

In addition to the poor quality of education, Keralite nurses also complained about the relatively poor work conditions inside Kerala. In a focus group interview, nurses talked about the high nursing vacancy rates in hospitals, which lead to a disproportionately low nurse-to-patient ratio and poor quality of patient care. In one hospital, nurses told me that, for every forty-five patients, there were only two staff nurses. As a result, Keralites who could afford it sought health care outside the state. Furthermore, many of the nurses who had trained and worked outside Kerala talked about the markedly different treatment they received from doctors and administrators in Keralite hospitals. Instead of being treated as equals and colleagues, they were shouted at and treated like subordinates.

Along with its relatively poor work conditions, Kerala is unique in the lack of collective action on the part of nurses in a highly politically mobilized society. As one nurse who worked outside Kerala explained, "Here they won't strike — they won't open their mouths. The problem is that the people working here either need their bond or they have gone abroad and they are coming back and working because they don't want to just sit at home. Salary is not a botheration [consideration] to them. So only we juniors are here for the salary, and most are only here for the time being. Most of us are here on a one-year contract. This is just a temporary thing, since most of us are planning to go to different places."

And despite the continuous stream of nurses going abroad, hospital administrations do not have to improve work conditions to retain even the minimal nursing workforce. Keralite hospitals rely on the three-year period of labor that nursing schools require of their graduates. Consequently, as long as the nursing schools are filled with students, Keralite hospitals constantly have a fresh batch of employees who can be paid very little, since their labor is defined as part of their apprenticeship.

One of my subjects summed up the reasons why she wants to immigrate, given the negative work conditions in Kerala: "Why struggle here and get no money? We can go abroad, make some money, and come back. Staying here, we don't get any respect and we don't get any money." Worsening work conditions in Kerala, coupled with great financial incentive to migrate, result in a transitory transnational nursing workforce with little motivation to fight for better conditions. However, the nurses mobilize to help each other through extensive nursing networks, underlining their exercise of connective autonomy in the immigration process.

WOMEN'S NURSING NETWORKS

From my interviews with nurses, I learned that nursing networks often formed even before aspiring nurses arrived at nursing school. Most often, prospective students would find out about the application process for emigration from existing networks of neighbors, relatives, or friends who had access to such information.[16] The friendships they built in nursing school and at work often determined where they would migrate and what type of job they would obtain.[17]

In some instances, the nursing schools in distant northern India put women in touch with other prospective students, initiating a professional network among the women. This was the case for Mrs. Eapen, who ended up traveling with ten of her classmates from different parts of Kerala on their initial four-day-long journey by train to the northern state of Uttar

Pradesh. It was with these women that she went to the national capital, Delhi, after graduation to seek out future prospects. Mrs. Eapen explained how each batch of graduating students depended on the previous batch of alumnae to help them:

> Our senior batches, they were all living in different hospital quarters in Delhi. So when we went for our interviews, we would all stay with them—two or three with each one, even though we were not supposed to, because they live in dormitories. It was just overnight, though. . . . When we got there, our senior batch would take us to the American embassy to file. To file, you really don't need to do anything, but they would help us. They would take us there on scooters or taxis. We [would] go and file and leave it there, and see what happened next.[18]

Mrs. Eapen used the same Delhi network in her emigration to the United States. Even though her cousin sponsored her, she chose to come to the city where a nurse friend from Delhi lived.[19]

Just as in Delhi, where the junior batches depended on the recent graduates, so those who emigrated first were invaluable to others trying to emigrate. Nurses in the United States wrote letters to India encouraging their friends to come and work in the United States. They told them how to go about applying for visas, warned them about preliminary interviews, and reassured them about finding jobs and living arrangements in the United States.

As a result, many of the women I interviewed chose, like Mrs. Eapen, to join their friends rather than relatives, even though the latter may have sponsored them. And sometimes this made it easier for relatives to sponsor nurses, because they did not always have to take on the burden of getting the new immigrants established. This was true of Mrs. Simon, who recalled that, while her husband's cousin had sponsored her, she did so on the condition that Mrs. Simon would live with her friends from nursing school. Migration scholars have found that, because migrating women depend on female-dominated networks, they are more likely to choose migration destinations where their networks are firmly established, and to choose occupations in which their networks have already established a niche (Kossoudji and Ranney 1984; Repak 1995).[20]

The help did not always go in one direction—from those already in the United States to those attempting to come here. For example, Mrs. Samuel explained how her former classmate in India helped her procure important paperwork: "The matron [nursing director] and the people in that hospital in Bombay did not like us going outside India. They were so mad that they wouldn't fill out the forms and send them back to me.

So I had to tell my friend Rosie, who was there in Bombay. She went directly to them and gave them some money and everything was done."

The strong friendships, sustained over large distances and long periods of time, sometimes appeared to become more like fictive kinship. For example, Mrs. Joseph's decision to emigrate to the United States was thoroughly influenced by one of her senior nursing schoolmates, whom she called Chechi, the term for an older sister. Mrs. Joseph recalled:

> By the time I went to Delhi, Chechi, who was already a nurse in Delhi, had gone to Kuwait. So what she did was to arrange with roommates to take care of me. They came to the railway station, and let me stay with them, even though it was difficult for them to accommodate girls from outside. . . . I finished my training in 1973, September. I had correspondence from Chechi in Kuwait. "Since everybody is going out of the country," she said, "why don't you file to go to the States?" She said this because her roommates who were helping me stay in Delhi, they were already in the process of going to the States. Even though my counselor—my so-called sister—was in Kuwait, she didn't want me to go to Kuwait. She said that is not the place for me. She encouraged me to file a petition to go to the States. She said that she would help me to do that without giving my family any burden. . . . I filed it, and within two months the tick form came. And then my mother died, and my Kuwait nurse-sister said, "Now you don't stay here anymore."

What is significant here is that the relationship between these two women took on a kinlike quality as Mrs. Joseph's friend assumed the role of the caretaking older sister and Mrs. Joseph submitted to her friend's wisdom like a younger sister. Use of the term *chechi* in this circumstance is not unusual, since formal kinship terms are used in Indian society when addressing elders, even when the individuals are not related. But clearly, Mrs. Joseph's friend took the responsibilities of this relationship seriously. She not only proactively counseled her to emigrate, but she also offered to help her financially so that the younger woman would not have to burden her family with the costs of emigration.

Such fictive kinships are not unique to the networks of immigrant nurses from Kerala. Mexican immigrant women have adapted the *confianza/compadrazgo* system to form fictive kinship relationships that help them maneuver in the alien environment of the formal workplace (O'Connor 1990). Cecilia Menjivar (1995a) learned that the Salvadoran immigrants she studied applied kin terms to members of their hometown on whom they depended for help in the process of emigration. Marixsa Alicea (1997) found that Puerto Rican migrants' fictive kinship ties, mostly the product of women's kinship work in the community, allowed people to claim they were related to almost anyone and to introduce friends in Puerto Rico as relatives to their children.

The nursing school friendships–fictive kinships that coalesced into transnational networks were sources of support to nurses but conceivably threatened others around them. Potential tension existed between the prescribed norms of dependence on husbands and extended-family members and the new pseudofamily relationships, which were strengthened by the process of immigration. Mrs. Thomas, for example, talked about how she avoided potential tension: "I obeyed my husband. My friend offered everything, but my husband wanted me to stay with his sister." Thus, Mrs. Thomas decided to stay with her husband's sister, with whom she was hardly acquainted, to maintain peace. Similarly, Mrs. Simon recalled that many women's friendships became strained when their husbands immigrated and could not get along with their friends.

In utilizing these networks, the nurses partly transformed the ground on which they stood, shifting from extended family channels of support to those developed in their professional ventures. Despite the difficult process of becoming incorporated into the nursing labor market in the United States, and the racism they faced, they continued to develop their professional identities by winning new respect for their own capacity to be better nurses in American hospitals.

Nursing in the United States

Indian immigrant nurses, like other foreign nursing graduates, must become credentialed as registered nurses (RNs) in order to work in the United States. The requirements for licensing have changed over time and vary from state to state. In the 1960s and through the early 1970s, as long as foreign graduates showed proof of a nursing education and a license from the home country, they could register to work in the United States. In the early 1970s, an increasing number of states in the United States began to require foreign nurses to pass state board exams to practice as RNs. Passing these exams became a major obstacle for many foreign nurses. The *American Journal of Nursing* reported that 84 percent of foreign nurses failed their first attempts at state boards in 1975, and that some of these continued to fail on consequent attempts ("Pre-immigration Tests Start in October for Foreign Graduate Nurses" 1978).

To respond to the dismal state board exam failure rates of foreign nurses, the Commission on Graduates of Foreign Nursing Schools, established in 1978 in the United States, administered screening examinations to aspiring immigrant nurses in their own countries. The exam significantly boosted the rate of success of foreign nurses who took the state boards to obtain their RN licenses.

Once foreign nurses were allowed into the country, they had to jump over a number of hurdles, in addition to obtaining registration, to become recognized as nurses. In U.S. hospitals and nursing homes, especially in the inner cities, they confronted a racialized division of labor, which I discuss in a later section. However, despite the discrimination and other obstacles they faced in the workplace, they gained a new sense of professional pride from their work.

BARRIERS TO INCORPORATION AND MOBILITY

For the nurses whom I interviewed, the state board examinations presented an extremely challenging impediment for many reasons. First of all, the exams were difficult given the Indian women's educational background. Besides the challenge of language comprehension, many were not familiar with the multiple-choice format of the exams. The five sections of the exam included psychiatric nursing, which was not a part of the required curriculum in India for most nurses at the time. Furthermore, as was determined in the late 1970s, the state licensing exams were culturally biased against foreign nurses, which also contributed to their low rate of success.

It was a financial burden for the newly arrived immigrants to meet the costs of taking the exam. Most worked as nurses' aides, making meager wages with which they had to support themselves and, in some cases, children and unemployed husbands. Paying exam fees became expensive for immigrants when the test had to be taken multiple times until they passed all the sections. And preparation for the exam was expensive because it required separate books for each of the sections and completion of coursework that was not a part of the curriculum in India.

Furthermore, the requirements for the exam were confusing to the immigrant nurses, and these requirements varied from state to state. Consequently, few nurses went to Massachusetts, where the exam was reported to be very difficult, and more nurses went to Texas, New York, New Jersey, and Florida (Williams 1996: 20). In general, the requirements included obtaining verification of their educational history in particular formats, which were not always easy to procure from Indian institutions. For example, according to Mrs. Varghese:

Even though you are a graduate from there, you have to pass the GED. I had graduated from high school and gone to college, so I did not want to take the GED, but I did not have a high school or college transcript. They don't accept the college certificate from India. They need everything in transcript form showing all the courses — physics, chemistry, et cetera. I sent a letter to my family and asked them to go and get a transcript from my college. But the rules are that they cannot send it to me. It has to go straight to Springfield. All these rules and regulations! Nobody ever told me. It took my school of nursing fourteen months to send my transcript. Somebody has to go behind the peons day after day to get them to send it. I had nobody there who could do that for me. It took some time for me to take the exam here.

In Mrs. Thomas's case, her husband had to go to India in person to round up all her paperwork before she could take the state boards.

Because of the difficulty and time involved in passing the state boards, most foreign nurses obtained jobs as nurses' aides in the meantime to make ends meet. Some states granted foreign-educated nurses interim permits to work as registered nurses if they had met the prerequisites for taking the next scheduled RN licensing exam. But in most states the only professional option for unlicensed nurses was working as a nurse's aide. (See appendix 2 for a description of different types of nursing jobs.) However, this meant that many foreign nurses ended up performing the work of registered nurses while getting paid nursing aides' salaries. Mrs. Eapen explained how this came about in her case: "I knew what to do. I knew how to change dressings. I studied in India, plus when the IV bottles were empty, I could change the IV solution for them if they were at lunch or they were busy. The things that I was not supposed to do as a nursing assistant, I was doing for the nurses. Either they asked me or I just had the free time and I used to do it." However, this practice made her very unpopular with her peers. The other nurses' aides did not like the extra work that she was doing, and they would report her to the administration, reducing the solidarity on the ward floor.

Many of the nurses I interviewed found it hard to work as nurses' aides for a number of reasons. It was emotionally difficult to do work that, in their eyes, had little to do with nursing. Mrs. Punoose told me that, in India, sweepers with no professional education did the dirty work, such as emptying bedpans. It was also physically demanding for the typically petite Indian nurses to lift heavy patients in and out of bed. Furthermore, they had to compete with American women — mostly African American nurses' aides — whom they perceived as having better language skills and physical capacities. Nursing home administrators were also less keen on hiring foreign nurses as aides because they feared, correctly, that foreign nurses were only waiting to pass their RN exams to leave for better opportunities.

For those who passed the exam, getting a job was not very difficult, given the shortage of nurses. Once immigrant nurses are licensed, they tend to work for more years than native nurses, who experience burnout and leave the profession earlier. However, even though immigrant nurses have long careers as nurses, few rise to managerial positions. In part, this results from the discrimination that does not allow immigrant nurses to rise to positions of leadership. Mrs. Lukos was an exception among the women I interviewed, because she was a nurse manager. Yet she too spoke about the difficulties of her position: "I have to do fifteen times more than what a white person does to survive as a manager. And my opportunities are also fifteen times less. . . . In order to get the next promotion as a vice president of nursing, I have to work fifteen times more. That's the system."

On the other hand, many immigrant nurses were not in a position to focus on career advancements, given their family obligations. Because the nurses I interviewed were supporting not only themselves and their immediate families but also an extended family in India, they tended to work long hours and use many strategies to earn higher incomes. For instance, they worked evenings and night shifts, which paid a higher premium. Or they worked double shifts and holidays, which often paid time and a half or double hourly rates. Furthermore, being a head nurse means more responsibility with very little compensation in the form of overtime pay or shift differential. Consequently, most of the immigrant nurses, who were already pressed for time, were not interested in additional responsibilities while facing the challenges of a racialized ward floor.

RACIALIZED EXPERIENCES ON THE WARD FLOOR: "REAL NURSES" VERSUS "REAL NURSING WORK"

Indian Christian immigrants are no strangers to discrimination. Since in India many of them worked in the north, they were minorities on two counts — as South Indians and as Christians. Consequently, a number of them expected to find a different experience in the United States. Mrs. Lukos described her sense of disappointment on this issue: "When I looked ahead, I didn't think that my kids had the same future that I did — because [the] majority [in India is] Hindu or Muslim, and Christians are just pushed aside. So I thought I should go to some country where people are treated equally, but it is not so great over here either. I was mistaken."

On the ward floor, immigrant nurses face discrimination by patients, doctors, and hospital administration as well as from their peers. Many of the nurses spoke of being rejected by patients who asked outright for white nurses, as happened to Mrs. George: "Some patients don't like us — our color. When that happens, we tell the patient that in all the other hospitals, in the 3 [P.M.] to 11 [P.M.] and the 11 [P.M.] to 7 [A.M.] shifts, it is only foreign nurses who work. There won't be any American nurses. And some patients will insist, 'I don't want you. I want a white nurse.' Then we tell them, 'If you want to find a white nurse, go ahead and look for one.'"

While Mrs. George described the racial element of the rejection, Mrs. Eapen's story pointed to another dimension of the rejection — namely, the questioning of their professional capacity. Mrs. Eapen worked on a floor where she and two other immigrant nurses covered the weekend evening shifts. In one incident she described, which involved another immigrant nurse as well, a patient expressed his lack of faith in her professional capacity: "So he said, 'I want to see a nurse.' We both had uniforms on. We both had our identification badges. So I said, 'We are nurses. My name is Susie and this is Nanny. We are both registered nurses.' He said, 'I want to see a real nurse.' So I said, 'We have our registration. We are registered nurses. So I think we are real nurses.'" After Mrs. Eapen explained to him that there was nobody else to help him, the patient came back to them later and apologized. Mrs. Eapen was skeptical about the apology, since she thought he had realized that he had no choice and needed them to take care of him for the next twelve hours. For the immigrant nurses who had to overcome many obstacles both in India and the United States in order to become nurses, it was especially painful to have their professional authenticity questioned.

Besides rejection by patients, the immigrant nurses had to deal with the racist assumptions of doctors and hospital administrators. For example, Mrs. Lukos talked about a discrepancy in how a nurse manager dealt with her and her American colleagues regarding a test required for all employees in the intensive care unit where she worked. The nurse manager singled out Mrs. Lukos with the warning that she could not work in that unit if she did not pass the test. Mrs. Lukos found that none of her American colleagues had received similar warnings. She surmised that "the nurse manager thought I am from a foreign country and I am not intelligent enough to pass." While Mrs. Lukos passed with the high score of 98 percent, she discovered that one of her American colleagues had failed the test and was still scheduled to work. She successfully challenged the nurse manager's double standard, and the American nurse could not continue working in that unit.

A number of nurses told me about doctors who complained they could not understand the nurses' English, even though nobody else had trouble understanding them. Although many Indian nurses have English training and English-language nursing curricula, fluency in spoken English can be challenging for many of them. For those who are fluent, their accent can present an added obstacle to communication. Unlike upper-class Indians, whose spoken English is often distinguished by a "British flair," middle- and working-class Indians, particularly those originating in rural areas, tend to speak English with accents identifiable by their particular linguistic background.[21]

Others nurses noted that doctors did not consult with them because they assumed that the immigrant nurses did not know what was going on. Mrs. Eapen complained about a number of instances where a doctor passed her by to ask her white colleague questions about Mrs. Eapen's own patients. When such mistakes happened consistently, the nurses felt that they were more than simply coincidence. Furthermore, a couple of the nurses told me that they felt that doctors and administrators were checking up on them behind their backs.

Another important group of people with whom the immigrant nurses had to get along was their American colleagues. One immediate problem for the immigrants was their lack of cultural capital, which made it difficult for them to interact socially with their peers. Despite not having a "language problem," Mrs. Philip explained, she had difficulty at work : "It takes courage to be with people and talk and laugh and joke like they are doing. I still feel the difference, being with white people, because I don't even understand them. Maybe it is my age difference with the group. Although they are at work, they talk about life at home, like their boyfriends and girlfriends, stuff like that, where I can't talk in that way with them."

This difficulty with social banter affects the nurses' integration into the workplace. Many complained of feeling isolated especially when they worked in the small private suburban hospitals of Central City. Mrs. Punoose, who worked in such a hospital talked about being the only one without any backup in a racially segregated ward floor. She said that the Filipinos there supported and helped each other, as did all the white nurses. Because she was the only Indian nurse, she felt alone. She felt that support is especially necessary in private hospitals, where there are few nurses of color and weak or nonexistent unions.

Mrs. Punoose's experience offers a sharp contrast to that of Mrs. Samuel, who worked in a large, public inner-city hospital. She described a ward floor that included nurses from mostly Asian countries — Indians, Filipinos, Koreans, and Thai — along with black and white American nurses. There were six nurses from Kerala who worked in her ward, and many more in the hospital. She said that the immigrant groups spoke in their respective languages at times, and that the others jokingly chided them for doing so. The social atmosphere described by Mrs. Samuel seemed strikingly different from that in Mrs. Punoose's hospital, but the two cases highlight the ethnic and racial lines of division among the nurses.

When facing devaluation of their work, and social segregation of the ward floor, the immigrant nurses I interviewed resisted by defining the work they did as "real nursing work" as compared to the nursing done by American nurses. The distinction goes as follows: Indian nurses are better at doing the "actual work of nursing" — the practical work of bandaging patients, checking intravenous tubes, and inserting catheters — whereas American nurses are good at "charting, writing, and sweet talking."

A number of the immigrant nurses, such as Mrs. Simon, complained that American nurses got away with not doing the "real nursing work." As she put it, "I see, like, a couple of nurses, not everybody — just a couple of nurses — they come and they sit and they talk, talk, and talk. But you hardly see them moving around and working — I mean, the real nursing job." When asked whether theses were immigrant nurses, she responded:

> No, these are white Americans. They will flirt around with white doctors — Blah, blah, blah, blah — I mean, we don't go for all these things. We come, do our job, take care of our patients, say, "Hi, I am so and so," and we do our job. The Americans have a way of saying, "Hi, honey, how are you? Hi, sweetheart." I mean, I have even seen nurses kissing the patients. We don't go for all that. And the patient likes that — the patient thinks, "Oh, the nurse — so wonderful she is." You know what I mean? Those nurses can act a lot. They get better feedback from patients. At the same time, we may be working hard and we may not be getting that much appreciation.

In Mrs. Simon's eyes, the American nurses can do less "real nursing work" because they are good at sweet-talking the patients and flirting with the doctors. While Mrs. Simon characterizes her partiality to "real nursing work" as a choice — "We don't go for all these things" — it is also clear that she would be less successful at kissing the patients and flirting with the white doctors. Thus Mrs. Simon and her ilk are limited to doing what she calls "real nursing work."

Second, Mrs. Simon contrasted "real nursing work" with "paperwork," which she characterized as preferred by white nurses. She talked about the ambulatory unit — where patients report before surgery — which she said was entirely made up of white nurses who mostly do paperwork. Because the patients in the ambulatory unit are not yet bedridden, they do not require much practical nursing care. Mrs. Simon described her own reticence to work in ambulatory nursing:

> I don't like ambulatory nursing because it's not really nursing — it's like more of a office-nurse type [of work]. Lot of paperwork — I really don't like doing paperwork much. I like to do real nursing. You know it's stimulating — watching the blood pressure and checking the patient's fluid levels. Things like that are more like nursing to me. Ambulatory [nursing] could be boring sometimes. Sometimes it could be so busy that it could make you confused, if you are not used to it. All the patients come, and so many people you have to send together to the OR [operating room]. You have to check everybody. You have to be careful — anything you didn't do, and they will call you. So originally the nurses were all white — in ambulatory, they are all white.

In this statement Mrs. Simon first identifies her distaste for working in the ambulatory unit as a choice. She prefers to do "real nursing," which is more stimulating than paperwork, but she then admits that doing all the paperwork in the ambulatory unit could be confusing for her. Consequently, she and other nurses like herself end up in wards where the work is physically more labor-intensive but requires less paperwork.

The notion of "real nursing work" points to a racialized division of labor that the immigrant nurses confront in the United States. If they fail to pass the state boards, they are forced to work as nurses' aides with other mostly minority women. With registrations in hand, not only are they more likely to be recruited for inner-city hospitals with other mostly Asian immigrant nurses but also they are more likely to work in wards where the work is physically labor-intensive and in areas with a high burnout rate for native nurses (Ong and Azores 1994). And despite the their limitations, the Indian immigrant nurses I interviewed, like Mrs. Simon, managed to find new empowerment in their vocation. Not only were they "real" nurses doing "real nursing work," but also they functioned as teachers and consultants on the American ward floor.

"DIRTY" NURSING REINSCRIBED: PATIENT CARE MANAGERS, TEACHERS, AND CONSULTANTS

Even though nurses were considered to be doing "dirty work" in India, few nurses, once they graduated and obtained staff positions in hospitals, had to clean up after patients. For example, many of the Indian nurses I spoke to recalled that there were ayahs or *methranis* in Indian hospitals — women who did the work of emptying bedpans and cleaning up after incontinent patients. In India, the "direct nursing work" — the dirty work — was left to nursing students, family members, and ayahs, whereas the staff nurse passed out medicine following the doctor's orders.

There is a clear hierarchy of care in Indian hospitals, where staff nurses are second in command after doctors and they maintain a distance from the dirty work as they move up the medical ladder. For women like Mrs. Punoose, it was a shock to find out that, in America, even "the nursing director will do the work of a nurse if it is necessary." The Indian immigrant nurses encounter a different philosophy and practice in nursing in the United States, as well as advanced technological resources that give them greater autonomy and a better estimation for their own capacity as nurses.

Many of the nurses I interviewed brought up "total patient care," a nursing practice that was different from what they had been accustomed to in India. As Mrs. Thomas explained, "Here nursing is about total patient care, the total well-being of the patient — mental and physical care of the patient as well as the patient's family. Back home you give medicines, that is all." The practice of total patient care requires nurses to be patient care managers. Not only must they respond to the patient's mental, physical, and emotional needs, but also they must represent the patient's needs to doctors, dieticians, pharmacists, and other caregivers in the medical team, as well as to the patient's family.

Total patient care was impossible to achieve in India, given the average nurse-patient ratio of one nurse to sixty patients. As a result, it was difficult for nurses to develop any personal relationships with patients. Mrs. Thambi observed, "I didn't know the patients' names. I didn't know who they were." Mrs. Philip noted that, in contrast, "here you have to be very polite to them and take care of them as a close friend."

Furthermore, many nurses emphasized their new role of teaching in their interactions with patients. Because U.S. law requires that patients be made aware of the effects of each medication and medical procedure, it is the duty of the nurse to keep patients informed. It is also the nurse's responsibility to question doctors and pharmacists in case of mistakes regarding the appropriate medications and dosages.

The immigrant nurses I interviewed spoke of having to take numerous courses to keep up with the changing medical field and fulfill their obligation as teachers. Mrs. Philip talked about how much more knowledgeable she felt about nursing as a result: "I think that I know more here than the doctors in India did. . . . I have taken a lot of classes. These are all special courses. . . . Yes, they teach us here. I did not know how to take an EKG [electrocardiogram] or look at an x ray in India, but here I do."

As patient care managers, as teachers, and as students, immigrant nurses are practicing their profession in new and varied ways. Mrs. Jacob put it best when she observed that, in the United States, nurses are like "consultants" and "patients are the beneficiaries." When I asked her to compare her experience as a nurse in India to that in the United States, she responded:

> It is much better here. I have the autonomy. I can make decisions. I can make an assessment. I am not carrying out orders like a robot. I think, and I put my education into what I am doing on a daily basis. There I cut someone's nails and hair because the staff nurses told me to. Over here I know why I am doing it, physiologically. You are improving your circulation if you massage the head. . . . Even though I am told to do it here also, I can make an assessment myself. I am not carrying out the doctors' orders here; I can question if something is wrong. Lots of autonomy.

As a consultant, Mrs. Jacob felt more empowered to autonomously make decisions and assessments in a way she did not feel capable of doing in India. But along with the increased autonomy comes additional responsibility and increased tension.

The legal aspect of nursing in the United States is a new feature for immigrant nurses that has also increased stress in their work experience. Mrs. Thomas verbalized the tension that comes with having to follow the letter of the law. As she put it, "Here, suing comes to mind first, before you do anything. So you have to learn to be very smart, to know the law. If I do this, it is not right. If I write this, I will be sued or I will lose my job. Here it is easy to lose the job. That makes you stressed, whereas in India you don't lose the job unless you really did something very serious, where people died or something like that. It is very stressful here, very stressful."

Despite the added responsibilities and the lower job security, most of the nurses spoke of greater professional gratification in the United States. With the help of better available technology, they feel a sense of accomplishment at being able to "save lives" more effectively. Mrs. Peter explained her improved evaluation of nursing: "Since we have heard the negative criticisms about nursing from our childhood, a part of that is still in our minds. Very difficult to get rid of it. After coming here, there is no way we can find fault with our profession. It is as equally important as other professions like [those of] doctors, physical therapists, et cetera. I don't see any difference."

Despite structural barriers posed by the difficulty of incorporation and by racial discrimination, immigrant nurses are able to find new professional self-worth through their work experiences.[22] As managers, teachers, and consultants in the United States, they have more autonomy in their work and feel more effective. However, this is not the experience of their spouses, most of whom experience downward mobility in the immigration process.

MEN'S IMMIGRATION AND WORK

Whereas, among most other groups that migrate to the United States, the men arrive first, in the case of the Keralite Christians I studied, the women, as nurses, came first and later sponsored their husbands and families. Typically, the men waited in India with the children until they were allowed to join their wives, who by then were working in the United States and supporting their Keralite households. In other cases, single women went back to India with their green cards and found husbands, whom they then sponsored as spouses. In this immigration experience, conventional roles were partially reversed for men and women (Williams 1988).

While the immigrant nurses experienced upward mobility and an increase in general status, especially due to their ability to sponsor migrating family members, many of their husbands became downwardly mobile and lost status in the immigration experience. These men experienced loss of status in two ways: with respect to the women in the community, and relative to their social and economic positions before immigration.

Relative to their wives and sisters who are nurses, Keralite immigrant men faced the prospect of perhaps never making as much money or gaining equivalent professional status. Although in India many of the women worked and contributed financially to the household income, they were not the primary breadwinners. Consequently, after immigration, men's lives became reordered—around the their wives' employment opportunities and family obligations.

A second way that men lost status was with respect to their social and economic positions before immigration. The difficulty in transferring Indian degrees, credentials, and work experience to the U.S. context often left the men in the position of having to start all over again. As immigrants in the United States, they had less access to the political and social structures of the wider society. Low incomes and unstable employment, usually in secondary-labor-market jobs, left many men with few opportunities for public participation and access to leadership positions. Men not only lost autonomy and patriarchal status in the immigration process but also lost their sense of belonging. They felt isolated in the United States.

NURSING-BASED IMMIGRATION

Since women were the primary agents of immigration, their husbands and male kin were dependent on them when they joined them in the United States. This dependence often went beyond the financial aspect to include social orientation in American society. Because they immigrated prior to the men, the women of the community were initially more proficient in dealing with the American society. Whereas some men married nurses with the intention of coming to the United States, others came because of their wives' initiative. For example, Mr. Peter told me that he had forfeited the opportunity to emigrate to Kuwait before marriage because he was doing very well in his bank job in Bombay and had hopes of getting a promotion and transferring back to Kerala. However, he changed his plans to follow his wife to the United States.

Two of the men I interviewed had not yet officially resigned from their jobs in India, even after twenty years of being in the United States. Mrs. Punoose described her husband's situation: "When he first got here and got into the car at the airport, he said 'I am only here for six months.' He had a salary of ten thousand rupees, and he did not want to lose that job. He wanted to go back and continue that job. But after six months, he sent a medical letter stating that he was temporarily unfit to work. Finally, he made the decision to resign, but since he could not send some paperwork, he has not yet resigned. . . . After all these years, he is still here. If he goes back, I cannot stay here." While Mr. Punoose planned to be here only temporarily, it was ultimately his wife's desire to stay that kept him here. Perhaps Mr. Punoose, who has returned several times to India, has not yet resigned because he is holding on to the hope of return.

Unlike their wives, who were much sought after in the employment market, the men had difficulty finding employment. Initially, the majority of the men were completely dependent on their wives, and then usually became only secondary providers for their households. In contrast, in India husbands and wives tended to have equivalently paying jobs.

Consequently, after immigration, the men I interviewed found that their lives were more likely to be ordered around their wives' work schedules and their children's needs. For example, both Mr. Thambi and Mr. Kurien dropped out of educational programs to take care of sick family members. In the absence of adequate child care, Mr. Papi quit a job to take care of his two children while his wife worked. Mr. Lukos spoke of his enduring remorse at not having furthered his education and career: "I got the job my second week here. That was a mistake. I should have waited and evaluated more, but I took a small job as soon as I could. They were nice people, but professionally it was damaging to me. . . . Also, because of taking up this job, I had to pick up the kids and be with the family, and I was forced to do that. That was very costly. I should have gone straight to school — does not matter what it was." The fact that Mrs. Lukos was working and going to school made it difficult for Mr. Lukos to go to school.

The men had to adjust their work aspirations to accommodate their wives' work schedules and work locations. Given that many families had only one car in the beginning, the men had to be available to drive their wives to and from work. Also, a nurse's job availability determined where the family could live. If nurses had trouble passing the board exams in a particular state, the men had to follow their wives to states where the exams were easier for them to pass.

Because women immigrated ahead of the men, they were able to sponsor family members in India before their husbands could do so. As a result, often the women's extended family immigrated before the husband's family did. Raymond Williams observes, "Tracing the network of an extended family or congregation often leads to an 'immigration matriarch' whose decision to immigrate ultimately led to a much larger community of family and friends being formed in the United States" (1996: 203). The family members required not only financial assistance for the journey but also help in getting established once they arrived in the United States. Consequently, there was some tension in the sponsoring family, as husbands felt resentful of resources being spent on the wives' families. Mr. Patrose gave his view on the cause for male resentment:

> So what happens is that, when they become citizens, these ladies try to bring their relatives. In most of the cases, they came ahead of us by two or three years. So they started to bring their relatives, and she is always supported by her small clan. The man becomes sort of isolated. Even if he brings his family, it is a little later than the wife's family. There is domination there. She has already sent money for their

> tickets. . . . All the spending is done by her. So wherever relatives have come, mostly only her family has come and his family hasn't. Nobody from his family is around. Then we know that, in that family, the domination is on the wife's side and less on the husband's side. . . . The attachment from the woman to her family is still there. Normally in India they can't show it. Here they are able to show it to their own family even after marriage. In India, you are 100 percent married to your husband. That changes. The attachment is less. . . . The American society has brought this to us. Basically that neighbor of mine is not worried about whether I am eating today or not. In the same way, I am not worried about him. That sort of individuality of society breaking into pieces is going on. In this particular case, the husband and wife become separated [have separate goals].

According to Mr. Patrose, that women gain additional support from their clan further undermines the men's already weakened position and increases their isolation.

Furthermore, a number of men talked about their own obligations to their natal families. Culturally mandated male obligations to the family include marrying off sisters, taking responsibility for the welfare of widowed sisters, and taking care of parents in their old age. For example, Mr. Thomas said that the main reason he came to the United States was to make money to provide a dowry for his sister. And in a cultural milieu where women are traditionally understood to be "100 percent married" to their husbands, the married woman is not expected to financially support her natal family. The use of resources to help her family takes away from what is available to help his family. Thus Mr. Patrose interprets the women's attachment to their natal families as being individualistic in an American sense, because the couple is not unified in carrying out their culturally mandated obligation to help the husband's family.

EMPLOYMENT AND UNEMPLOYMENT: NO STATUS, NO SECURITY, AND "TIED TO A STAKE"

Upon immigration, most men attempted to find a "small job," as Mr. Lukos did. After acclimating themselves to the new social and work settings, they would attempt to find better paying employment through Keralite immigrant networks. Because their degrees, credentials, and work experience were not always recognized in U.S. workplaces, the men had to retrain themselves in new professions, take secretarial and clerical jobs, or do manual labor to contribute to the family income.

Most of the men I interviewed went from doing physically difficult jobs to easier jobs that required some training, such as electronics, respiratory therapy, and x-ray technology. Some took advantage of programs made available by the Comprehensive Employment and Training Act, which provided job training for the unemployed.[23] Raymond Williams, in his study on immigrant groups from India and Pakistan, says of Keralite Christian immigrant men: "Most of the men who followed their wives took positions in machine shops or factories, or used the connections their wives had in the hospitals to get training as medical technicians" (1988: 108). In an informal survey and in interviews I conducted at St. George's, many men were hesitant to disclose the exact nature of their work and used such vague terms as "business" or "office" when asked about the nature of their employment, illustrating their discomfort in relation to this topic.

Whereas preexisting nursing networks established in India provided the nurses with information as well as help in getting jobs, most of these women's husbands did not have ready-made and lasting support systems such as these. For example, Mr. Elias explained the difficulty presented by not having preexisting networks when he noted, "When you come to this country, you are alone all the time. How do you make your connections? That is very hard. So our own Kerala people helped me get a job."

Mr. Elias's work history demonstrates how he depended on other male immigrants from Kerala to move from job to job. He found a job as stock boy in a furniture store with the help of an immigrant friend. After working there for three months, he got a job as a packer and messenger in another company with the help of another immigrant acquaintance. While there, he befriended another Keralite immigrant, who helped him find his third job, as a worker at a shipping dock. Although he made a lot of money at this job, he wanted to further his education and consequently left this job. Again Mr. Elias turned to his immigrant acquaintances for information, but he ran into the limits of the newly formed network. As he put it, "I wanted to go to college, but nobody knew how to do it, because there were not too many Indians there. So I, who came from India, how would I know how to go to college? It was very hard. . . . Nobody knew anything in those days — 1976. I ask one person how to do it, and he says, 'I don't know.' Then I ask the next person, and he will also say he doesn't know. . . . After two years, I figured out how to enroll in college." Mr. Elias's experiences highlight the shortcomings of the networks available to the immigrant men. Not only were the men all equally unaware of how to access resources in this society, but also they were in the same tertiary job market, floating from one unsatisfactory job to the next.

The sociologist Cecilia Menjivar, in her engaging book about Salvadoran immigrants in the United States, found a similar weakness in the networks of those she studied. As she puts it, "When all members of one's network live in highly constrained conditions, links to multiple social fields that could create social capital are practically nonexistent. . . . Thus our attention should shift from reifying the notion that immigrants achieve benefits through informal exchanges with relatives and friends toward examining the structure of opportunities that determines if immigrants will have the means (and what kind) to help one another in the first place" (2000: 156). The "structure of opportunities" available to the men in my study channeled them into particular areas, such as technical or medical fields. For example, Mr. Mathew explained how a Keralite nurse who was a supervisor at a nursing home became the point person of an immigrant network for men: "All the Malayalees that come from Kerala first go to her for a job. . . . A lot of men would apply for other jobs in factories and places like that while they were working in the nursing home. And when they got jobs, they would quit the nursing home and go."

Because they had to accept whatever job was available to them initially, many of the immigrant men had to abandon any status-related reservations that they had about doing manual labor or other such jobs. Because manual labor paid more than clerical work, it was more lucrative for the immigrant men. Furthermore, there was a leveling of status in the beginning for all the immigrant men, since even the professionals — such as the physicians or dentists — could not work in their professions without passing their registration exams. As a result, even physicians and dentists were working as cashiers and security guards. It was while reflecting on immigration as a status-leveling experience that Mr. Samuel observed, "There is no status here, period. . . . You can't say that I don't do that kind of thing, because you have to eat and you have to pay the mortgage. There I could say, 'I don't care for that job. I don't want it. That is too cheap.' Here there is no way to say that."

While the men were willing to take any job, there was very little job security in their postimmigration employment. Over a quarter of the men I interviewed who came as the husbands of nurses lost their jobs after ten or fifteen years of working for a company because of downsizing or relocation of the company. In the recession of the early 1980s, the ebb and flow of the U.S. economy more immediately affected men in the secondary labor market. As Raymond Williams explains:

> In the early 1980s many who had gained a foothold in the lower rungs of the ladder lost their jobs in the recession that hit the northern cities in the "rust belt" and the southern regions due both to the oil crisis and the recession in the aeronautical industry. A congregation in Houston began construction of a new church building, and six months later half of the congregation had lost their jobs, primarily the men. Such job insecurity was novel for men from India because,

although India and especially Kerala has a high unemployment rate, those who have jobs keep them for life without lay-offs or dismissals. (1996: 203)

As these men compared their work situation to that in India, many complained about the lack of unions or about weak unions in the United States. Mr. John, whose job was a casualty of the Reagan era, spoke about the lack of freedom in the United States:

Even though we say America is a democratic country, really it is not. In India we have all kinds of freedom. What can you do of your own in this country? We are working here. Do you have any guarantee? We don't have any guarantees at all. However smart you are, they can fire you any time. But in India this kind of situation is not there. If you have a job in India, and you have three hundred and sixty-five days' experience, your job is secure. Nobody can do anything against it. Here unions have no validity. . . . If you look deep into the system, you can see the flow of slavery current underneath. The common masses do not realize it. They are using the people.

After working for thirteen years in electronics, Mr. John was laid off and was not able to find another job. At the time of the interview, he had not found another job and was training to become a chauffeur.

Like Mr. John, Mr. Samuel saw the lack of job security as connected to a systemic problem. In comparing his current employment position to his past in India, Mr. Samuel also underlined the lack of union strength in the United States: "There in India, once you are in the register — especially in government and factory jobs but no matter what job it is — once you are in the attendance register, you are a unionized person. No matter what you do, your job is guaranteed until you retire. Here no matter how they polish it, . . . there is no security."

Mr. Papi, who worked at a mental institution, felt there was discrimination at his workplace. Given his background in India as a union organizer, he decided to do something about it. He attempted to garner support to start a union. However, his position was terminated, and he believes that his interest in starting a union may have been a cause.

The lack of job security led a number of the men to speak of a broader sense of insecurity and isolation that they felt in the United States. For example, Mr. Samuel spoke of the absence of a safety net:

When it is good, everything is good here. When it starts falling apart, this is the worst place. If you are in India, when you fall apart, there will be neighbors, friends, relatives there. Here there isn't anybody. That is the difference. That is my feeling. There is no safety net. In India, with all the relatives — even if they don't help or do anything, I always mentally feel like there is somebody behind me to back me up. Always there are people with me — relatives — somebody is there. Here, I always get an emptiness in the depth of my mind. As long as you are okay, healthy, your job is there; everything will go smoothly, and you are safe.

Even if his relatives were not necessarily in a position to help him, Mr. Samuel knew that he was not alone in having to face his problems. He misses the sense of connectedness built into the basic social framework in India.

Others, like Mr. Markos and Mr. Thomas, spoke of the absence of a social life. Mr. Markos remembered his life in Kerala where, after a day's work, there was always an opportunity to relax and speak with relatives and neighbors. In the United States, his sole confidante and friend was his wife. He missed the members of his extended family and commented that, while he was better off financially in the United States, he felt that he had "lost everything." Mr. Thomas, who was a union organizer, spoke about his isolation: "I was a person who was always working with people and walking around, doing public works. So my nature was like that, and now I feel that I am tied to a stake."

My male subjects are not alone in their marked feelings of isolation. The Salvadoran male subjects in Cecilia Menjivar's 2000 study also told her about feeling depressed and lonely. Menjivar hypothesizes that gender ideologies shape the way men and women use the networks available to them. She found that men were more likely to talk about the sharing of material resources than about getting moral or emotional support from other men. Prema Kurien (1998), in her work on South Asian immigrants, similarly found that the loss of same-sex networks after immigration forced Indian immigrant couples to depend much more on each other than they had in India. Likewise, the men I interviewed were less likely than their wives to look for emotional support from their networks. Consequently, men felt alone and disconnected socially.

For men, immigration brings a very different set of experiences than for their spouses. Because they follow their wives, who have stable employment, their work aspirations must come second to their wives' employment requirements. Unlike their wives, who are supported by a network of nurse friends as well as by family members they sponsored, the men do not have such preexisting connections to help them. Unlike their wives, they experience downward mobility and a leveling of status in their search for employment. Low job security leads to a decreased sense of autonomy and control over their lives. Furthermore, they feel alone and without safety nets in a rather precarious existence in the United States.

Conclusion

While the new earning power of the Keralite nurses was welcomed by their families, it also created some confusion in Keralite Christian society. According to tradition, obligations and responsibilities to loved ones governed all relationships within the family. Parents were obligated to pay dowries for daughters and give designated gifts to grandchildren when daughters came home to deliver their babies. Sons were responsible for the welfare of parents in their old age. Brothers were responsible for the welfare of sisters and their children, especially if they were widowed. Wives were "100 percent married" to their husbands and attached to the husband's family. And the husbands, who were sons and brothers, had culturally binding obligations to their natal families. The new earning power of the nurses was a disruptive force that challenged the given nature of such obligations to the family and, consequently, to society.

As the nurses exercised their newfound autonomy in collective ways, they also challenged gender and class norms within the family and society. Consequently, they were able to contribute to the growing democratization of the moral framework of the family and society. Within their natal families, they were pioneers in demonstrating that a daughter is not a burden. They were often selfless in their attempts to help siblings and extended-family members, underlining the value of all women. They contested the assumed rights of husbands and husbands' families over wives, using their selfless desire to help their own natal families as the moral ground for this challenge.

Their relative independence and financial autonomy placed them in a position to question societal gender and class norms. In a society where dowry is still the norm, nurses commanded a market power that allowed them to refuse to pay dowry or at least speak against the practice. It was their ability to emigrate to many parts of the world that made them desirable partners, even across class lines. Some potential suitors overlooked the "menial" nature of their work because marriage to a nurse would give these men the chance to emigrate. In this way, too, nurses pushed the envelope of given gender and class norms.

Whereas nurses' entry into the labor market, migration, and work experiences in the United States helped them gain autonomy, they experienced it within the context of connectivity—of a self fundamentally understood only within relationships and obligations. Rather than simple autonomy, they gained connective autonomy in the immigration process. As already noted, the terms of the existing debate about the effect of migrant women's labor participation on women's status assumes a narrow notion of autonomy. Migration scholars might be well served if they pay attention to the differences in the very notion of self and the fluidity of boundaries between people that motivate people to act in ways that may not be recognizable when one uses a more delineated notion of the individual.

Nurses' husbands' experiences of immigration appear to be the antithesis of the nurses' experiences. These men not only depend on their wives in the immigration and settlement process but also must play second fiddle to their wives' careers. They have neither a familial clan nor fictive kin networks to help them in the settlement process. Their work experiences highlight both their insecurity and the absence of safety nets that is inherent in a postindustrial capitalist society. The men lose both autonomy and connectivity in the immigration process. Their downward mobility raises questions about what happens in the domestic sphere and how men compensate for their loss of status.

CHAPTER 3

Home

Redoing Gender in Immigrant Households

Given the status of immigrant nurses from Kerala as primary breadwinners, and the initial financial dependency of the husbands who follow them to the United States, what changes in the household division of labor can we expect to find? With the growing participation of women in the paid labor force, the household division of labor has been a subject of increasing scholarly attention in the last two decades (Berk 1985; Hochschild 1989; Brines 1994). The intellectual debates concerning how men and women negotiate reproductive labor fall across the spectrum. While some argue that women are still burdened with the "second shift" — doing housework despite working outside the home (Hochschild 1989) — others claim that men have taken on more of the housework over the past few decades (Bianchi et al. 2000).

These divergent perspectives on male and female participation in household labor are anchored in theoretical explanations that also run a gamut, from rational choice theories to social constructionist understandings.[1] Most of the empirical research in this area points to the differing time constraints and relative resources of men and women to explain the division of labor (Shelton and John 1996). The time-constraints argument promotes the view that the division of labor is a rational process based on the work that needs to be done and the availability of the individual. The relative resources explanation points to power differentials between household partners, where the more resources a person brings to the household (such as earnings), the less domestic work that person does.

In her study on economic dependency and household work, Julie Brines points out a weakness in rational choice, economistic models (1994). She finds that "the more a husband relies on his wife for economic support, the less housework he does." Brines explains the breakdown of the logical rules of economic exchange by suggesting that dependent men are not only "not doing" housework but also are "doing gender." That is, in the face of cultural norms that equate masculine competency with work and providership, dependent men may feel as though their gender identity is threatened and therefore be less likely to do "women's work" in the home. Thus the production of gender can take precedence over the most economically efficient production of household commodities. Following Brines, one would expect that all husbands of nurses would resist housework in the interests of doing gender. But I found that the Keralite immigrant men and women in my study relied on a variety of strategies in dividing household labor and in resolving tensions between gender ideologies and lived reality.

It is important to recognize the difference between what people say is their gender ideal and the reality of gendered practices, especially in the marital relationship. The sociologist Arlie Hochschild (1989) distinguishes between gender ideologies and gender strategies to make the point that there can be contradictions between the two. A person's gender ideology has to do with his or her understanding of manhood or womanhood and how that person identifies with masculine or feminine ideal types. Gender strategies, on the other hand, are plans of action that individuals adopt to reconcile their gender ideology with lived reality.

The most common point of reference for the gender ideologies of the couples I interviewed was Kerala. Some women held ideologies that contested the Keralite norm, and they attributed these ideologies to American societal influences. Another point of reference for gender ideologies was religion. Some women talked about the importance of obeying husbands as a religious obligation. In some households, there was a fit between ideology and lived reality, whereas in others there was dissonance. But both men and women used different gender strategies to sustain the fit, or to adjust for the lack of fit, between ideology and lived reality.[2]

Given the men's initial economic dependence on nurses, how do Keralite immigrants deal with the challenge of dividing household labor? What variations exist in the ways they divide household tasks and child care? What gendered ideologies and strategies do they use in the production of gender after immigration?

I choose to define the household division of labor along three dimensions — namely, child care, housework and cooking, and financial decision making. These three dimensions correspond to the analytic categories of class and economic factors, status and sociocultural factors, and power and relations of power. Among the twenty-nine couples I interviewed in their homes, when it came to decisions about child care, economic factors such as whether the couple could afford child care or obtain shift work mattered most. Similarly, housework, especially cooking, was clearly linked to status, in that this was a gender-specific task relegated to women within the household. Financial decision-making issues — such as whether both partners had equal say in money matters — tapped into relations of power. This list of dimensions is neither exhaustive nor mutually exclusive, but rather it provides broad categories useful in examining the division of household labor.[3]

In my interviews, I looked for differences in how each couple dealt with dividing household labor.[4] In Kerala, the division is strictly demarcated. That this was so in the natal homes of the immigrant couples that I studied became apparent when I asked them to describe the marital relationship and the division of labor in the households of their parents. Because the mothers of all but one were homemakers, household chores, child care, and cooking were exclusively in the maternal domain, whereas financial affairs, breadwinning, and the disciplining of children fell within the paternal realm. I next asked them about the division of labor in their own households in the United States.

Based on their responses, I categorized the households into four types. On one end of the spectrum is the traditional male-headed household, where the men do the financial decision making and the women do the rest of the domestic labor. On the other end is the anomalous female-led household, where men are not present or active and the lion's share of the labor falls to the women. In between these two categories fall two more types. The first is the forced-participation household, which appears to be similar to the traditional household except that the exigencies of immigration have forced the men to take an active role in child care. The other category is the partnership household, where the couple shares domestic labor in a relatively egalitarian fashion.

A number of factors explain the variation in the division of labor in these households. I focus here on three primary factors that are significant in shaping the division of labor in all the households. First is the pattern of immigration — whether the husband or wife is the primary immigrant. Second is the immigrants' relationship to the U.S. labor market. Third is the couple's access to help with child care, especially from Kerala.

Table 2 shows that these three factors affected the four household types in different ways, with the approach to child care having the greatest variation.[5] It is important to note here that I am not trying to generate a tight causal model. Rather, this table represents some identifiable patterns in the household division of labor that I observed, which can be associated with certain shaping factors.

To explain the variations in the division of household labor, I present each of the four different types of households in turn. After examining the factors that explain the division of labor in the household type, I present an archetypal family who best represents it. Then I look at how the couples who fall into this category deal with the different dimensions of the division of labor—namely, childcare, housework, cooking, and financial decision making.

Traditional Households

The eight families that can be described as traditional households followed the Keralite norm of maintaining gendered domains in the division of labor. The wife was responsible for the cooking, cleaning, and child care. The husband was the patriarchal disciplinarian and had the final say in the arena of financial decision making.

Relative to the other categories, traditional households stood out in a number of ways. First of all, their pattern of immigration was opposite of the norm in the community. In only one of these couples did the wife immigrate first and later sponsor the husband. In four of the cases, the men came first and later sponsored their wives. Two of these couples came together, and in one case, each partner arrived independently, and later met on a return to Kerala when family members arranged their marriage. On average, these couples immigrated earlier than the families in the other categories, since most did not immigrate on the basis of nursing. Five of the couples came on the basis of student or professional visas not related to nursing.

What is also distinct about this category is that the men were not downwardly mobile like the men in the other categories. Seven of the eight men had a master's degree or higher from Kerala or the United States. Six of the eight men held professional jobs in the United States, and almost all of them were paid as much as or more than their wives. Likewise, while five of the eight women had at least a bachelor's level or higher education, only two held professional positions in the United

TABLE 2. Variations among Household Types

Household Types	Shaping Factors		
	Immigration Pattern	*Relationship to Labor Market*	*Arrangement for Child Care*
Traditional	· Men are the primary immigrants	· Men have high status · Women have lower or equal status	· Women stay home · Kids are left in Kerala with relatives or at boarding schools
Forced-participation	· Women are the primary immigrants	· Women have high status · Men have lower status relative to their jobs in India and to their wives' jobs in the United States	· Men are forced to participate · Couples work alternate shifts · Some child care help is available in the United States or Kerala
Partnership	· Women are the primary immigrants	· Women have high status · Men have lower status relative to their jobs in India and to their wives' jobs in the United States	· Men participate · Couples work alternate shifts · There is little outside support
Female-led	· Women are the primary immigrants	· Women have high status · Men are absent, not active, or have low status	· Women are mostly alone · Relatives and the community provide some support

States. Of the three women who had been nurses in India, only one worked full-time in the nursing field. The high level of education of the members of this category corresponded to their relatively higher-class backgrounds in Kerala. Only one of the eight couples came from an impoverished background, whereas the others had been middle class or upper-middle class in Kerala.

Finally, unlike the other households, these families had a variety of options when it came to child care. These included having the mothers stay home to raise the children, sending children to boarding schools in India, and leaving them with relatives in Kerala. Such distinctive features of immigration and background allowed these families to maintain a traditional division of labor in the household.

THE ITOOPS

The Itoop family is highly representative of the traditional household. Thirty years ago, Mr. Itoop left Kerala as an ambitious young man with a dream to continue his education. Leaving behind his young wife and three children, he came to a college in the United States in 1970 to get his second bachelor's degree in computer science and business administration and eventually a master's in business administration. While he had "money, property, and everything" in Kerala, he was not content. Earning a bachelor's education in physics had instilled a fascination with the United States, and he wanted to see "NASA and the spaceship going to the moon and things like that."

Two years later, his wife joined him, after enrolling their children in a boarding school in Kerala. For Mrs. Itoop, the trip to America was not the fulfillment of a dream. In fact, her dream had been to go to college and become a teacher. However, her father had other plans for her, especially when Mr. Itoop's family approached him with a marriage proposal. Consequently, at the age of eighteen, she married Mr. Itoop, who was eight years her senior. When she joined her husband in the United States, he was still a student. In order to support the household, Mrs. Itoop, who had never worked for pay a day in her life, found a job in a factory. After her husband completed his master's degree in business administration, she quit her job. She did not like her factory job and eventually got a secretarial job.

Despite meeting his educational goals, Mr. Itoop had a very difficult time finding a job. It took him two years to find a job as the chief administrator of a nursing institution, where he still works. After seven years of separation from their children, the family was reunited when the children permanently emigrated to the United States in 1977. However, the arrival of the children brought some changes in the workload, especially for Mrs. Itoop.

The Itoops, like many middle- and upper-middle-class families in India, had a lot of help in the management of their daily lives back home. For Mrs. Itoop, the transition from life with her natal family to life with her husband was not a big change in terms of domestic duties. Before marriage, she claimed, "at most we had to take the dirty plates to the kitchen. We had servants to do that. . . . I was lazy to do even that." When the Itoops set up their own home after their marriage, Mrs. Itoop had what she described as an easy life, despite having three small children. She credited the servants for this, especially one particularly "smart" woman who "used to do all the cooking, cleaning, and also took care of the kids. She was very capable. She used to bring me coffee in bed."

However, life in the United States was a stark contrast for Mrs. Itoop. She complained that here "we have to do everything in the place of servants. Everything! Buy groceries, get everything together, cleaning, and everything. We have to go outside and make money too." With the exception of the activity of making money, Mrs. Itoop had to do everything else for the household herself. Mr. Itoop recalled how difficult it was for his wife: "The men back in India, they don't think of such things — helping in the kitchen. So, I was continuing just like that, and she was continuing in her own way as an Indian woman. She never complained. But gradually, I realized that it is not nice to take advantage of the situation. So, I started to help her."

Mrs. Itoop admitted that her husband became more helpful, especially after the children left home and she and her husband had more time on their hands. For instance, she explained that, if her husband came back early from work, he would make tea or cut vegetables, but that she still did all the cooking. Not only did she not mind the cooking, but also she was critical of the young women of the second generation who did not cook for their husbands. As she put it, "We struggle so much to cook for them. That is how we feel. Do you think today's youngsters will do that? 'You are tired and I am tired too.' She will sit down, and if he wants [food], he has to make and eat it. That is the attitude."

She points to American culture as the causal factor behind the shaping of women who are not "subdued." When I asked her what it meant to be subdued, she pointed to some American women who worked with her, as examples of those who were not subdued: "These women consider their own opinion to be most important. . . . All my women bosses are divorced. The attitude they show at work is the same as the one they show at home." She also mentioned nurses in the Indian community as examples of women who were not subdued, who try to control their men. For Mrs. Itoop, "classy" women were subdued, and neither the nurses nor her female superiors at work fit into this category.

Correspondingly, Mr. Itoop had what he called a "dictator feeling" that paralleled Mrs. Itoop's gendered calling to be subdued. Especially when it came to financial decision making in their household, his "dictator feeling" decreed that "I make my decisions, and that is none of her business." In practice, however, he did discuss decisions with his wife. Mrs. Itoop admitted that if there was a difference of opinion, they would talk it over and her husband would "make her agree" with him, since he was the final decision maker.

Mr. Itoop was also the final decision maker in the important decisions of their children's lives. When it came time to arrange the marriage of one of their sons, Mrs. Itoop recalled, she was keen on a particular young woman for her son. They found out later that Mr. Itoop's prudent rejection of the proposal saved them from a bad match. She used this as an example to illustrate why both she and her children acquiesced to Mr. Itoop's superior decision-making capacity. Much like the Itoops, the other families in this category followed a rigidly gendered division of labor.

CHILD CARE

Because the traditional families did not emigrate specifically so that the women could take nursing jobs, the majority of these women were not the primary breadwinners. As a result, with respect to child care they had more options relative to the couples in the other categories. For instance, four of the eight women in the traditional households did not work outside the home and thus could care for their young children. The other four couples sent their children either to boarding schools or to relatives in Kerala for periods of time. But in all the traditional immigrant families, the responsibility for the children fell on the women, whether they stayed home to raise them or worked outside the home.

The men expressed in a number of ways the assumption that their wives were the primary caretakers of their children. Explaining why his wife did not work outside the home, Mr. Mathen stated, "She is raising my kids. I shouldn't say my kids — our kids." While he very quickly corrected himself to say that the children also belonged to his wife, Mr.

Mathen's patriarchal authority over his wife and children was always assumed in his statements.

Her husband forbade Mrs. Paul, a registered nurse, to work after their first child was born. Unfortunately, he lost his job soon after. When he could not find a job after three months, she decided to go to work against her husband's wishes. At the time I interviewed her, she was staying at home to care for their two children while her husband ran a real estate business to support the family.

Mr. Zachariah talked about the child care issues of their household in the past tense, since both their children were grown up. He regretted having sent their first child to daycare, saying that he and his wife should have adjusted their shifts, as was common with other two-job families. But his wife was not like the other "girls," who were able to work and take care of their children at the same time. Consequently, she quit work to stay home with the kids after their second child was born. Mr. Zachariah did not discuss his own untapped potential to help with child care but pointed out his wife's relative limitations.

Whereas the men in this category were clear about their wives' exclusive child care responsibilities, the women were more ambivalent. For example, Mrs. Zachariah's perspective on the issue of child care was different from her husband's: "I threw away my good jobs because of the kids." For Mrs. Zachariah, it was a series of career compromises that finally led to her staying home to raise the children. After she got married, she wanted to continue her education and get a master's degree in nursing. But instead she decided to let her husband continue his education, since they could not afford for both of them to be in school. When her first child was born, she "threw away" a good job to be closer to home. Finally, she stayed home after the birth of her second child and found it extremely difficult to find a job again when the children were grown.

Similarly, Mrs. Cherian, who has a master's degree in natural science from India, chose not to work outside the home because both she and her husband agreed that she should stay home to raise the children. After the children had grown up, she tried to find work but was unable to do so, because her field had changed dramatically in the fourteen years that she was away from it. She instead found a clerical position, where she did not have the opportunity to apply her education.

While the men, such as Mr. Zachariah, focused on their wives' responsibilities and limitations, most of the women talked about missing the support of family members and the servants they had had in India. This lack led some of the couples to leave their children with family members in India, especially during the early childhood stages. Once the children were older, they were brought back to the United States or sent to boarding schools in India.

HOUSEWORK AND COOKING

Traditionally, cooking and cleaning in Keralite society has been clearly demarcated as women's work. In fact, the men I interviewed talked about being shooed away from the kitchen by mothers and sisters. Consequently, the majority of men in this category comfortably admitted to never helping their wives, resting on the assumption of a permanently gendered division of labor. For some, it was a matter of pride, as in the case of Mr. Cherian, who differentiated himself from many men in the church because he did not cook or clean at home.

There were a few exceptions, such as Mr. Itoop, who had started to cut vegetables and make his own tea and sometimes even wash dishes because he wanted to help his wife and not take advantage of her. Close to retirement and with the children out of the house, Mr. Itoop had more time to show such appreciation for his wife. Mr. Zachariah, however, had no choice in the matter. His wife became extremely ill a few years ago and had to be hospitalized for an extensive period. He was forced to learn to cook and clean, especially since she never completely recovered from her illness.

Another exception was Mr. Mathen, who claimed that he did a lot of work both inside and outside his home. In fact, he claimed not only to help his wife with the cooking but also to be able to cook anything by himself. When I asked him how many times he cooked in a week, he said that there was no fixed number. Rather, he cooked only when he felt like it. His wife, a full-time housewife until very recently, was responsible for every meal, but he might help her if he was in the mood. He did not like to clean the house, especially the bathrooms, so this was also her responsibility. It turned out that Mr. Mathen felt he did a lot relative to his father, who never entered the kitchen. Mr. Mathen, who had emigrated to the United States by himself for his college education, had been forced to learn to cook in order to fend for himself. Thus, in his marriage, while he was not responsible for the cooking, he felt that his potential capacity to do things around the house was greater than the norm in Kerala.

As in the case of Mr. Mathen, Kerala was the point of reference for most of the women in this category. For example, Mrs. Itoop used the division of labor embraced by her relatives in Kerala to explain why it was culturally justified for women to be responsible for domestic duties in a two-job household. As she put it, "Back home, even if there are servants, things are the same. Women work too. . . . Nowadays, to live, both must work. If you compare things, the women back home struggle four times more. They are up at four in the morning. There will be two or three school-age kids. You have to bathe, feed, and dress them all. The men will be lounging around. The women do everything. They make breakfast, feed everyone, pack [lunch] for everyone, and pack for themselves, and run. Often, they have to catch a bus to get to the school or the bank." The memory of her own family's experiences as well as the present lived reality of her female relatives that she witnessed on her trips back home prompted Mrs. Itoop to make the statement "This is our culture. It has always been like that."

While all the women in this category would identify with Mrs. Itoop's cultural credo, a few of them articulated awareness of alternative ways of thinking. For instance, Mrs. Stephen, a medical doctor, told me that her workload increased tenfold after immigration, especially without servants. When I asked if her husband had helped her, she said, "Not enough. Not according to the standards here, but then back home we never had to think about it. He didn't have to help me there." While she accepted her husband's failure to help her, she was also aware of a different set of American standards that she could use to assess his failure.

Similarly, Mrs. Paul, a full-time housewife, was aware of how difficult it was for some of her professional friends who got no help from husbands in the domestic arena. She speculated that, had she gone to work, she might not have had the same peaceful atmosphere at home. She was grateful that she did not have to work in order for the family to get by, since she did not think that her husband would have helped. While she recognized that the men in the immigrant community were used to the Keralite norm of not helping, she reasoned that they needed to help out more, given the different circumstances in the United States.

FINANCIAL DECISION MAKING

Unlike the child care and housework, the decisions regarding finances are traditionally in the male domain. All the men in this category saw themselves as the final decision makers, much like Mr. Itoop. Mr. Mathen, however, felt that, even though he made all decisions, he was better than his father because at least he discussed decisions with his wife.

Mr. Cherian had a different perspective on such spousal participation in decision making. He complained of feeling compromised: "In India, men control everything. Here it is impossible. . . . Here both husbands and wives work. Over there the ladies stay home, so they don't know what the hell is up. So here we have to discuss with them. Otherwise they don't feel that equal." For Mr. Cherian, immigration brought a sense of loss of control over his children and a loss of the social status in the community that should have been his, based on his family's status in Kerala. Having to discuss financial decisions with his wife was another instance of loss of control, despite the fact that he made the final decisions.

Like Mrs. Itoop, the other women in this category deferred to their husbands when it came to financial decision making. They offered religious, cultural, and practical justifications for why men should be in charge. They seemed to believe that things had improved, given that they were better off than their mothers. But ultimately, as Mrs. Stephen explained, when she disagreed with her husband about financial matters, "he laughs and says that he will think about it, but that is the extent of it."

For Mrs. Paul, her husband's leadership was mandated by her religious beliefs. But she was aware that other alternative conjugal models could be the source of marital discord: "I was a religious type, so what I learned was that I should not challenge my husband's authority, but learn to live under his authority. Life unlike this would be hell. We know many people in America who have quite a bit of money. . . . When they are registered nurses, then they earn more than their husbands, and there are problems in the household. They lose their peace."

Mrs. Itoop believed that her husband should be in charge, even though she claimed that she understood and could handle all their financial affairs very well. This was because she believed that women should be "subdued," since it was both culturally appropriate and a practical tactic. As she explained, "We should be subdued, and want the family to be successful. Men feel that we should listen to them. That gives them satisfaction."

In Mrs. Itoop's assessment, women are stronger than men. In fact, she believed that many women play the traditional role to keep their men happy: "I know a lot of women in our society; many of them are very capable, more so than the men. Some don't show it that much. . . . They [the women] are very smart. They give more importance to their husbands."

In conclusion, families like the Itoops sustained their traditional division of labor after immigration because of a number of factors. The primary immigrant status of the male, and his positive relationship to the

U.S. labor market, maintained the considerable status gap between husband and wife. The various options that these households had for child care, including that of having the women stay home full-time, further supported the traditional division of labor.

For these traditional households, there was a fit between their gender ideologies and postimmigration lived reality. As the Itoops portrayed it, the "subdued" woman and the man with a "dictator feeling" complemented each other. It was relatively more difficult for the women of the traditional households, who relied on a variety of gender strategies, to sustain this fit in the face of postimmigration changes. Without the additional help of servants or relatives in the United States, women in traditional households "threw away" good jobs or chose not to work, because they felt exclusively responsible for the domestic realm. And while immigration and entry into the U.S. labor market may have made them more ambivalent about the traditional division of labor, many of these women continued playing a traditional role to keep their men happy.

Kerala became the reference point by which they justified their level of participation in household labor. For example, Mr. Mathen felt that relative to his father, he did a lot of work around the house, while in actuality his wife was still doing the lion's share. Or Mrs. Itoop, reflecting on the current "second shift" struggles of her female relatives in Kerala, postulated that immigrant and second-generation women should accept their cultural obligations to do likewise. For these traditional households, Kerala was the measure by which they assessed and adjusted to the changes in their lives.

It is important to note that, with only one exception, none of the women in the traditional households were full-time nurses. When wives are nurses, and men have lower status in the U.S. job market, there is a reluctant accommodation in the household. When men have to participate in child care, forced-participation households occur.

Forced-Participation Households

As in traditional households, in the eight families who fell into the forced-participation category the wife did the cooking and cleaning, and the husband was in charge of the finances. Where they differed was in the area of child care. In these households, the husband was forced to share child care duties because the couples did not have the choices that were available to the traditional householders.

The women in this category were the primary immigrants, and all of them immigrated to work as nurses. Unlike in the traditional households, these couples experienced a gendered reversal in their relationship to the U.S. labor market. All the women in this category were registered nurses, except for one who was in the process of taking her board exams and another who did not pass her boards and who worked as a medical technician. The men in this group ranged widely in their educational and occupational backgrounds. Four of the eight men had college degrees from India, although only one, an engineer, was able to get a job suited to his credentials in the United States. Most of the men were doing technical or clerical work. The majority of them had uneven job histories, with periods of unemployment and moderately successful attempts to start their own businesses.

These couples subscribed to the traditional division of labor in the household, but the men were forced to contribute to child care because they had few other choices. They were not able to survive on a single income, and in some cases, despite leaving children for periods of time in Kerala, the men still have had to participate in child care in a substantial way. The Thambi family exemplified the challenges faced by the forced-participation households.

THE THAMBIS

Mrs. Thambi's emigration to the United States was the fulfillment of her father's dream and the fruit of his planning. She became interested in nursing as a ten-year-old after she got her first vaccination. As she recalled, "You know, when you get vaccinated, you get a bump. Well, my sisters would do the poking [they pretended to give shots], and I would bandage it up. From then on, they said I should be a nurse, and I agreed." After her nursing training, it was her father who "talked a lot and thought a lot about America." In fact, it became a family enterprise to find a way to send Mrs. Thambi, the eldest of eight children, to America. Her brother searched newspapers and magazines for advertisements put in by American hospitals and sent inquiries to them concerning job openings for his sister. Her father found a friend in America who was able to sponsor her, and she emigrated to the United States in 1975.

A year after her arrival, she went back to Kerala for an arranged marriage. Mr. Thambi, who was working in the United Arab Emirates, had two bachelor's degrees, in physics and education. He had been a high school science teacher in North India and had emigrated to the United

Arab Emirates as a bank employee. A year after their marriage, he joined his wife in the United States. Unhappy with his first two jobs here, as a security guard and a cashier, he tried to study respiratory therapy but had to drop out of the program because of the illness of one of his children. Finally, after working as a data processor for a period, he found a new job as a computer operator.

The birth of their first child, Julia, brought a critical change to the lives of the Thambis. Julia was born with life-threatening problems. Treatment included multiple surgeries and eventually a kidney transplant. Julia needed care and attention twenty-four hours a day. The Thambis worked out their schedules so that one of them was always home with the children. They could not afford to have Mrs. Thambi quit her job, since she was the primary breadwinner. But Mr. Thambi told me that it was really important to him that his wife be home when the kids came back from school. Consequently, he chose to work an evening shift to allow his wife to be there for the kids in the evening.

The Thambis worked out a seemingly traditional division of labor in their household. However, there was a self-conscious and forced nature to this arrangement. Both were aware of the shift of power in the relationship and made concerted efforts to match their practices to their traditional ideology. For instance, Mrs. Thambi asserted that she was exclusively responsible for the cooking and cleaning because her husband "does not know how to cook or clean." Because he did not know how to make coffee, she had to wake up earlier to do this for him before she left for work at five-thirty in the morning. She had given up on trying to teach him, since he refused to learn.

Yet there is a corresponding way in which Mrs. Thambi also refused to learn something. She told me, "He does not know the ABCDs of cooking. On the other hand, I don't know anything about billing." When asked if that was by choice, she replied, "Maybe I don't want to learn." When pressed further, she responded, "I don't like it. . . . I just go to work and get my paycheck. I don't even know how much I make a year. I don't want to know anything about money."

Later in the interview, as we discussed the different experiences of men and women in the immigration process, Mrs. Thambi's comments illuminated the reason for her self-elected ignorance regarding money matters. She said, "I think they [the men] feel a little insecure when they don't have jobs. If they don't have jobs — If they have jobs, I don't know. . . . If he [her husband] makes much less money, he may [feel insecure]. I never give him a chance to feel that way." When I asked how she thought she did this, she replied, "I mean—I don't know—in the first place, I don't talk about salary—'You make this much?' or 'I make this much.'" I asked if her husband took care of all the money issues, and she said, "Yeah, I don't ask him about that. I don't tell him about that. When the income tax comes, I ask, 'So how much did I make?' I don't know exactly how much I make. I don't know where the bank accounts are. Like sometimes I say, if something were to happen, I don't even know where the bank is. I don't think he feels that way [insecure]." When I asked whether she consciously made an effort to not make him feel that way, she replied that she did.

Despite Mrs. Thambi's concerted effort to not participate in financial matters, her husband was aware that his wife's working outside the home had changed the balance of power relative to how it would have been in Kerala. He said that he was trying to run his household like his father ran his natal household. Perhaps this is why he said, "I really like it that I don't think that she has any idea about financial matters. . . . I don't know if she ever paid any attention. I really never heard her." He was not sure how much his wife knew about financial matters, but he liked to think that she did not know much. However, Mr. Thambi struggled to articulate why he felt the need to be in control of their finances: "Ours is a male dominated society, right? I always like to get a little more money than her. I don't know why I like it. . . . It's not the money itself. When she makes more money, I feel a little inferior. I don't know why. . . . I want to manage the home in a comfortable way. I want to be the head of the household. I like it that way. I don't know why. I am not sure about it." Mr. Thambi's desire to be the head of the household is much like Mr. Itoop's "dictator feeling." But Mr. Thambi is a lot less comfortable with it, especially given his awareness of male domination and his wife's bigger paychecks.

Mr. Thambi's headship is something that Mrs. Thambi accepts. Before marriage, her father was in charge of her life and she sent all her money to him to help the family. After marriage, she was not able to send as much money as she wanted because, "once you are married, they own you." While her husband supported her in sponsoring the immigration of her seven siblings, it became a problem when she wanted to send money every month to her parents.

Her relationship to her natal family and her desire to keep sending them money was one of the issues they had to confront. She resolved it by deciding that all women had this problem after marriage, and that it was not right on her part to want to do more than other people. She accepted that framework because she believed that women should always be subservient to their husbands. This belief is similar to Mrs. Itoop's notion that women should be subdued, but Mrs. Thambi had to deliberately change her behavior to match her ideology, especially regarding financial decision making. While she believed in the traditional division of labor, she was not able to maintain the traditional ideals when it came to child care. Her husband confirmed that looking after the kids was the main change for him relative to his father's role in the natal family.

CHILD CARE

While some of the traditional families immigrated at a stage when their children were older and could take care of themselves, all of the forced-participation families had to face the problem of child-care arrangements for their infant offspring. The most typical solution employed by these couples was to juggle their work schedules so that one of the parents was always home. Because shift work is available to nurses, many women I interviewed worked evening or night shifts while their husbands worked during the day, or vice versa.

Three of the eight families opted to take their infant children to India, where grandparents or other relatives took care of them for a few years. For instance, Mrs. Joseph left her kids with her husband's parents for two years while she studied for her nursing license exam. A couple of people talked about how relatives they had sponsored were able to help out with child care, as was the case for Mrs. Peters. However, a majority of the couples, especially the men, complained about the difficulty presented by child care.

Couples lived like strangers for years — hardly seeing each other, as one handed off the child care baton to the other between work shifts. But sometimes rearranging schedules did not take care of overlapping periods when the children needed supervision. Mr. and Mrs. Papi found themselves in such a predicament. For a while they relied on the generosity of neighboring Malayalee immigrant families who were in the same boat. Eventually, because they could not work out their scheduling overlap, Mr. Papi had to quit his job and look for one that would accommodate their child care needs.

It is interesting that the overwhelming majority of the families in my sample did not use nannies, housekeepers, or day care centers. In my observation, financial considerations and discomfort at allowing outsiders in their homes, caring for their children, were reasons for their not relying on such help. Furthermore, as one commentator contends, "Religious, cultural and linguistic traditions thus prevent such South Asian families in the United States from using McDonald's, European nannies, or microwave ovens as comfortably as a white family, even if they can afford it" (Shah 1998). Consequently, they got around these obstacles by adjusting shift work or by leaving children with family or friends in Kerala or the United States.

These are not uncommon strategies for immigrant communities. Studies of West Indians in the United States indicate that these immigrants often leave their children behind in the home country with relatives or friends, relying on what Isa Soto calls "child fostering" and Christine Ho refers to as "child minding" (Soto 1987: 131; Ho 1993: 36). Among Latina immigrant women, Pierrette Hondagneu-Sotelo and Ernestine Avila (1997) found a pattern of "transnational mothering," where women leave their children behind in their home countries and work as nannies in the United States, taking care of other people's children.

The men I interviewed talked about their involvement in child care as one of the biggest changes relative to their own fathers' roles in the household. Mr. Elias exemplifies their view when he yearned for a past where mothers were the exclusive caretakers of children: "Back home, taking care of the kids means, when they get back from the school, ask them to go and study. That is it. Here you have to change diapers, give them bath[s], help them dress, and the day is gone. Back home, even if the father and mother are there, mother stays at home and father works outside. Mother takes care of the kids. Mother is the one who forms the character of the kids. Here, the mother works outside the home, and so that is left to the father. That is the biggest difference here. Back home it is the mother's sole responsibility. Isn't it? . . . Here it is the opposite."

Additionally, in Kerala, the role of the disciplinarian was the jurisdiction of the father. It appears that the mother may have taken over some of this role in the U.S. setting. In an informal discussion I had with four immigrant nurses, children's disciplining became a topic of discussion. All the women agreed that the kids came to them for permission to do things, but that this was the cause of conflict with husbands, who were consistently more conservative, especially when it came to daughters. Mrs. Varkey theorized that perhaps mothers were better able to relate to their American-born children because they studied American psychology for their registered nurse licensing exams, which enhanced their understanding of American culture.

Living in a culture where children are encouraged to question authority, the immigrant first generation has to tolerate attitudes and behaviors in their own children that are disrespectful by Indian standards. It is especially poignant for the fathers in this category, who not only lose their unchallenged patriarchal status but also become partially responsible for forming the character of their children. This raises a question: if child care is forced upon the husbands, what is the consequence for the other dimensions of the household division of labor? Does it mean that the men reassert their authority even more emphatically in the areas of housework and cooking and financial decision making?

HOUSEWORK AND COOKING

For all of these families, cooking and housework was clearly designated as female labor. The most popular standard of measurement when it came to male cooking skills was the ability to make a cup of coffee. Many of the men claimed coffee making as the sole item in their repertoire of cooking skills. Whereas Mrs. Thambi asserted that her husband refused to learn to make even a cup of coffee, Mr. Thambi, like his contemporaries, claimed coffee making as his only cooking skill. While the truth about Mr. Thambi's coffee-making abilities may never be established, it is clear that his wife, along with all the other women in this category, was responsible for the cooking.

Like Mrs. Thambi, most of the women accepted their role as the food preparation specialist in the household. They gave different reasons for their exclusive expertise in this household task. For example, both Mrs. Varkey and Mrs. Elias cited their husbands' busy work schedules as the main cause for the men's lack of interest in cooking. As Mrs. Varkey explained, "Engineering association meetings. He is very busy with this."

Mrs. Peter gave a number of reasons for her husband not knowing how to cook. At first she said that he had no interest in or talent for cooking. I asked if it was true that she would not let him into the kitchen as he claimed. Finally, she expanded on her resistance to her husband's presence in the kitchen: "It makes me uncomfortable to see a man cook. He is not used to doing it. I don't think he has any experience doing it."

Mrs. Papi was more forthright about her reasons for not wanting her husband to cook: "Everyday I have to cook something. If I am sick, he will cook. Otherwise, I will do everything. I don't like him to do it on a daily basis. . . . When I am not here, for the kids he makes [meals]. This is not the way men in our country behave." She believed that, to keep up tradition, she could not let her husband cook. But she was sometimes forced to ask him for help, given the lack of auxiliary support from relatives or servants in the United States.

Mr. Papi was unique in this category because he liked to cook. He often cooked with a group of men for church functions. But he recognized that his wife did not like him to cook every day. Furthermore, he claimed that she enjoyed cooking as creative release from the tension of work. Consequently, he limited himself to helping her on special occasions.

Whether it was because men like Mr. Thambi refused to learn to cook, or because others like Mr. Papi had to restrict themselves, in this category of immigrant households, cooking was a female preoccupation. However, other types of housework seemed to be less rigidly cordoned off in these households. Washing dishes and laundry were examples of tasks with which some of the men acknowledged helping women. Mr. Joseph explained why this might be the case: "When she has to work, she has to go. I have to take care of the home, and take care of the kids. Some of my friends, they have to cook. Some of the ladies work two jobs. . . . The man of the house may not have a job. So they take care of the kids. They even cook. I didn't have that kind of hardship. When my wife was away at work, I used to change the diapers, wash the dishes once in a while. These things are not acceptable back home, but there is no choice." Relative to some of his friends, who had to cook, Mr. Joseph felt that his lot was not so bad, which perhaps made it easier for him to occasionally wash dishes.

FINANCIAL DECISION MAKING

Like cooking, financial decision making was a clearly gendered task among the forced-participation households. Both men and women noted that women would bring home paychecks but that their husbands endorsed the checks. They claimed that the women did not even know how much they made. This pattern was consistent with Mrs. Thambi's claims about not knowing anything about financial matters.

What was striking about the women in this category was that, with one exception, they did not talk about disagreements with their husbands regarding financial matters. Mrs. Peter was representative of the women when she described how she and her husband dealt with financial matters. After her marriage and his arrival in this country, "everything shifted to him. He had the responsibility to become the head of the household. That is the way that I thought. So I handed over everything to him. . . . He thinks that he is the man and he should take care of me. That is the way he thinks."

While the women in the traditional household category, like Mrs.

Itoop, also adhere to the model of male leadership, they talked about disagreements and critiqued their husbands. They seemed aware of alternate, American, standards of spousal involvement and compliance by which they could judge their husbands. They justified their own behavior as owing to religion, culture, or practical strategies. In sharp contrast, the women in the forced-participation category consistently resorted to espousing what seemed like the party line: " I don't know how much I make. I don't even sign my paycheck." It seemed as if they, like Mrs. Thambi, had self-consciously decided on a hands-off policy when it came to finances.

Some of the women expressed their good fortune at having found trustworthy and cooperative husbands who were also good money managers. For these women, the measure of the goodness of their husbands was the extent to which they let the women help their natal families. For instance, Mrs. George observed, "I am really lucky. I have no complaints. If I need to do something for my family, if they are in trouble or something, he helps them. My sister needed some money, and he gave it to her. You know, some Indian men, they don't do anything for the wife's family. He is not that type."

The one exception was Mrs. Elias, who seemed to be frustrated by her husband. Even though she felt he gave her what she needed, she was dissatisfied with the unilateral decisions he made regarding the investment of their money. Mr. Elias agreed that he made all the decisions and did not take his wife's opinions into account, partly because she did not have the confidence he possessed in financial matters. She complained that he regularly sent a lot of money to his relatives in Kerala and even constructed a house there without consulting her. She felt that he loved his relatives in Kerala more than his own children. But even she presumed his headship in the conjugal relationship.

For the men in this category, forced involvement in child care and to some extent in housework undermined their sense of themselves as men and as heads of their households. Additionally their headship became even more vulnerable when their wives earned more than them on average. Consequently, the men compensated by exerting their patriarchal privilege in refusing to do household labor other than child care.

Mr. Papi attempted to justify a tenuous ideology of male headship when he said, "In family life, my thinking is always that the man should be the leader. That does not mean that he should flaunt his power. She is equal to him, but still, you know, that man should be 'first among the equals.' Somebody has to take leadership, and in the ancient world, history shows that man has always had this role." On one hand, Mr. Papi relied on historical tradition to argue that men have always been the leaders in the home, yet he was faced with the reality that his wife was equal to him. Like Mr. Thambi, he struggled to establish a justification for his leadership, leaning on the weak proposition that he was first among equals as a result of his gender privilege.

In conclusion, for the forced-participation households, the primary immigration of the women, their relative success, and the stability of their jobs challenged the traditional power dynamic in the household. The men's difficulty with finding jobs and maintaining stable employment in the United States underlined the precariousness of their positions as traditional heads of the household. Their position was further jeopardized when they were forced to get their hands dirty doing child care instead of doling out doses of patriarchal discipline from a symbolic distance.

Whereas there was a fit between ideology and practice in the traditional households, there was dissonance in the forced-participation households. Mrs. Thambi and others like her responded to the dissonance by adopting the gender strategy of ignoring the reality of their relative economic success. By not knowing how much they made and by not signing their paychecks, these women consciously chose to play down what threatened their traditional ideology and their husbands.[6]

Despite such efforts on the part of their wives, men such as Mr. Thambi and Mr. Papi were ill at ease as head of household. They struggled to articulate why they should occupy the position. Some, like Mr. Thambi, had to give up plans for education, and others, like Mr. Papi, had to work out child care arrangements for their households. Faced with the reality that their jobs or career goals were secondary to those of their wives, and that they consequently became responsible for child care, these men had difficulty articulating their positions as head of household.

The reversal of status between husbands and wives in the forced-participation households compelled both to make adjustments against ideology, but the tension between ideology and practice remained unresolved. There is another response to the reversal of status between husband and wife — namely, that the ideology itself shifts to egalitarianism.

Partnership Households

The eight households that make up this category took a different approach to the division of household labor. Each couple shared the housework and cooking, the child care, and the financial decision making. They talked about this sharing as a necessary and logical adaptation made in the face of changes in lifestyle resulting from immigration.

The men were very involved in raising their children, and they did not complain about it. In a couple of cases, the men seem to cook more frequently than their wives. None of them claimed headship of the household, despite their being raised with this prevalent ideology in Kerala.

As in the forced-participation households, the women in this category were the primary immigrants, and these couples also experienced a reversal in status with respect to the labor market. All the women were registered nurses. Two of the eight had bachelor's degrees in nursing from India. One had gone on to get a master's degree in public health. On average, they were positive about their professional status. In contrast, almost all the men felt extremely negative about their occupational experiences in this country, and most experienced a loss of status at work.

The majority of these families did not leave their children in India or get much help from their relatives. In fact, only one couple left their children in Kerala with their parents. Consequently, the men did not have much choice but to contribute to child care. Perhaps as a result, these couples were more dependent on each other and seemed to be better friends with each other, as in the case of the Eapens, who exemplified the compromises of the partnership household.

THE EAPENS

Unlike Mrs. Thambi, who began by playing nurse in childhood, Mrs. Eapen harbored a different dream. She wanted to become a teacher, but financial obstacles prevented her from pursuing this career. Even had her parents been able to manage the fees for the teacher's training course, they did not have the huge sums of mandatory "donation" money required for her to obtain a job in Kerala. Consequently, she made a practical decision and chose a nursing education in North India, where a job was guaranteed upon graduation. But even before she and all her fellow graduates looked for jobs locally, they filed for employment immigration visas at the American embassy and other embassies. In a little over a year, she got a job in the United States, and she arrived here in 1976, after being sponsored by her cousin.

Three years later, she was back in Kerala because her marriage had been arranged with Mr. Eapen, who was himself waiting to emigrate to Kuwait. Because he could not find a job in Kerala despite a bachelor's degree in mathematics, his sister had promised to take him to Kuwait. After marriage, he emigrated to the United States and tried his hand at a few jobs, and ended up doing manual labor in a factory.

Mr. Eapen had a difficult time with this transition. His wife, who had not yet passed her licensing exam to become a registered nurse, was working as a nursing assistant. She became pregnant soon after his arrival, and he had to continue working to help make ends meet. When she finally got her license two years later, Mr. Eapen was able to quit the factory job. He was unemployed for a few years while he studied respiratory therapy part-time, but ultimately he got a job as a respiratory therapist.

Despite some improvement in his work conditions, he was unhappy with the quality of life in the United States, which he described as being full of tension. The biggest points of tension were child care and family life. Like many couples, he and his wife arranged their work schedule in alternating shifts so that somebody was always with the children. But, as he explained, this arrangement left him unsatisfied: "When the husband is at home, the wife is at work. When the wife is at home, the husband has to work to adjust to the kids and their child care. So where is the family life?" They did not like the option of giving their children to a baby-sitter, so they managed themselves. In fact, Mr. Eapen claimed that he enjoyed taking care of the children, but that the quality of their family life suffered.

Another point of tension for Mr. Eapen was the work that he had to do around the house. As he explained, "Here I had to do cooking. I had to do the cleaning—I don't mind doing that. I know some Indian men are thinking they don't do this work. I do it. . . . If she will end up having to do everything, she cannot do it, right?" Here, he expressed his discomfort at being caught between the prescription that Indian men "don't do this work" and the practical reality of the limitations of his wife's time and energy after working nights.

His wife elaborated on the "tension" that her husband experienced: "Here life is more frustration, more tension. . . . Because my husband, he had three sisters and he was the one son—I think he found it more difficult here. He said he made a mistake. He should have never come here." In spite of the fact that Mrs. Eapen understood her husband's tension, her assessment of the conditions of work in the United States led her to expect a democratic division of housework:

> In India, you leave the dishes in the sink; the lady comes and washes. Here you can't do that. Because you work — everybody works, so everybody has to help. Before I go to work, I leave everything neat and tidy, so I expect the same thing when I

come back from work too. Because I don't want to work eight-hour [evening] shifts [3 P.M. to 11 P.M.]. . . . That is really hard; the floor where I work, it is so damn busy. Sometimes I don't get out even [at] midnight — two o'clock in the morning. So I don't want to come [at] two o'clock in the morning to find out [that] the whole sink is full of dishes.

Just as they shared child care and housework, the Eapens were democratic in their financial decision making process. Mrs. Eapen said she was fortunate in finding a responsible man who did not waste any of their hard-earned money. She did, however, complain about Mr. Eapen's penchant for being overly generous. She was concerned that others might take advantage of him. He knew that she disapproved, so he did not always tell her about his openhandedness.

As a result, she had to set limits concerning his spending habits: "Couple of incidents happened, so I told him, 'I don't like the way you do that. If you are going to do that, it's not good for our family life.' I straightforwardly told him, so after that he didn't do it again. I said, 'I work hard, you work hard. It's our money, not only your money and my money. We have a combined account and everything. If you want to do something, even though I may not like it, you can still always tell me before you do it.'"

Mr. Eapen planned to go back to Kerala after saving money for five or ten years. But his wife and children were less keen to go back. In his truly democratic way, he said that they could do whatever they wanted, but that he hoped his wife would eventually go back with him to a less tension-filled life in Kerala.

CHILD CARE

While the couples in the forced-participation category had some support from Kerala as well as some baby-sitting help here, most of the partnership-household couples had no help. The exceptions were two families who received intermittent help from family members that they sponsored. Most families resorted to alternating their shift work to provide child care themselves. Like the Eapens, some did not like the idea of using baby-sitters, and others could not afford baby-sitters, as was the case for the Samuels. After working the night shift for seven years, Mrs. Samuel switched to the day shift when their younger child reached school age. Because both parents left very early for work, they had to depend on their seven-year-old to look after herself and her younger sibling. As Mrs. Samuel put it:

I didn't have any baby-sitting for them. We didn't have money for that, and besides, there was no baby-sitter available. My daughter was very responsible. If you gave her the key and showed her how to open and close the door and how to go to school, she would do it. She used to wake my five-year-old up, get him dressed, and drop him off at the kindergarten. . . . They would go to school, and come back at three o'clock. Sometimes when we came back, the door was left wide open as if somebody was inside. My God! We would take a step inside and call out to them "Are you in there? Did you lock the door?" And they would say, "Oh yeah!"

Like the Samuels, the Punooses relied on an older sibling to look after younger ones. The Punooses emigrated to the United States when their first two children were very young. They left the children with grandparents for two years. Eventually they had another child, fifteen years after the oldest child was born. Even though the older children helped take care of the baby, the Punooses still worked alternating shifts.

A number of the couples were used to having a lot of help in India, as is the case for most middle-class families. For instance, in the Lukos family, neither husband nor wife was used to doing any work at home. Mrs. Lukos described their life before immigration: "Each of my kids had a nanny, and the servants were there to cook. He never did anything. He just went to work and came back. I never did anything personally. . . . That changed tremendously. He started doing child care. It was important that he participate, and I learned too." Mr. Lukos agreed with his wife's assessment of the change: "In India, I never did any child care. . . . Here I used to help in every way. Since she had to work the night shift, I had to do plenty of work, and she had plenty of time with the kids."[7]

The Markoses were another family who had had servants and babysitters in India. Moreover, Mrs. Markos's mother, who was in Kerala, offered to take care of their children after the family's emigration to the United States. But Mrs. Markos had refused her mother's offer. As she explained, "We have solved our problems ourselves. Never bothered anybody." Mrs. Markos's desire to not trouble anyone and manage their own problems was an underlying theme expressed by some other couples in this category.

HOUSEWORK AND COOKING

Juggling cooking and cleaning along with work and child care was a challenge for all these couples. But cooking was easier for two of the men than for the others. These two had lived away from home in their bachelor days and had some experience fending for themselves, and even admitted to enjoying cooking.[8] For example, Mr. Thomas, who left home at sixteen for technical training in North India, maintained that he did most of the cooking in the house. His wife concurred that he not only cooked but also did most of the heavier cleaning.

Mr. Samuel also asserted that he enjoyed cooking and did it on a daily basis for his household. Because he had to live on his own in North India for about six years, he learned to cook for himself. He was glad to have this skill because he could use it for the benefit of his family and friends. As he put it, "I don't think it is degrading myself, or cheap, to do housework and things like that." Rather, he assumed a leadership role in communal cooking efforts at church functions and other community events.

While his wife appreciated his talents, she complained that he cooked and entertained too much. She observed, "All the time, he has a lot of company here. Cousins, friends, and everybody. He cooks and invites everybody everyday. Chicken fry, fish fry, chicken curry—something everyday. So I don't cook too much." According to their division of labor, Mr. Samuel did the cooking, and Mrs. Samuel did most of the household cleaning.

Mr. Thomas and Mr. Samuel were exceptional in their love for cooking. Most of the men in this category learned to cook against their preimmigration instincts. For instance, Mrs. Philip described the initial shock and consequent adjustment in her household as her husband started to help her with the housework:

> I came first, and after eleven months my kids and my husband came. O God! That was the time I was studying for the psychiatric courses [for the licensing exams] and we had little kids. My husband did not do any work. By 4 A.M. I had to get ready, get the milk ready. At that time, I had a newborn baby. Then I went to work. At noon I needed to go to classes at [the] hospital. I took the bus there. By 10 P.M., I would come home and see all the dishes, the kids sleeping in dirty clothes. My husband then was not used [to it] and did not know how to do the work. I managed for about two weeks and then burst out crying. I was like a mad woman. I told him that I get up at 4 A.M. and, between work and school, get back at 10 P.M. . . . If I have to cook and clean till 12:30 A.M. at night, how long do I have to sleep? This is when he realized how I was doing all the work. So he slowly started to help and do the chores around the house. Things started to get better after a month.

Similarly, Mrs. Markos reminisced about the metamorphosis of her husband: "He was not a very good cook. He only knew how to make rice.

Now he has learned everything. In the beginning he was not very good. . . . He never washed plates after eating. After some time of marriage, he has changed. He is a very understanding person."

The Punoose's worked out an arrangement where Mr. Punoose did everything but the cooking. Mrs. Punoose admitted that she did most of the cooking, but that her husband helped her whenever necessary. She stated, "From the day he came here, he was doing all the cleaning. We both work together, and in emergency situations he helps me." Mr. Punoose also did all the grocery shopping for the household. He and the other men in this category recognized that their wives needed help, and they were able to adapt to the exigencies of postimmigration life.

FINANCIAL DECISION MAKING

What was striking about the partnership households was that, as they spoke about financial decision making, both men and women presumed a democratic process. The women were especially straightforward in their affirmation of a shared ownership and responsibility for financial matters. Mrs. Eapen put it best when she said, "I work hard. You work hard. It is our money." Thus she felt justified in setting limits on her husband's generosity with their money. Why are these women so different from some of their contemporaries despite having very similar backgrounds? Why do their husbands go along with the changes despite coming from traditional homes?

The women pointed to the postimmigration cultural and structural contexts to explain why their households were democratic about financial matters, especially relative to men's behavior in Kerala. For instance, Mrs. Thomas explained why she was primarily in charge of the finances in their household:

> Most of the things are still under my name — it did not change — phone bill, credit cards, and all other things. He is not good at checking and writing, but he used to do it when it was necessary. He managed. When he had some problem and he could not do it, he would give it to me. I am better at talking in English. When you come from a rural area of India, there is a problem in talking. There was only Hindi in that part of the country where he was working. So I took the responsibility of dealing with all kinds of matters. He has picked up a lot now, so it is less of a headache for me.

Having immigrated before her husband, and having acquired better linguistic skills, she was in charge. The new conditions shifted financial responsibilities to her, so she was not only participating in their financial affairs but also in charge of them.

Immigration also brought changes for these families because of their contact with American society. As previous research among immigrants reveals, the social organization of work exposes women to middle-class American values and gender roles. Scholars have found that, among Central American immigrants (Menjivar 1999a) and Caribbean immigrants (Grasmuck and Pessar 1991), women's work as nannies and domestics exposes them to the private lives of their employers and what they think is the American model of relationships, which leads women to alter their own relationships, making them more egalitarian.

In a similar vein, Mrs. Philip noted that many of her nurse friends had changed as a result of interaction with their American coworkers.

> They learn more. They are not the servile women, and they talk back to their husbands. They are not like slaves. They have more freedom. The country has changed them. . . . An example: I give my paycheck to my husband, and he gives me ten dollars to go and spend. Then they [American coworkers] ask you, "Why? You are working. You make the money. Why do you have to go and ask him?" Then the women think about this, and they start to feel that they should have more freedom, and they start living that way. . . . I have eight family friends here. All of them are aggressive and different from when they came here. . . . But husbands have changed also. They realize that the women are working like them, and take this into account.

Not only had the nurses changed, but also their husbands had been forced to change when faced with their newly "aggressive" wives. Like the Korean immigrant women in In-Sook Lim's study, the women in such households seemed to depend on "psychological resources such as pride and honor" — which the Korean women gained after immigration, as they became aware of the magnitude of their contributions to their families (1997: 49).

In addition to interactions with American cultural practices, structural conditions of American financial transactions also encourage democracy in a couple's financial decision making. Mrs. Punoose gave one example when she explained why she argued and fought with her husband about financial matters in a way very unlike her mother: "My father deals with everything. My mother does not know anything. She knows just cooking only. My father, whatever he does, he does not even tell to my mother. . . . Yes, she never argued. But here we have to. Here you can't do anything yourself. If you buy, both of you have to sign. Both are working and both are responsible for the payment. Everything should not be in one person's name. It won't happen anyway. Everything is shared." When asked if she thought that was better, she replied: "I think that's better. If everything goes to one person, you end up with nothing. Everything is not controlled by one person. Everything is equal. Equal responsibility. If I need money, I have money. If he needs money, he has money."

Mrs. Punoose pointed to the structural conditions of financial transactions in the United States that allow for the participation of both husband and wife. While a woman may choose not to sign her own paycheck, she has to participate in all major credit-based transactions, such as the purchase of a home or car. Especially because her salary may be the larger and more stable of the two, in most cases her husband would need her to cosign for all loan applications related to major purchases. Thus, Mrs. Punoose could confidently assert, "Everything should not be in one person's name. It won't happen anyway." Consequently, she underlined the fact that both members of the couple became responsible for payments. The new structural conditions of postimmigration finances imposed equal ownership and equal responsibility on the couple, which contributed to the required participation of the women in the financial matters of the household. While some women, like Mrs. Thambi, might choose to just sign on the dotted line, women such as Mrs. Punoose liked the fact that they and their husbands had equal responsibility for and control over their shared financial investments.

In conclusion, the partnership households were very similar to the forced-participation households, given the women's primary-immigrant status and relative employment success and the men's difficulty in the U.S. labor market. These households received very little help from Kerala relative to the traditional and forced-participation households. Unlike in forced-participation households, the husbands' participation in child care in partnership households did not lead to the reassertion of their patriarchal status in the other areas of the household division of labor. Rather, they responded to the changes in postimmigration life in an egalitarian manner by extending themselves and sharing in all the responsibilities of domestic life. Often following the lead of their wives, husbands in the partnership household transformed their gender ideology to fit with the new reality. Consequently, as in the case of traditional households, ideology and practice were once again synchronized in the partnership households.

The Eapens exemplified this process of ideological transformation. While both Mr. and Mrs. Eapen probably started out with traditional expectations of marital roles, their starkly different postimmigration circumstances led them to adopt egalitarian ideologies to match their new reality. Certainly Mrs. Eapen and the women of the partnership household cohort were more forceful than their husbands in their espousal of egalitarianism. As Mrs. Philip recalled, the women of the eight couples she knew closely became "aggressive and different," leaving behind their "subdued" selves. But their husbands, like Mr. Eapen, changed despite being haunted by the knowledge that "Indian men don't do this kind of work."

But whereas Kerala was the main reference point for traditional and forced-participation households, the partnership family seemed to be more immediately influenced by the cultural and structural conditions of life in the United States. For example, while all the households faced similar changes in the postimmigration structural and cultural context, the couples of the partnership households referred to these new circumstances as factors to explain the changes in their lives.

Female-Led Households

The five households in this category fall on the opposite end of the spectrum relative to traditional households. For one reason or another, responsibility for the housework, child care, and financial decision making fell disproportionately on the shoulders of the women. No one family represented this category, given the various reasons this anomalous type of household existed. Of the five households in this category, one merited inclusion because of the literal absence of the man, two were included because of the unreliability of the men, and two because of the extreme dependence of the men on their wives.

The women in this category were the primary immigrants, with the exception of one who was sponsored by her immigrant husband after their arranged marriage in Kerala. As with forced-participation households and partnership households, the women were better situated than their husbands in the U.S. labor market. All of the women were registered nurses. Of the three employed men, two worked in the nursing field but in auxiliary positions, and one worked in a factory. The fourth man was unemployed, and the fifth had passed away.

In four out of the five households, relatives in Kerala helped care for the children. In two cases, grandparents had come for extended stays. In another case, a sibling immigrated with the explicit intention of providing child care.

These households' pattern of immigration, relationship to the labor market, and access to extraconjugal child care made them similar to households in the forced-participation category. However, the differences in how the men in these families responded to postimmigration conditions resulted in female leadership in all aspects of household labor.

ABSENT MEN

Mrs. Jacob was an extremely unusual person in the immigrant community, not only because she was a widow, but also because her deceased husband was a white American. From the time she was a young girl in her village in Kerala, Mrs. Jacob had different ideas about what she wanted to do with her life. She was enamored of the consumer items she saw people bring back from the city — items like sweet-smelling soap.[9] As a little girl, she used to sit in a corner and pretend to talk in English to herself. Her desire to speak English and find the sweet-smelling soap inspired her to pursue a career in nursing, a decision intolerable to her father, a prominent politician in their village. So she ran away to Bombay — a journey of three days and nights — to look for educational opportunities.

Eventually, she got a bachelor's degree in nursing, which placated her father, since it was a college degree. She first emigrated to Kuwait, where she worked for three years before traveling on to the United States. Unlike most other immigrants, she did not connect with the Malayalee community. She eventually met her husband through a roommate, and they married against her parent's wishes. Unfortunately, three years after the marriage, he was diagnosed with a terminal disease; he died a few years later. Left with two young children to raise, Mrs. Jacob went on to get her master's degree in community health and supported her family as a single mother.

When I interviewed Mrs. Jacob in her home, I noticed a plaque on her bathroom wall that represented her position on marital gender relations. It said something to the effect that, if God had meant for Eve to rule over Adam, he would have used a bone from Adam's head to create Eve. If God had meant for Eve to be ruled by Adam, he would have used a bone from Adam's foot. That God used a bone from Adam's rib signified that God wanted Adam and Eve to be equal partners. From what Mrs. Jacob said about her marital relationship, the third scenario best described her marriage.

When I asked her to compare her relationship with her husband to her parents' relationship, she said, "My mother was very subdued. She went along with whatever my dad said. . . . She did not have anything more, and there was no gratification. My husband and I, we would discuss and plan. If I wanted to do something on my own, I did not feel like I had to ask him for permission. Whenever I was going to be late, . . . I did not have to get permission." Mrs. Jacob told me that one of the main reasons she ran away from home to become a nurse was that she did not want to end up like her sister and her mother. Her sister had been forced to get married at a very young age because a dying grandmother wanted to see one of her grandchildren get married. Mrs. Jacob thought that it had been "cruel" that her sister, who had wanted to attend college, had been deprived of the chance to do so because of her early entrance into matrimony.

After her husband died, Mrs. Jacob was left with the difficult task of caring for her children. While she was able to handle the financial and household responsibilities, she found that she needed help raising her children. Consequently, she sponsored the emigration of her sister and family to the United States to help her. She also joined the immigrant Orthodox Church and had her children baptized there. She described this experience as "very hard. That is when I knew the meaning of swallowing your pride. I didn't want my girls to not have any identity at all." Without her husband, she felt less comfortable among his friends and sought support from the more familiar immigrant community to bring up her children.

Unlike most of her contemporaries, Mrs. Jacob left home with the explicit intention of finding a more egalitarian option than being in a marriage like that of her parents, where her mother was "very subdued." She started her family life in a partnership household with her husband; but with his death, she was left to head her household on her own.

UNRELIABLE MEN

Unlike Mrs. Jacob, neither Mrs. John nor Mrs. Kurien had to run away to become nurses. They went with the full knowledge of their families and with the intention of helping their families. Both were the eldest daughters of their families, and both had multiple younger siblings. Coming from poor families, they told their husbands before marriage that their intention was to continue helping their natal families. That they had to negotiate this matter points to the cultural expectation that a woman, once married, belongs to her husband's family. In both cases the husbands failed to keep their end of the premarital agreement, and this contributed to spousal conflict.

Mrs. John tearfully told me about the betrayal of their pact: "When the proposal came, I told him, 'I am the eldest in the house. I have to support my family.' He said it is okay. He can do everything for me. After marriage, he changed totally." She bitterly observed that he might have agreed to her conditions before marriage only because he wanted to come to the United States.

Similarly, Mrs. Kurien thought her husband had agreed to help sponsor her family members' emigration to the United States. However, although she was able to bring them over, he made it very difficult for her to support them once they had arrived. For instance, her sister had to pay him to be able to live with them. However, his mother and a number of his sisters, whom they also sponsored, stayed with them at no charge. One of her husband's nephews got in trouble with the law, and her husband took the nephew's side against Mrs. Kurien because of his loyalty to his family.

This was the last straw for Mrs. Kurien. She decided that she would take a different strategy in helping her brother emigrate to the United States: "I was determined to help my brother, no matter what my husband said. I became more outspoken then. My husband made me more outspoken. So I told him, 'If you want to say anything, say it to my face, because I am going to help my brother. If you agree with it or not, I don't care a bit. You can go to hell.' And he was more cooperative."

In addition to reneging on their preimmigration pacts, both Mr. John and Mr. Kurien were unreliable financial managers and did not participate in child care and household duties. Mrs. John constantly had to work double shifts in order to earn overtime money, since her husband had been unable to hold down a job after he was laid off eleven years earlier. She told me that her husband would not even use the microwave to heat up food she prepared for him. She used to do that for him but recently had become too tired to continue it. She remembered the days when she would have to cook for his many friends, who were always over at the Johns' house drinking and playing cards.

What irked Mrs. John even more was the way her husband had mishandled their money. He was prone to making expensive purchases on their credit cards without consulting her. Once he put the house up for sale, and she had found out about it only when the real estate agent called to ask if he could come by with a potential buyer. Another time Mrs. John's husband bought a car and called her from the dealer's office to ask for her signature. She refused, but when the car dealer showed up at her door, she relented and signed. Without contributing anything to the household, her husband used to burden her with his whimsical purchases. She told me that she used to believe she had to obey her husband, but that she no longer believed this.

Mrs. Kurien had a similar litany of criticisms about her husband. While he may have taken care of the immediate needs of the children when she was at work, he did nothing else in the house. She complained, "Very seldom did he ever cook. I still remember when I went away for a couple of days and came back, all the dishes were in the sink. . . . He doesn't even know where his own clothes are. . . . I go and do my night shift, and then I have to cook breakfast and wake up my husband and feed him. . . . He won't even make a cup of coffee."

Likewise, when it came to financial affairs, Mrs. Kurien had to change her ways in order to deal with her husband's incompetence. She said that she used to give him her paycheck and had not even known how much money they had. But he invested in the stock market, lost a lot of money, and never told her about it. This prompted her to take greater control over their finances. Interestingly, she sees his losses in the stock market as an answer to her prayers. As she put it, "When his family came, all these problems came with them and I just couldn't take it. I had to work. I had to take care of him. I had to take care of the kids. It was all just too much. I just wanted to kill myself. And then I prayed like I used to do as a child. I asked God to make him more understanding. And I think that's how he lost his money."

Both Mr. John and Mr. Kurien were aware of the difficulties their wives faced. For instance, Mr. John noted that it was difficult for his wife to work both inside and outside the home, yet he admitted that he helped her only occasionally, and only when she asked for help. He observed, "Nowadays she is tired—getting sick. Otherwise there is no problem. I am thinking that I should do a little more work for the house. It will be good for her. . . . But since I don't have that kind of routine experience, I don't do it. Something else will come up, and I will go for it." Mr. Kurien also observed that, because his wife took care of all the cooking and household labor and then went to work, "it is very stressful for her. I know, but there is no choice." When I pointed out to him that there was another choice, that he could help her, he said he had very limited time.

Apparently, both these couples began with the traditional division-of-labor paradigm, in which the men were in charge of decision making and the women did most of the other household labor. Along with feeling betrayed by their husbands' failure to honor their preimmigration agreements, these two women were also dissatisfied by their husbands' failure to properly manage their common finances. As a result, the women had to take greater control over household finances, as well as be responsible for the child care and the housework.

DEPENDENT MEN

Similarly, Mrs. Simon and Mrs. Mathew had to assume a disproportionate share of the household labor, but for different reasons. Their husbands were present in their households, and both were employed. However, both were extremely dependent on their wives, and the latter did the lion's share of the household work.

Mrs. Simon was working in India as a nurse when many of her neighbors and coworkers started emigrating to the United States. She wanted to see if she could make it here, and she felt that her children would have better opportunities in the United States. However, her husband did not have the same ambitions and did not want to leave India. Eventually he relented. After immigration, Mrs. Simon established herself as a registered nurse, and her husband secured a blue-collar job.

Mrs. Mathew immigrated after her arranged marriage with her husband, who was already in the United States. His brother and sister-in-law—a nurse—had sponsored Mr. Mathew, who, in turn, had returned to Kerala to look for a nurse to marry. Even though Mrs. Mathew had not liked him, she had married him for the opportunity to come to the United States. His significant limp, a result of childhood polio, probably contributed to Mrs. Mathew's dislike of her husband's looks. However, she wanted to help her parents, who were not financially secure. Mr. Mathew, who had graduated from high school in Kerala, became a nursing assistant upon immigration. His newly arrived wife also started as a nursing assistant, but she soon passed her exams and became a registered nurse, while he continued as a nursing assistant. His limp did not allow him to try for other jobs that would require greater physical capability.

Both these women were responsible for all the cooking and housework. Mrs. Simon worked two jobs, which meant that she worked every day of the week. She cooked for her family in the evenings, after work. She described her struggle with her husband, who expected her to be with him at all times when she was not at work:

> Saturday mornings are the only mornings I get to sleep in, but he expects me to get up at 6:30 in the morning and make an Indian breakfast—get up and move around. He doesn't want me to sleep once he gets up—that's always his nature.

He says women should not sleep in the daytime — it's bad, and you know. And finally he got tired of telling me. . . . I said, "No matter what you say, I have to sleep in, and I have to sleep in the morning. . . . If you are that hungry, you can have bread or hot cereal." So he doesn't bother me nowadays too much.

Likewise, the labor of child care was the responsibility of the women. According to their wives, both Mr. Mathew and Mr. Simon were not very patient with their children. Mrs. Mathew had taken over child care because, as she put it, "He gets upset with the kids easily. I don't like it when he starts yelling at the kids, so I do most of the child care."

Mrs. Simon found that her husband was authoritarian and tried to control his children like his father had controlled him. But Mrs. Simon intervened in his disciplining, because she believed that such an approach did not work. Consequently, he accused her of spoiling the children. I overheard the Simons' college-age daughter announce to her mother after church that she would be going to see a play with her friend. When her mother told her to ask her father about it, the daughter quipped, "As if he wears the pants in the family." Both Mr. Simon and Mr. Mathew were unable to adapt to circumstances where the patriarchal authoritarian role did not work with children. Consequently, their wives had to take on a greater responsibility in the care of their children.

Finally, both women felt they had the greater responsibility in making and carrying out the day-to-day decisions in their households. In talking about her household, Mrs. Mathew said, "I do feel that I can do many things now, whether it is going places or making decisions about taking the children to the doctor or anything. In fact, he tells me to do everything on my own, so I end up doing it all on my own." I had the opportunity to witness what she meant when I was at the Mathews residence. She decided against his wishes that they would go to church after my interview. I watched as she told him what to wear and what clothes the children should wear. And she drove them to church — which is extremely unusual for most of the families, since the men usually drive. Mr. Mathew's physical disability may have made it more difficult for him to drive.

As for Mrs. Simon, she felt burdened by her husband, who needed her presence for most activities. She stated, "My husband always makes decisions with me. He doesn't want to make decisions by himself. Like even if I tell him, 'You go and do it,' he won't do it. He still wants me to go with him. Even if he wants a T-shirt, he doesn't know how to go and do it. He wants me to go with him, and I have to say, 'This is good for you — take it.' That's the type he is." Perhaps this was the reason he evaded my multiple attempts to set up an interview with him separately, even though he seemed happy to talk to me whenever he saw me at church or during visits at his home.

Whether unreliable, dependent, or absent, the men in this category left the women with the larger share of household labor. For the most part, these families emigrated to the United States with traditional expectations concerning sharing the work of their households. The exception was Mrs. Jacob, who immigrated with the express intention of finding more egalitarian options than those available to her in Kerala. For this group of women, their domestic experiences in the United States with unreliable and extremely dependent or absent men created a dissonance between ideology and practice.

The dissonance was severe in the case of the unreliable men because it was caused by the complete breakdown of the "patriarchal bargain" found in traditional households (Kandiyoti 1988). Both Mrs. John and Mrs. Kurien were in tears as they told me that their husbands had failed to honor the bargains they had made at the time the women emigrated. Furthermore, not only were these men unable to do their share of household labor, but also they became obstacles in the way of their wives, who were trying to do it all on their own. As a result, Mrs. Kurien recounts, she told her husband to go to hell because he made her assume such a burden.

Rather than adjusting to ideology, as in the forced-participation families, the women of the female-led households, for the most part, rejected the ideology that did not correspond to their lived experiences. In the face of dissonance between ideology and practice, they realized that the dictate to obey one's husband no longer applied. However, these women were unable to adopt a new ideology that that would fix the dissonance, as did the couples in partnership. They continued living with the contradictions of female-led households, where they were not socially supported and not rewarded for their headship as were the men in the traditional families. Yet as pioneers, they had to come up with strategies that worked for them, all the while carrying the burden of husbands who were unreliable, dependent, or absent as domestic partners. Some of these women turned to relatives in Kerala or the Keralite immigrant community for help, especially with raising their children.

Conclusion

One of the biggest changes that Keralite immigrants in general face upon arrival in the United States is the change in the domestic sphere. All the couples have to find a way to deal with a new set of circumstances without the accustomed and readily available help from relatives and servants. Dividing labor and child care issues presents a challenge, particularly for the families of nurses, given the men's initial economic dependence on nurses. The husbands of nurses find it difficult to "do gender" in their customary ways, as a "routine, methodical and recurring accomplishment," given the vast changes they encounter after immigration, both in their work and home lives (West and Zimmerman 1987: 126). Because household tasks often become occasions for the "reaffirmation of one's gendered relation to the work and to the world," the already "dependent men" have trouble doing work that labels them as women (Berk 1985: 204). And since doing gender is not an individual performance but an interactional process, many nurses have to overcompensate by "doing gender" in the home to counterbalance their breadwinner status.

Yet among the couples I interviewed, I found variations in how families negotiated this challenge. As I noted earlier, the postimmigration gender relations in these households were shaped by such factors as the couples' immigration pattern, relationship to the labor market, and access to child care. But gender relations were also the result of the couples' level of success at resolving the tension between gender ideology and practice in their lives. I found that the choices these families made from those available to them put them in four categories.

In the traditional households, couples like the Itoops had a larger set of options available to them, which allowed them to maintain a traditionally gendered division of labor. Half of the women did not work outside the home, especially when their kids were younger, which relieved their husbands of child care and household duties. Other couples left their children at boarding schools or with parents in Kerala to alleviate the pressures of housework and child care. In all these households, men continued to be the primary breadwinners and to be in charge of financial decision making. If men felt compromised, it was relative to the ideological standards in Kerala. In practice, their lifestyles were not very different. Women voiced awareness of alternate standards by which they could judge men; however, they did not demand change. Overall, there was little inconsistency between the gender ideology and practices employed by these couples, as seen best in the Itoop household.

In the forced-participation households, like that of the Thambis, men experienced the greatest change in the area of child care. Some families received help from Kerala, but in most the men had to fit their work schedules around child care. Not only were they actively involved in forming the character of their children, but also they had less patriarchal authority in the United States. In most cases, the men had to share some of the housework, although they drew the line at cooking. Because all the women in this category were upwardly mobile nurses, and the majority of the men had become downwardly mobile after immigration, husbands and wives had to face disparity in their paychecks and job status. It was with unsteady voices that Mr. Thambi and the other men claimed headship over the household; their wives claimed ignorance in financial matters. In this category, the fit between gender ideology and lived experience was tenuous, although the women, like Mrs. Thambi, made concerted efforts to create a fit.

In partnership households, men and women shared the domestic labor, and they saw this sharing as a logical and necessary adaptation to postimmigration circumstances. None of the men complained about having to take care of their children, and Mr. Eapen even claimed to enjoy it. Most of these men could do much more than make coffee — the standard threshold for men's cooking skills. However, although some men said they enjoyed cooking, most did it because they had to.

What was striking about the partnership category was the democracy presumed by both men and women when it came to financial decision making. There were many possible reasons for their egalitarianism. The women in these households spoke of being influenced by American society and noted that it had, in turn, led them to aggressively demand changes from their husbands. The men were all downwardly mobile. As families, they had less help from Kerala and consequently fewer connections. As a result, these couples were more dependent on each other. Perhaps this explains why the men were more willing to follow their wives' leads and to alter their traditional gender ideologies to fit with the new realities of postimmigration life.

The final category consists of female-led households, where women had the disproportionate burden of responsibility for household labor for a variety of reasons. Men were absent from these households because of death, were partially present but unreliable, or were extremely dependent on the women. As a single mother, Mrs. Jacob was able to handle the financial and household responsibilities by herself. However, she needed help with child care and followed the same strategy as most of the other immigrant families. She looked to relatives in Kerala and was able to sponsor her sister's emigration to the United States. She also looked to the immigrant community in the United States, which was a type of extended pseudofamily for most of the immigrants.

The wives of the unreliable men started off within the traditional paradigm, but their experiences of betrayal by their husbands and the breakdown of the "patriarchal bargain" changed them, making them more assertive women. As a result, they had greater financial control. Their desire to help their families — their connections to Kerala — acted as the impetus behind their immigration and the changes in their marital relationships.

In the case of the dependent men, the women would have liked for their husbands to participate more actively and autonomously. But the men continued to take a backseat in the day-to-day decision making, leaving their wives no choice. When the men did participate, they acted as patriarchal authoritarians with their children. When this parenting strategy did not work with the children, these men were unable to adapt to the different circumstances. As a result, their wives had to take over for them. In all the female-led households, the women had to let go of their traditional ideologies in the face of absent, partially present, or incompetent partners. There were no clearly viable resolutions to the tension between ideology and practice for these households.

On a spectrum of change, the traditional households had made the fewest changes and the partnership households had made the most changes, in terms of the fit between gender ideologies and lived experience. All the immigrant men were forced to do at least some work that their fathers would not have dreamed of doing. Furthermore, they faced the loss of patriarchal status in relation to their wives and children, coupled with a general loss of status in the wider U.S. society. With the new circumstances of postimmigration life, most of these families were forced to make some changes in the domestic sphere. Of particular interest are the ways that changes in the household were translated into a greater need for male participation in the communal sphere of the church.

CHAPTER 4

Community

Creating Little Kerala and the Paradox of "Men Who Play" in the Church

The change of seasons was in full swing early one November, heralding the approach of Advent in the church. The priest's announcements at the end of the service on the first Sunday in November included an invitation for those interested in Christmas caroling to join and practice with the church's carolers. I had been attending the church as a visiting researcher only since June, and I was unfamiliar with their practice of caroling. I turned to Anna, who sat next to me, to ask if she were going caroling. She smiled and replied that she would like to go, but that in their church only the men caroled. I expressed my surprise, since I had never heard of any such restrictions on caroling participation in the Indian Orthodox Syrian Christian tradition.

Over the next two Sundays, Anna and her friends discussed among themselves, and with the priest, their desire to participate in the caroling. These conversations led them to approach the men during the practice session. There was a tense moment of silence as the fifteen young people—mostly teenage girls clutching their head coverings—faced their fathers, who were practicing songs in their native language, Malayalam, that they were planning to sing during the church's annual caroling party. The men seemed surprised that the young people wanted to accompany them. Anna, one of the older girls, approached her father, a drummer in the group, to explain. As her peers carefully watched, he brushed her off, saying, "Not now. We'll talk about it later." The men continued their practice session as if the teenagers were not present in the sanctuary. Ironically, although the first generation of immigrants often worry about how they will keep their children involved in the congregation, in this instance they clearly did not want to include their children. The men remained reluctant to comply with the girls' request, but in the end the priest intervened and persuaded them to take the young women along. Nonetheless, the men resisted the girls' participation every step of the way.[1]

Many immigrant communities in the United States face the problem of maintaining their ethnic traditions as their children absorb American culture. Indian Christians manifest just such a concern, which they express as the fear that their children will succumb to what they see as the secularism and immorality of American society (Williams 1988). Unlike the majority of Indian immigrants, Indian Christians come to the United States with the expectation of being a part of the majority in a "Christian land," but find themselves alienated from the morals of "Christian America." These fears, as well as the desire to re-create a community in a land of strangers, propel Indian Christians to "attempt to preserve personal and group Christian identity by establishing Indian churches in the United States" (Williams 1988: 104).

Immigrant religious institutions tend to have special classes and programs to teach the next generation about their religion and culture and to motivate them to participate in and maintain their religious institutions into the future. To judge by the Sunday school classes, the vacation Bible schools, and other special programs organized for the socialization of the youth, this Orthodox congregation of immigrants from Kerala was no exception.[2]

Consequently, I was surprised to observe the anomalous adult resistance to the teenagers' desire to participate in caroling, a church-sponsored social event without any special ritual or cultural restrictions. Why did these parents, who normally insisted on involving their children in the ethnic space of the immigrant church, resist their participation in caroling? The answer lies in the fact that it was mostly young girls, not boys, who asked to be included.

The men's attempt to maintain caroling as an adult male preserve had to do with this congregation's specific immigration history, which involved a relative shift in status between men and women in the family. To understand the incident, we have to consider the importance of the congregational space for the immigrant men. Postimmigration loss of status for the men had led to a greater male need for public participation and leadership opportunities. The immigrant congregation is an arena par excellence for meeting such a need, since it is a communal sphere where male headship is reinforced.

I begin with my ethnographic impression of the service and congregation at St. George's, followed by a discussion of why the church and religious identity are particularly important to Keralite immigrants. Next, I argue that an increased male need for participation after immigration may be part of the impetus behind the extension, creation, and redefinition of male roles in the congregation.[3] Furthermore, there is a reproduction of traditional female behavior in the immigrant congregation that is overseen by a church hierarchy invested in maintaining the status quo. Surprisingly, challenges to the hegemonic order come from upper-class women from traditional households, progressive priests, and the second generation, whereas the majority of the women, who are nurses, seem to go along with traditional expectations. Finally, the men's very attempt in the congregation to recover status lost as a result of immigration becomes the basis for a loss of status. Ironically, in asserting male privilege within the church, they become stigmatized as emasculated, lower-class men because of their connection to nurses.

The Importance of Religious Identity among Keralite Christian Immigrants

The congregation stands with bare feet in the sanctuary at St. George's, since it is considered to be a holy space, much in the tradition of Indian religious spaces. As the worshipers trickle in for the Sunday morning service, they leave their shoes in the foyer or the basement. The church building is shaped like a T. The chancel, containing the altar, is at the end of the leg of the T, and the priest faces the front—away from the congregation. The wall behind the altar that the priest and the congregation face has a stained glass window with a cross and white dove figuring prominently in it. The chancel is veiled and unveiled at particular times in the service by means of an ornate curtain. The curtain and the priest's vestments are made of the same highly embroidered and brightly colored material.

The main altar is flanked on both sides by two small altars with shrines dedicated, respectively, to the Virgin Mary and Saint Gregorios, a bishop of the church who was canonized after his death. Devotees can light votive candles and donate money in the collection boxes placed in front of the paintings of Saint Mary with baby Jesus, on the left, and Saint Gregorios, on the right, each of which measures approximately five feet square. The altar area; the ornate curtain and garments of the priest; the paintings of the saints; the twelve tall candles on the altar symbolizing the twelve disciples, with a prominent cross in the middle; the incense; the chalice for the Eucharist; the special bells and noisemaking devices for different parts of the service, all make for a sensually evocative and aesthetically provocative experience.

The whole service can take from three and a half to four hours. Most of the service is either chanted or sung and is conducted with the congregation standing. While the traditional church in Kerala does not have chairs or pews, since people stand and sit on carpeted floors, most Keralite immigrant churches in the United States, such as St. George's, have pews. A male member of the congregation plays a synthesizer, but there is no official choir. Traditional Keralite churches had no choir, but it is not uncommon now to find them in the churches in Kerala. At St. George's, the women seem to be unofficially responsible for carrying the singing during the service.

The service does not change from Sunday to Sunday. Rather, the liturgy is always in the same format; the translation of most of the service into Malayalam from Syriac is a relatively recent event. While neither Bibles nor hymnals are necessary for the service, and while most people know the service by heart, there are copies of the service book in Malayalam in the church and English transliterations of the service so that the non-Malayalam-reading youth can follow along. After the official service, the congregation files by the priest — first the boys and girls, followed by the men and women, respectively. They place their monetary offerings in a plate, and the priest blesses them by touching a cross to each one's forehead as each crosses himself or herself.

A long carpet that runs down the center of the church physically separates the sexes. The younger boys and girls stand at the front of their respective sides. The women and girls have their heads covered. Almost all the women wear saris, a traditional Indian dress, the end of which can be raised and draped over the wearer's head. Some visiting grandmothers wear the traditional women's outfit from Kerala, which predates the sari. Young girls tend to wear Punjabi *salwaar kameezes* (a North Indian outfit made up of pants, a loose top that hangs to the knees, and a long scarf), or they wear Western-style skirts and dresses and bring scarves to cover their heads. In contrast, the men and boys wear almost exclusively pants and shirts; the occasional visiting grandfather wears the typical Keralite white *mundu* (sarong) and shirt. In her study of Hindu Indian immigrants in Pittsburgh, the sociologist Aparna Rayaprol found a similar divergence in the clothing choices of the two sexes. As she notes, "The dress code symbolizes the reality that immigrant women more than men are considered the custodians of religious and cultural tradition" (1997: 78).

The majority of St. George's congregation is made up of Indian-born adults from Kerala. It is difficult to give an exact membership count, since the Indian Orthodox Church categorizes membership per nuclear family unit and not per adult. The adult males in the family are the official representatives of the family, and typically only the man's name appears in the church roster. In the very rare cases where there is no male representative, the woman's name appears on the roster, but she is still ineligible to vote in public meetings since suffrage rights belong to financially contributing males over twenty-one years of age. While 101 families were listed on the roster, I estimate that about 400 people — adults and children — attended services.

The children include both the American born and the "1.5ers" — those born in India who emigrated to the United States while between the ages of eleven and thirteen. The youth who attend church range from the very young to those in high school. The college-age and post-college-age youth are conspicuously absent. This is not unusual among immigrant religious congregations. For instance, the sociologist Karen Chai (1998) reports that several studies on Korean immigrant churches estimate an attrition rate for post-college-age youth as high as 90 percent, a phenomenon one pastor labeled a "silent exodus." There seems to be a similar trend at St. George's, a concern voiced by several parents and the priest.

The majority of the congregation appears to be between the ages of thirty and fifty, with equal numbers of men and women. While members of St. George's come from different regions of Kerala and have diverse customs and church practices, such regional differences are not apparent or cause for conflict at St. George's. Within Central City, members are spread out over the metropolitan area and travel long distances to come to church. Such devotion is an artifact of both the postimmigration need for community and the traditional importance of religion in the lives of Keralite Christians.

Because of the highly heterogeneous nature of Keralite society, with its large numbers of Hindus, Muslims, and Christians and even a small Jewish community, religion has traditionally been an important identity marker for Keralites. Furthermore, the history of colonization in Kerala contributed to the importance of religion in this region. Especially in the case of the Orthodox Christians in Kerala, "the true Orthodox Christian faith" frequently had to be defended from the Protestant and Catholic influences of the colonizing Portuguese, Dutch, and English. While the denomination one belongs to becomes an important source of identity, this privilege is reserved for males, as women are expected to join the denomination of their husbands upon marriage.

In Kerala, the church one belongs to is the essential basis for social life. One immigrant man I interviewed explained to me why a person had to belong to a church in Kerala:

> In our home [Kerala], if we don't stay in a church, it is a great problem. If we have children, we need to baptize. If we die, they won't bury you. When you go to get married, that is a problem. We will be brought down. You have to obey and go along with them. We have to go along with the church or we become people without anything. If a death happens in your family and the church does not do the burial, where do you take your dead body? Do you understand? That is the problem. So you have to obey and get along over there.

The same man explained why it is different in the United States: "See, here, there is more freedom. If I don't want to go to one church, I can go to another church, or I can stay away from the church. The church will not put any force on me. . . . Here it is not like that. . . . We can do whatever we want. It's okay if we don't go to church. It's okay if we stand up against the church. The church cannot bring us down or bend us. There, it is not like that."

Raymond Williams, in his book on immigrant Indian Christians, makes the same point when he notes, "Migration removes individuals from social constraints and frees them to chart new paths that would not be viable for them in their previous residence" (1996: 98). He identifies several ways in which Indian Christian immigrants can strike out on their own: they can reject the Christian religion and turn toward the secular, marry someone of another faith and change religions, or participate in an American local congregation that has no immigrant ties. But, as he sums it up, "no way exists to determine who, where or exactly how many they are" (1996: 99).

Despite there being "more freedom" in the United States from the dictates of the church, most immigrants report higher levels of church participation. The role of the church as the main source of community life continues in the United States and, in fact, has become more prominent because few venues exist where Keralite immigrants can cultivate social ties. Among the alternatives in Central City are three Keralite cultural organizations that provide space for Keralite immigrants to socialize. There are informal sports clubs, which offer a source of community, particularly for younger men in the community. There are also some professional associations, such as one for Keralite engineers and others for graduates of particular nursing and medical schools. But cultural gatherings and professional meetings occur less frequently and consistently than the weekly opportunities for fellowship provided by the church.

Consequently, for Keralite Christians the immigrant church remains the main space for social life. Most of these immigrants continue to depend on the church to conduct their marriages, baptisms, and funerals and to bless their new homes and cars. The immigrant lay members I interviewed reported a significant increase in participation in church life after immigration. Because immigration is often a "theologizing experience," as the historian Timothy Smith calls it (1978: 1175), the increased participation of immigrants in religious institutions can be partially attributed to the alienation inherent in the immigration experience. For the Keralite Christian men who experience a markedly alienating immigration process, religious institutions such as St. George's provide an arena inherently structured to cater to their need for community and involvement.

The Extension of Male Prerogative: The U.S. Congregation as Male Turf

Several factors coincide to make the immigrant congregation an ideal space for male participation and leadership. In Kerala, leadership roles in the church are reserved for socially and economically prominent male members of the community, so that lay leadership is associated with high status. For the immigrant male members suffering from a loss of status, St. George's becomes a logical space to exercise leadership that is communally associated with high status. Second, many immigrant congregations endeavor to forge a social and religious space in the new setting that reproduces what has been left behind in the imagined homeland (Herberg 1960). In many ways, St. George's attempts to produce an untainted little Kerala for its members. As Mr. Varghese put it, "The church is a community—it is a place where once a week or once a month you can share your sorrows or happiness." The church becomes an important proxy for the missing extended-family relationships that make up the fabric of social relations in Kerala, especially for the men, who suffer greater losses in the immigration process.

The congregation offers leadership to some men and a sense of community to others. More generally, and this is the third compensatory role, the congregation has always been a place of male privilege. Orthodox gender ideology and practices in Kerala allocate ritual and administrative duties to men. The gender hierarchy in the Orthodox Church is starkly delineated and enforced, as best exemplified by the physical separation of the congregation by sex. Women have no official roles in the three-hour-long Sunday morning service, other than joining in communal responses and hymns. Only men and boys can be altar helpers or assistants to the priest, after they have been consecrated as deacons or acolytes. They can formally lead the congregation in responses and enter the altar area, which is off limits to all women and girls. In the U.S. congregation, men continue to assume all administrative duties, as members of the managing committee and the board of trustees of the church.

Thus, the immigrant congregation offers a unique setting for men to restore their lost identity, their self-esteem. To compensate for demotion in the labor market and the family, they use the church to assert their leadership, develop a sense of belonging, and secure their exclusiveness. The congregation, however, does not merely reproduce gendered patterns found in Kerala: it appropriates those patterns in order to deepen and extend male prerogatives. This reactive intensification can be found in three areas I have already mentioned: the search for leadership leads to the phenomenon of congregation splitting; the need for communal belonging calls for new activities for men, such as food preparation on public occasions; and the claim to exclusiveness is displayed in the organization of caroling.

Congregational Splits: The Propagation of Male Roles

One way of expanding the opportunities for leadership is to multiply the number of congregations by physically dividing existing ones.[4] While not conventionally understood as a response to the devaluation of men in work and family life, splitting, as it is called, certainly addresses it. The tendency for congregations to split over nondoctrinal issues is a growing concern raised by many church leaders. While I do not have the exact number of congregations that have formed as a result of splits, informed church members at national meetings indicate that splitting is a common pattern in most metropolitan areas where there is more than one congregation. For example, in Central City the first congregation, established in 1972, split twice, engendering two more congregations — including St. George's, which in turn split once more, as noted in fig. 1. At the local level, splits serve the needs of both individual laity and immigrant priests.

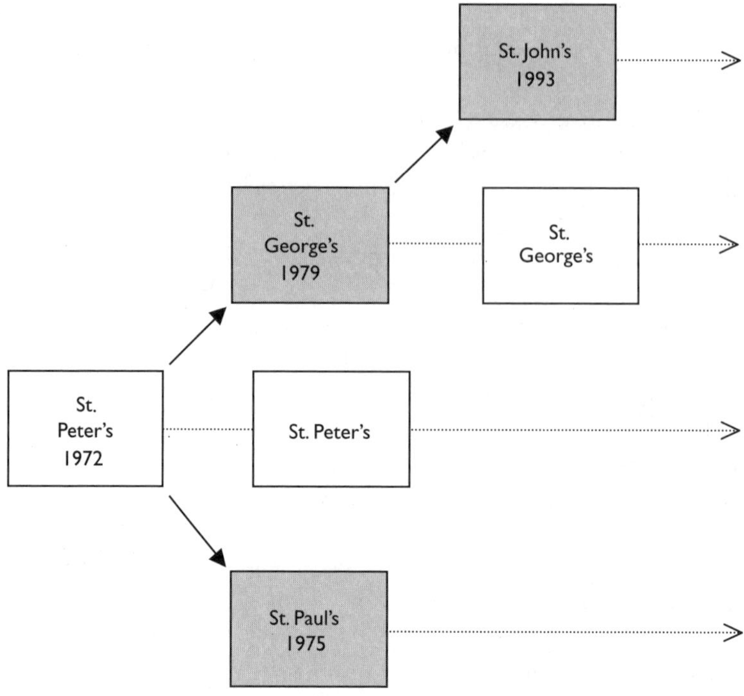

FIGURE 1. The history of congregational splits in Central City.

At the national and international levels, the proliferation of congregations appears to have benefited both the administrations of the American diocese and the mother church in India.

Splits in immigrant congregations allow more male members to participate actively in church affairs.[5] Because the split-off groups tend to be small, the vigorous participation of men becomes crucial to the survival of the split-off congregations. Mrs. Simon told me that her family had left their first congregation to join a split-off congregation because her husband was given the chance to serve at the altar there. She elaborated that her husband did not get along with the priest at their home congregation and, therefore, did not serve at the altar. The priest of the newly formed congregation had "compelled" them to join.

The people involved in such splits seemed to feel a sense of importance as key players shaping events. For example, Mr. Kuriakose, who was hesitant at first to speak openly of his involvement in the group that eventually split off from St. George's, became markedly animated as he gave the following account of the prominence of his own role:

> Well, before the split they came here. Everybody was in this room. Father Mathen was sitting there. All the people who left—they were all here. And Father Mathen told us what he was going to do. Of course, he suffered a lot. He said, "I am going to resign." At that time, I suggested that we buy some time—one or two weeks. But Father Mathen's very strong supporters in the group made him resign. The same day, in a conversation, one of the people in this group [the splitting group] was saying that we might split again. Even after going [from St. George's], we will split again.

When asked why this person made this statement, Mr. Kuriakose said, "Well, that is the pattern. That's how this history goes. It was like that every time we split."

Many of the church members I interviewed experienced the splits in the congregation as extremely painful times. Mr. Peter gave this touching description of his experience of the most recent split at St. George's, when Father Mathen left with a group of members to form a new congregation: "Because we used to all be together—Father Mathen and all the members—now it is heartbreaking to have to choose the group to which you will belong. . . . For a few Sundays I went to Father Mathen's service. Then I came back here. Actually, I was telling my wife that my heart is bleeding. I think there is nobody else in the church who is as terribly sad. Those people were dear to me too, and so are these. This was a terrible thing that happened to me."

Mrs. Simon's comments about her husband exemplify why, despite the painful consequences of church politics, church participation is so important for immigrant men. "As for me," said Mrs. Simon, "I told my husband, 'Don't join all these [political] parties and groups in the church. Just go to church, pray, and come back. Why go for these parties? I don't like that.' He [her husband] says, 'I have to have a niche here somehow. What can I say to all these guys that turned against me? At least I have three to four people with whom I can talk now.'" Without extended family or friends in the United States, having a niche becomes crucial for many men as the congregation compensates for the missing family relationships that are present in Kerala. Consequently, for the individuals involved, splits in the congregation are as emotionally disturbing as conflicts and separation within the family.[6]

The phenomenon of increased splitting is also facilitated by the manner in which the mother church in India handles the immigration of priests. Instead of being sent by the church to serve a congregation for a specified period of time, the priests come like other immigrants, sponsored by relatives. Often priests are married to nurses and suffer a loss in status similar to that of immigrant men in their congregations.[7] Furthermore, because most congregations cannot afford their upkeep, the priests cannot be full-time priests and must find a second job. In several interviews, respondents suggested that the "Sunday" priests were partly responsible for the prevalence of schisms, since it becomes an important identity issue for the immigrant priest to have a congregation for whom he can conduct mass, thus enabling him to maintain his vocation.

Income is another incentive, in the form of a monthly congregational contribution as well as individual donations. Therefore, priests may help engineer the splitting of congregations. If there is a thriving congregation in a particular area, and a new priest emigrates there, chances are that within a few years he will find a dissatisfied group of people in the existing congregation who will precipitate a split.

Interestingly, the larger institutional politics of the Indian Orthodox Church appears to have played a part in the phenomenal incidence of congregational splitting in the United States. Father Elias, a veteran in the American diocese, gave this opinion on the issue of congregational splits: "Most of them — a number of congregations started because the priest had a problem with the congregation, so they went away with a number of people and started it, which is because of a lack of discipline in the church. And the bishop encouraged it, unfortunately, because of ulterior motives." When asked what he thought these ulterior motives were, Father Elias replied, "To tell the world that he has so many congregations in his jurisdiction. I have not seen any effort on his part — again not to be considered as a negative criticism; just my observation — to resolve a situation where a congregation was going to be split. He indirectly encouraged splitting. He always said 'The more you have, the better you are.'"

It is widely held that the bishop who resigned as head of the diocese of the United States in 1992 was attempting to promote a separation from the mother church in India, so that he could become the leader of an independent church in the United States. Part of his alleged strategy was to encourage the splitting of congregations in order to have a greater number of congregations under his jurisdiction.[8] The mother church ostensibly did not discourage the tendency for congregational splits, since it meant an increase in mandatory dues and revenue for the church.

COLLECTIVE COOKING: THE CREATION OF NEW MALE ROLES

If forming new congregations provides new leadership opportunities, the creation of new roles within a congregation fosters a sense of belonging for men. For example, those activities typically seen as female responsibilities, such as cooking and serving food, are assumed by the men at St. George's and practiced on a weekly basis, as well as on the major feast and festival days.

In Kerala there is a tradition of male leadership in cooking for wedding banquets and other social events where food must be prepared for large groups of people. However, there are few occasions for serving food in the congregational setting. The typically large congregations in Kerala do not have weekly refreshments after the service. Because worshipers in the United States often travel a great distance to attend Sunday services, and because the social and fellowship aspects of congregational life are much more central to the immigrant congregation, refreshments and whole meals after the service are the norm in this country.

The men at St. George's appear to control the public part of this process, from the planning of meals to the collective preparation and serving of food in the church. Each week, men make the coffee and take charge of serving refreshments and meals. Typically, I would see six to seven men discussing politics and other matters in the basement kitchen while waiting for the coffee to brew. There was clearly no need for six to seven men to make coffee or put out the snacks for the day while the service was going on upstairs. That these men gathered in the kitchen to do so points to the importance of this alternative space for male fellowship.

When the priest announced one Sunday that people were needed to bring food for the meal on a particular festival Sunday, it was the men in the congregation who volunteered. On Christmas Eve, as on other special occasions when a meal had to be prepared for the worshipers, men gathered in the church kitchen to cook the collective Christmas meal. Several women gathered near the kitchen as they waited for the Christmas Eve social program to begin. While some sat quietly talking among themselves, others peeled onions or cut garlic while watching the men cook. The women appeared to be more of an audience for the men, who joked around as they cooked, cleaned, and decorated the hall for the festivities.

At one point, a man left alone in the kitchen lamented in jest that he had been deserted much like Jesus on the cross to take the blame for cooking. Later the men reminisced about the days before the most recent split at St. George's, noting that they had lost a couple of expert male cooks to the split-off group. Clearly, cooking for church functions had become institutionalized as another opportunity for male participation.

The women's lack of participation in public cooking does not mean they do not cook for church functions. In fact, in the case of potlucks or other occasions where food is not cooked in the church kitchen, it is likely that the women prepare the food at home, even if it is their husbands who stand up to volunteer what will be brought. For example, on one festival Sunday, as Mrs. Patrose and her husband arrived, the latter carried a pot of food for the communal meal taking place that day. I was standing with a group of women when one of them teasingly suggested that Mrs. Patrose's husband was doing the cooking these days. Mrs. Patrose immediately assured us that she had done the cooking, and that he was only carrying the heavy pot because of her bad back.

I had the opportunity to ask a number of the men how they felt about cooking for the church. It was clear from their answers that they valued the communal nature of the activity despite the low status attached to communal cooking for church events in Kerala. As Mr. Samuel explained, "I never did anything in India, you know—cooking and things like that. . . . Members of the church—poor people—are there to do it. It kind of looks small. The tradition over there is that, if you go and cook for the church, you will look—you are cheap or small in the society. They look down on that. Here also, maybe people think about it, but I don't care. Here nobody cares about anybody, you know. . . . It was really fun when the other church people, when we were all together [before the split]—it was fun to do things like that."

For the men, therefore, participation in this regular public ritual produces a collective identity more significant than any misgivings about the low status of cooking and serving in general. Male initiative in the serving and preparation of food seems to be present to the extent that it happens in a collective public process that allowed for male participation in a group of their peers. If splitting propagates new leadership roles, and cooking and feeding the congregation creates a sense of belonging, caroling is partially a way of establishing the church as male territory.

CAROLING: THE REDEFINITION OF ROLES

While Christmas caroling in the United States is an activity traditionally available to individuals and groups without institutional affiliations, in Kerala it is mainly a church-sponsored activity. Besides having the overt function of spreading "the good news" of Christmas, caroling is also a means of raising money for the Sunday school group of boys who generally participate in this activity. In Kerala, caroling groups from different churches make the rounds of the neighborhood, visiting the homes of members and nonmembers, where small donations are an expected part of the visit.

In the United States, the Keralite Christian congregations continue the practice of forming caroling groups, which go to the homes of members and nonmembers, including Hindus in the Keralite immigrant community. They are bringing the "good news" in the form of carols often written in the tunes of Malayalam film songs.[9] The tacit understanding is that each home they visit will donate money to the congregation. These donations are an important source of income for the congregation. For example, in 1994 the donations from caroling made up one-third of St. George's total income for the year.[10] This is a point of pride for many of the men who participate. Over several weeks, the caroling groups put in long hours and cover extensive areas of a typical metropolitan region.

Caroling not only is an opportunity for passing on "the good news" and for fund-raising for St. George's but also promotes exclusive male participation and camaraderie. As mentioned earlier, in Kerala the caroling group of the Orthodox congregation tends to be made up of young people from the Sunday school chaperoned by Sunday school teachers. The caroling group at St. George's departed from this Keralite convention in that only men took part in this activity.[11] In making caroling an exclusively adult male activity, members of St. George's redefined a role traditionally assigned to boys in Kerala.

After the young people at St. George's first made public their interest in caroling, the priest asked me to organize the group and direct their singing. With the staunch backing of the priest, nine teenage girls, three preadolescent boys, and I were able to accompany the men a few times. Because of my gender, relative youth, and role as organizer, my presence prompted some adult male reactions that gave me insight into the boundaries drawn around male participation. An incident that occurred as we traveled between homes for caroling demonstrates the men's discomfort with the gender of those challenging the boundaries.

There were about six male carolers packed into the two front rows of a rather large van. The girls and boys and I were jammed together in the back. We did not have proper seats, since the back seats had been folded down to make additional room. I was trying to teach the young people a new Malayalam carol that they could add to their repertoire. They did not have much trouble picking up the carol, which was sung to the tune of a classic Malayalam film song. I noticed that a few of the men were paying attention to our singing in between their conversations. The words of the song were unfamiliar to them, but they started chiming in at the refrain since it was a classic and a catchy tune. Then one of the men said, "Next year the kids will be able to do it [caroling] on their own." Another said, "Yup! That's all we are good for now—to sing the refrain." After a while, he added, "I guess Indira Gandhi is still in power."[12]

The interaction in the van demonstrated the men's awareness that their territory was being infringed upon when the young people started learning the Malayalam songs. Many of them had complained about their children not speaking Malayalam.[13] Yet in this instance, some of them appeared intensely uncomfortable listening to their offspring singing in the language. The comment that "that's all we are good for now—to sing the refrain" sounded like a lament about losing their last stronghold. The subsequent comment about Indira Gandhi still being in power may have been directly inspired by the majority female presence among the young people and especially by my role as the organizer.

By accompanying the youth and directing their singing, I was able to observe that caroling was primarily a male bonding experience not only for the men singing but also for those listening. Furthermore, I witnessed how caroling was organized by men for men. The camaraderie of the carolers came from their normally exclusive male membership (the few times the youth were allowed to join them constituted an exception), from the style of the singing, and from the illicit drinking among some of the carolers, which had to be hidden from the priest who accompanied them. In addition to building a fraternal bond among the singers, caroling also seemed to be aimed at meeting the approval of the male heads of the households and inspiring their benevolence in the form of donations.

Caroling parties were normally made up of twenty to twenty-five men, including a couple of drummers and tambourine players, someone dressed as Santa Claus, and the priest. The men were extremely animated as they clapped their hands and sang at the top of their voices. They usually stood around in a circle rhythmically moving together and, at critical moments, throwing their bodies forward to match the beat. It was a highly physical experience, and the carolers appeared exhilarated as each song inevitably built up to a crescendo. The style of their performance seemed reminiscent of the Keralite folk singing that accompanies boat races; only men participate in the boat races.

At the typical home, the family was usually awaiting our arrival, given that the caroling coordinators had called ahead to notify them of our itinerary. Usually the priest and other leaders of the caroling party would address the men in the household and shake hands with them. The women and children of the household remained in the background, listening and preparing refreshments for the group. The men of the household in turn addressed the carolers and communicated the good wishes of the family. Finally the men of the household gave the donation check to the leader of the group at the end of the singing.

In the homes of congregational members, the male hosts often had additional duties. Sometimes these men would personally direct the caroling group to the homes of Keralite immigrant neighbors, often not church members, who had agreed to a visit from the caroling group. Thus the men of the congregation were intimately involved, as both performers and hosts, in the success of the caroling venture.

In addition to engaging male participants in the singing, hosting, and donation collecting, the caroling venture also gave each of them an opportunity for display, comparison, and measurement of progress, especially of the financial type, in the wider Keralite immigrant community. Caroling provided an annual chance for community members to exhibit their new homes or the successes of their children to others in the community, who acted as the touchstones by which they gauged their achievements. Discussions about property values, long-term plans for a return to India, and the pain of losing children to extracommunity marriages made up the exchange as male hosts and carolers interacted with each other.

The importance of having the man of the house present in the home receiving the carolers became clear one night when, despite an appointment, the male householder was absent and the carolers decided to change plans. Upon finding that this man would not be home for another half hour, the carolers altered their itinerary despite the inconvenience. The fact that the carolers decided to wait, even though his wife and the rest of the household were perfectly capable of receiving the glad tidings and making a donation, suggests the significance of the man's presence as host and audience.

Along with being fun, it was a lot of hard work for the men who had to commit to the grueling caroling schedule. Over a period of three weeks, the group went out caroling on Thursdays and Fridays from early evening to the early hours of the next morning, even though many carolers had to work the next day. On weekends, the group started caroling as early as two in the afternoon and often did not finish until two the next morning. They covered large distances in a single night, going out to distant suburbs.

When I asked them to reflect on their experience of caroling, many of the men mentioned that waiting up for the caroling group to visit one's house is an essential part of the Keralite Christmas. As Mr. Samuel put it,

"It is an old tradition. During Christmastime everybody is expecting caroling to happen. If there is no caroling, you don't feel like it is Christmas. That is the way. We are used to that." Mr. Samuel clearly saw his participation in caroling as serving the community, since it would not feel like a Keralite Christmas without the singing.

For immigrant Keralite men, the immigrant congregation is an important space for participation, given their downward mobility with respect to the workplace and the domestic sphere. Along with the propagation of existing male roles via the splitting of congregations, and the creation of new roles within congregations, the redefinition of caroling as a male activity is a way that the church sphere has become more firmly established as male territory. While men turn to the immigrant congregation as a space of participation, the church, in turn, depends on the men's participation to fulfill its functions as a vital community center and a replacement for missing extended family.

It is important to reiterate that, by participating in the congregation, the men not only are compensating for their own loss of status but also are filling an opportunity vacuum created by a growing community. The church is a central institution that brings together a growing immigrant community. Several people told me that the first thing they did after immigration was to locate the immigrant congregation, where they met other immigrants and procured help to begin the process of settlement. The men's large contributions of time and resources are essential to the survival of the congregation.

It is especially important to look at the church's role as a substitute for members' extended families left behind in Kerala.[14] During happy times and sad times, individual members share the events of their lives with the church family. Beaming parents bring huge birthday cakes for the whole congregation to celebrate their child's important first birthday. A housewarming party is usually a communal celebration that takes place after the house-blessing ceremony conducted by the priest. Death or illness — even of relatives in Kerala — summons up an immediate network of support. Church members gather together at the home of the grieving member to offer spiritual consolation and material support.

Given the alienation that most immigrants feel away from their homeland, it is understandable why the church family becomes so important. For the men, it is more so: this is the one space where they are inherently endowed with the right to civic participation, and where they are the representative heads of the household. Mr. Elias put it well when he said, "Back home, if someone is visiting, your relatives will invite you. If there is death, your relatives will invite you. . . . For the death anniversary of a loved one, you would invite your relatives to your home and serve food. Here, since you don't have relatives, the church members become your relatives. Your friends become your relatives. So church is the center of social events. Cooking, serving, cleaning, and everything — we are like one family."

Maintaining extended-family ties is hard work. Somebody has to do the necessary work of cleaning and setting up for family events, and of cooking for and serving the family. Despite the negative connotation attached to cooking and cleaning in the church in Kerala, Mr. Elias and others like him are able to cook and clean in the immigrant congregation because they are doing it for their extended-family members.

The Reproduction of Female Roles

As in India, women have no ritual roles in the immigrant congregation. So as not to distract men, women and girls must cover their heads during the service. Typically, they receive communion and final blessings only after the men and boys have taken their turn. Because they are viewed as polluting by nature, the women in the church cannot enter the altar area or touch the garments of the priest. Because the consequences of their sex include menstruation, they are believed to be capable of defiling that which is holy and so are barred from contact with all that is holy.[15] The traditional importance of this prohibition is illustrated by my own experience with a priest in another church: he almost dropped a heavy table on my foot while I was helping him move it, because I had accidentally stepped on the altar.

Women also do not have many formal leadership positions available to them in the administration of the church. As mentioned already, only males over twenty-one years of age have a vote in meetings of the general body. Typically, women do not hold administrative positions other than in the areas of child education, food production, and church-sponsored women's groups. For instance, women may become Sunday school teachers, but they cannot be elected to the managing committee of the congregation. The church service or prayer group for women offers them some administrative positions, but in every congregation the president of this group is the priest.

THE ROLE OF THE CHURCH: AN INVESTED HIERARCHY

Both ideologically and practically, the Indian Orthodox Church in the United States is heavily invested in reinforcing a traditional hierarchy in the social relations of the family and the congregation. The husband's position as head of the family mirrors and reinforces the hierarchy that places the priest over the congregation, the bishops and church administrators over the priests, and the administration of the Keralite mother church over the U.S. diocese.

It is especially important at this historical juncture for the church to emphasize the traditional hierarchies, since it appears to be losing organizational control in the U.S. diocese. The splits in the congregations point to the loss of control over their congregations that priests face, and that the American diocese faces with respect to the priests. Furthermore, the mother church in Kerala was troubled by the dissension in the American diocese following the alleged attempt by a bishop to break off ties with the mother church and form his own church. Despite the presence of a new bishop as head of the diocese, a number of renegade congregations support the former bishop and refuse to follow the dictates of the mother church. Facing such challenges, the church finds it all the more important to emphasize traditional order and hierarchy.

This became evident at the 1995 annual national family conference sponsored by the American diocese, where a large number of families from St. George's were also present.[16] The theme of the conference was the Orthodox family. The organizers had invited an American Orthodox priest to be the keynote speaker for the three-day conference. This man, Father Rudolph, told the audience that he had left the Baptist church because he found American fundamentalism too unorderly. He had converted to Orthodoxy, attracted by the inherent orderliness in it.

The particular topic for the morning was titled "The Mystery of Marriage." Father Rudolph explained that the Christian marriage is a symbol for heaven. As scriptural reference, he quoted Ephesians 5:22: "Wives submit to husbands . . . as the church is subject to Christ so also." He spoke at length about how men are called to love their wives as Christ loved the church, and women are called to respect men. He then described this order, spelled out to the Ephesians by Apostle Paul, as representing the order in heaven, reflected within the order of the Trinity. He explained that there is a hierarchy in the relationship between the Father, Son, and Holy Spirit. For example, one could never imagine Jesus or the Holy Ghost challenging God's authority. Even though there is equality, there is also a hierarchy that creates order. The unity of the Trinity is in the Father, and there is order because the Father is in control.

Similarly, in marriage there must be order. Father Rudolph argued that, while modern feminism claims that "the wife is just as good as the husband," he believed that this is the recipe for the breakdown of order. He said that wives should voluntarily submit to their husbands. There should be no doubt as to who is in charge. The husband may not necessarily be smarter, better, or more spiritual, but God created this order, just as he created order in the kingdom of Heaven. Father Rudolph then reasoned that this order should also be present in the hierarchy of the church. He noted that he was placed under the authority of the bishop of his diocese, and that he had to submit to the wisdom of this bishop. Even if he did not agree with the bishop, he obeyed him in order to maintain order.

Traditional Christian theology tends to emphasize the unity of the trinity as three persons in one, but rarely does it mention a hierarchy in the relationship of the Father, Son, and Holy Spirit. Father Rudolph's interpretation of the Trinity as a hierarchy not only buttressed male headship in the immigrant family but also served to reinforce all the hierarchical relationships within the church.[17]

Sermons given by visiting bishops at St. George's and other venues for the various church events that I attended often spelled out appropriate gender roles and characteristics. One bishop, on Annunciation Sunday, highlighted the initial fallen condition of all women via Eve and the redemption of women through the Virgin Mary's attributes of passivity, patience, and total obedience. He then contrasted Asian women, with their ideal "patience and goodness," to American women who do not have these qualities. Another bishop, commenting on the increase in marital problems in immigrant families, advised women at a national church conference that they must be long suffering. Even if their husbands were to lose their tempers and abuse them, they should be patient even as Christ was and not give up on the relationship. These sermons by the bishops contained significant patriarchal ideology representative of the church's allegiance to traditional gender hierarchy.[18]

Literature on the Asian Indian immigrant community reveals that immigrant Indian religious and cultural organizations tend to construct an exemplary "model minority" public face that does not allow for the expression of the diversity of gender models in the community (Bhattacharjee 1992; Dasgupta and Dasgupta 1996; Ralston 1996b; Kurien 1999). Instead, the dominant construction of Indian womanhood that is sanctioned by the community is that of the pure, virtuous, and self-sacrificing wife and mother, similar to the bishop's model woman. The immigrant Hindu women whom the sociologist Helen Ralston interviewed told her the temple was the last place they would go for help in case of domestic violence, mostly because of temple functionaries' patriarchal perspective on domestic violence. As Ralston theorizes, "Patriarchal structures produce androcentric religious ideologies which constitute, legitimize and reproduce relations of domination, subordination and exploitation of women" (1996b: 15).

Besides patriarchal gender ideologies, practices supporting male primacy and headship were also preserved in the communal life of the immigrant congregation. There are three occasions on an average Sunday morning when members of the congregation come to the front of the church to receive blessings from the priest during the service. First, people who want to receive communion will come up to receive prayer for the absolution of sins. Then there is communion. Finally, at the end of the service, the congregation files by the priest as they place their weekly offering into the collection plate and he blesses them by touching his cross to their foreheads. For all these occasions, the men go first, followed by the women. On one Sunday at St. George's, after all the men who had lined up had received the prayer of absolution, the priest started working through the waiting queue of girls and women. One man who had changed his mind about receiving communion came up to the front and immediately cut in front of all the women who were waiting. This man's behavior points to the unspoken rule that men have precedence. All parties concerned assumed that the man, despite having missed his turn, must have the right-of-way before the women.

Another way that male primacy is publicly reinforced in the congregation is through the assumption that male heads of households make decisions about financial contributions. At a general-body meeting I attended, when the secretary read the minutes from the previous biannual meeting of the general body, he addressed the group as "gentlemen" despite the priest's explicit invitation to the whole congregation to participate in the meeting. Copies of the financial report had been made only for the men in the meeting, even though many women usually attend such meetings. This became especially clear when women without men accompanying them—widows or women whose husbands were not present—raised their hands to indicate that they needed a copy of the report. They received one only if there were enough left after all the men had gotten their copies.

Sociological theory leads us to believe that, when a church in the U.S. religious market enforces a patriarchal order from above, women will either escape it or challenge it (Warner 1993). It is not surprising that immigrant women have no greater participation in the church than they do, given the gender ideology in the Orthodox tradition. Yet, there is growing evidence that women in fairly conservative, orthodox traditions of Islam have increased opportunities for participation after immigration (Haddad and Lummis 1987), as is true for women in a number of other religious traditions (Ebaugh and Saltzman 1999).

Among South Asian immigrants from non-Christian traditions, scholars find that women tend to increase their level of participation after immigration (Lessinger 1995; Ralston 1996a; Rayaprol 1997; Kurien 1999). For example, in her study of a South Indian Hindu temple in Pittsburgh, Aparna Rayaprol found that women have subverted the private/public dichotomy that assigned them to the private, domestic sphere by actively seeking after and obtaining elected positions. They have assumed power in the temple organization that, in India, was exclusively the domain of men. Similarly, Prema Kurien argues that women play a more crucial role in the United States in defining and transmitting culture and ethnicity. Consequently, at the household and local-associations levels, women are able to reinterpret the patriarchal images more in their favor and assume greater leadership positions. Given this trend among other South Asian groups, why do Keralite Christian nurses, being upwardly mobile professional women, not demand such change? It is largely their profession that shapes their response to the extension of male prerogative in the immigrant congregation.

THE ROLE OF THE NURSES: SELF-PATROLLING COOPERATION

Irregular nursing work schedules and shift work make it difficult for most of the immigrant Christian Indian women to consistently attend church and other affiliated activities such as the women's group meetings. This problem was illustrated in a discussion during one general meeting when I sat with women as they participated in their own running commentary on the proceedings. One suggested to another that she run for the position of committee member. After some joking about how she would be kicked out of the church for doing so, she suggested to her friend that they run for the position as a team. As she explained, "When you're working, I'll sit on the committee; and when I'm working, you can sit on it."

At the same meeting, when any decision was made after a belabored discussion, some of the women would start to clap spontaneously, as if to let the men know that it was time to move on to the next topic. One of them said, "This is our job — to clap." But it also seemed that they did not take the meeting very seriously and were getting tired of waiting for their spouses. One woman explained her disengagement from the church politics: "I don't like too much involvement. . . . I don't like the quarreling and fighting in the church. That is the only place where I get a little peace. If there is fighting there as well, I cannot tolerate it."

Since shift work was a common solution for the childcare problem, this work arrangement impinged on women's ability to participate extensively in congregational life. Consequently, I observed many women looking sleepy during the long, three-hour Sunday morning service after having worked all night. I saw other women hurriedly collecting family members and belongings after Sunday service to make their afternoon shifts on time. Many of the women were not motivated to stay after church for meetings and other activities. Whereas male participation in the church expanded after immigration, women's participation was cut back because of their busy work schedules.

Part of the reason why nurses go along with the status quo is to compensate for their increased status in the immigration process in the work and domestic spheres. Because it is known in the community that nurses tend to make more money than their husbands, the women have to be careful to not be seen as too assertive, for this would risk censure not only for themselves but also for their husbands. One woman related a telling incident concerning a woman who spoke up during a meeting of the general body. In Kerala, women are not allowed in the churches during general-body meetings, which occur about twice a year. In the United States, because families travel long distances to church in one car, women and children often attend meetings with the men, but women do not participate in decision making. The reaction to the woman who chose to voice her opinion in one such meeting was immediate, and it remained etched in the memories of the many people who referred to this incident when I asked them if women spoke up in church meetings. Mrs. Itoop told me, "Women don't give opinions [in church]. Haven't you noticed? I remember once in a general-body meeting, a woman stood up and talked. Oh, the commotion that created!" When I asked Mrs. Itoop what happened, she responded, "A man said to her, 'Women don't talk here, so sit down!' . . . Isn't that humiliating? If she kept quiet, she wouldn't have been humiliated. Whatever they say, I keep quiet. If you say something, they will say, 'That woman is terrible — she expresses her opinions when men are discussing things.' . . . The men will judge you."

After referring to the same incident, Mrs. Philip bemoaned the fact that it was still not acceptable for women to speak in public in the immigrant community: "I don't think that this mentality will change in this generation — unless you take all their blood and wash it out." She explained her own disinclination to vocally participate in the general-body meetings: "In fact, I have felt like talking at times, but I know that they [the men] are going to talk about me." When asked whether they would talk about her or her husband, she said, "You know what. They will talk to the husband and say, 'See how your wife is.' This leads to a fight at home. But when they [the women] are at work, they argue and talk, but because they don't want a fight with their husbands or people talking, they just keep quiet [in church]." If Mrs. Philip were to speak up in church, she would risk not only public humiliation but also a loss of face for her husband and conflict at home. Given these disincentives, the women find alternative spaces, such as the workplace, for their discussions.

Because nursing is a marker of deviant femininity, it may be even more important for nurses to be circumspect and stay within gendered boundaries in church, to guard their carefully forged respectability. Mrs. Mathai, who left home at the age of sixteen to study nursing, explained why she is still afraid of having her reputation maligned in communal settings such as church:

> If some girl was sent for nursing, the feeling was that she was lost. But people just made up those things. Even now our people are like that. If I speak to somebody, even though I am married our people will make up things to say. They don't look at age. They will say whatever they want, especially our men. Even if we smile at somebody or say hi, immediately that information goes to the Indian store, and they start talking about you. It is just like in Kerala — that's how our people are. There are many stories like that around here. This is why I don't send my daughters anywhere without their father. I am actually scared.

Mrs. Mathai was referring to a loss of moral reputation when she spoke of nurses being thought of as "lost." The need to guard her reputation still limited Mrs. Mathai's movement within the immigrant community, just as in Kerala. Even her daughters' mobility had to be monitored to prevent the soiling of their reputations.

Another woman told me that, when she first came to the United States, she did not go to an immigrant church because she did not have a car. She was afraid to ask for a ride from the families that attended church, because she did not want anyone to gossip about her being friendly with the men who might give her rides. She explained that she and her single immigrant nurse friends "tried to stay away from such problems till we settled down with husbands. We never gave people a chance to talk like that."

This concern about moral reputation among immigrant women is not unique to the Indian nurses I studied. For example, Menjivar (2000) found that female immigrants from Central America also tended to limit or avoid accepting favors, such as rides, from unrelated men so as to avoid misunderstandings and gossip in the community. According to the sociologist Yen Espiritu (2001), concern about morality, particularly regarding women's sexuality, is a common feature of racialized, minority groups like immigrant communities. From her research among Filipino immigrants, she posits that the "virtuous Filipina" is constructed against the image of the immoral Western white woman. She argues, "Because the control of women is one of the principal means of asserting moral superiority, young women in immigrant families face numerous restrictions on their autonomy, mobility and personal decision-making" (2001: 417). Anannya Bhattacharjee (1992) also makes a similar point about the importance of the model of the pure woman in the construction of Indianness for South Asian immigrants. This issue becomes even more relevant for immigrant nurses who, like Mrs. Mathai, carry the additional burden of fighting against the existing sexual stigma connected to their profession.

Women police themselves in terms of their bodies, as manifested in their concern over the clothing they wear and where they stand in the communal space of the church. In an informal conversation, Mrs. Mani, whom I met at a national church conference, told me that she agonized over what to wear in front of the bishop, whose home in New York she had to visit frequently. She was one of the main national officials of the women's group and often had to deal with the bishop's secretary, who was a priest. She described her complicated process for making decisions about what to wear on the days she had to go to the bishop's house. Whereas she usually wore a skirt and blouse to her nursing job, on the days she went to the bishop's home, she either wore an Indian outfit or took a change of Indian clothing with her to work, after having discussed the choice with her husband.

She then told me about an incident in her church that showed how conservative "our people" are. Once when her daughter wore a nice, dressy pair of pants to church, the priest's wife pulled Mrs. Mani aside and asked her why her daughter wore pants to church. Mrs. Mani's reasoning in the matter illustrates the detailed patrolling of the female body. She said, "Yes, my daughter tucked her shirt in her pants, but wearing a skirt with your blouse tucked in and wearing pants — both ways your behind is visible to the same extent."

The silence of the women in the church and their insistence on following scripted norms of femininity appear to be compensatory behavior designed not only to offset their husbands' losses in immigration and underline their own respectability but also to establish their families as acceptable in the eyes of the community. The sociologist Marjorie DeVault (1994) makes the point that, when women do the work of wife or mother — that is, when they take on assigned social roles — they are producing the family. Rather than taking the "the family" for granted, she argues that doing the work of wife and mother — such as feeding the family or monitoring the children's correct social behavior — produces family life. Discourses on family life — informed by culture — prescribe different ways to "do family." Individuals who follow the prescriptions end up producing a socially acceptable family.

To some extent, in the families of nurses, the assigned social roles that produce family are in crisis, and as a result, "doing family" is also full of tension. One way of relieving the tension is for men and women to have a space where they publicly "do family" in the culturally assigned ways. For example, Mrs. Patrose was "doing family" when she insisted that, although her husband was carrying the heavy pot, it was indeed she who had concocted the food within. Similarly, Mrs. Mathai's and Mrs. Mani's concern about their daughters' behavior and clothing in the community reveals their keen awareness of the importance of their mothering responsibilities and the fact that how they handle these responsibilities reflects on their families.

While most nurses did not have formal leadership roles, in interviews they spoke of less visible ways in which they participated in church life.[19] For instance, Mrs. Eapen displayed a sense of ownership when she recounted how much money different people in the church had contributed to the building fund. She spoke about how she recently had pledged two days' worth of her pay when the priest asked for financial help for the church. Mrs. Lukos revealed that one of the first splits in the history of the congregation happened in her house, and that she was the one who had called the bishop to tell him the news, since she knew him from India.

From my interviews at St. George's, it was clear that the female members' opinions about the permitted level of participation varied. Some of these women were satisfied with the status quo; others would have liked to have more active roles and a public voice in the congregation's decision-making processes. Nurses' work schedules make it difficult for them to consistently attend church activities. Additionally, their upward mobility and alleged deviation from cultural norms of female propriety motivate the nurses to compensate by purposefully maintaining the expected gender norms in communal spaces such as the congregation. As a result, in the public space of the church there is a relatively successful reproduction of gender relations as even the second-generation females are patrolled by their mothers and other women watching to make sure that gender norms are followed. This reproduction, however, is not happening without some resistance.

CHALLENGES TO HEGEMONY: NON-NURSES, PROGRESSIVE PRIESTS, AND THE SECOND GENERATION

At the same conference where Father Rudolph spoke about the hierarchy in the Trinity, the women's group meeting discussed what was appropriate clothing for young women to wear to church. The bishop's final comment was that girls under twelve could wear pants to church, but that older girls would have to be more modest about their clothing. There was a lot of discussion about how much skin could be shown and what constituted tradition and modesty.

After this discussion, I had tea with some women from St. George's. One woman complained that standards of modesty were hardly fixed. She recalled that during her childhood in Kerala a questionable change in fashion had been facilitated by its adoption by upper-class women. Sleeveless blouses were deemed risqué until rich upper-class women started wearing them to church. She noted that many of these women were very fat and had big, fleshy upper arms that were visible when they wore their sleeveless blouses. Nobody in the church hierarchy said anything about this skin-revealing attire. In recalling these upper-class women from her childhood, she was making the point that some women could get away with breaking norms.

Within the context of the immigrant church, it was the women who were not nurses who led any attempts to change the status quo. For example, at another national church conference, one session focused on the role of women in the church. One woman spontaneously assumed leadership and wrote up a petition asking for suffrage for women in church affairs, which she passed around for signatures from those present. She was from a well-known family in Kerala, related to the bishop in charge of the American diocese, and a full-time homemaker in the United States. Her confidence in taking such a public stance had as much to do with her family background and proximity to the male power structure as with the fact that she was not a nurse. And the most vocal protest to this petition came from some nurses who wanted to maintain conventional gender roles.

At St. George's, an attempt to change the gender segregation of the Sunday service similarly occurred during a women's group meeting. Responding to the problem that children were not behaving themselves during the service, the priest suggested that perhaps they should sit with their parents. Dr. Stephen, a woman who is the vice president of the women's group and a medical doctor, took this opportunity to endorse the idea that families should sit together as a group. Mrs. Papi, who was sitting next to me, muttered that the Orthodox Church was not ready for this type of change. She turned to me and said that "our men" would never agree with such a suggestion. I asked her if the women would agree. She said that she would not feel comfortable with men and women sitting together. She then stood up and registered her dissent, stating that it was not Orthodox tradition to mix men and women together.

Dr. Stephen argued that the Orthodox tradition in Kerala used to place all the men up front and the women behind them, in the sanctuary. Then some women complained, and tradition changed to allow men and women to stand side by side, in two sections. She concluded that there was no biblical basis for determining where people stand in church, and that there was nothing unorthodox about families sitting together. Mrs. Papi murmured that it was not only the Bible that people must follow; they must also follow what the church fathers taught. One woman turned to her neighbor and said, "Sunday morning is the only time in the week that I get a chance to sit by myself in peace, and I don't want to be sitting with my husband." The priest brought this discussion to an end by suggesting that they drop the issue, since he did not want to start a problem in an already fragile political environment.

At a later date, when I asked Dr. Stephen about this meeting during an interview, she seemed to still find the incident preposterous: "What's this idea that men have to sit here and women have to sit there? It's just ridiculous. It's stupid. But of course our priest said, 'No, let's not do it,' because he knew that they would send him away, and they would probably send me away packing too." Despite Dr. Stephen's assessment of the situation, the nurses who resisted this change would not agree with her. For Mrs. Papi, it was concern about the opinion of the men that added to her own discomfort and justified her dissent. For another woman, Sunday morning was the only time she had for herself—away from children, husband, and work—and it was not in her interest to change this arrangement. Neither of the women with upper-class social capital was successful in bringing about the changes she had desired. Interestingly, their attempts were overruled not only by the church hierarchy but also by the other women, most of whom were nurses.

It is instructive to look at the experiences of other women of color in the United States to understand why women can be motivated to submit to formal male leadership and uphold traditions that are ultimately oppressive to them. For example, the sociologist Belinda Robnett (1997) found that, in the civil rights movement, black women left formal positions of leadership to the men because they believed that black men had more obstacles to overcome and, therefore, had greater need of the status that leadership conferred. One female former leader of the Student Nonviolent Coordinating Committee said:

> I am now in my own research looking at the religious women, the churchwomen, and of course there is no place where women are more subordinated than the church. But some of that . . . is that, because of the ways in which Black men have been demeaned, because there were no places in which Black men could give leadership with dignity except those places which were controlled by the Black community, and that would be the Black church and the Black movement organization. . . . So in that sense, I think that there has been an attitude of support for Black male leadership by very, very strong, assertive Black women. (1997: 42)

Robnett concludes that, for the black women, gender identity was determined by their racial identity, so that the women's support for formal male leadership should not be understood as false consciousness. Instead, it must be appreciated in the context of a racist, white patriarchal society, in which black women yielded to male leadership. Similarly, it may be argued that the Indian nurses who resisted Dr. Stephen's initiative for change were also reacting with an awareness of the importance of the church space for their husbands, who did not have access to status-bearing positions in the wider society, and the strong possibility that the men would perceive the initiative as threatening.

Along with the upper-class women who are not nurses, priests also have the potential to introduce change — perhaps, more successfully — as was the case at St. George's. Whereas most priests, being the husbands of nurses, are wedded to the traditional gender hierarchy, there are exceptions like Father John, the vicar at St. George's. An unmarried, retired professor, Father John had an extremely egalitarian outlook. His sermons often started out as discussions of a Socratic nature. He never spoke from the pulpit but always walked down to where the children sat in front. He started out by asking questions of children and adults, men and women.

Often, women enthusiastically responded to his questions and expressed appreciation for his style of teaching.

While not directly challenging the official stance of the church regarding the participation of women, Father John's sermons critiqued the social oppression of women in the community. He strongly objected to the custom of dowry and the coexistent devaluation of girls in the community. One Sunday, he portrayed the unequal relationship between husbands and wives as a problem. He stressed that marriage was meant to be an equal relationship between two people, not one where a man finds a woman to be a slave, as many of the men in the community may have assumed. Many women laughed at this, and I saw a couple of women nudging each other. He said he knew that there were cases of men abusing their wives both emotionally and physically, but that he did not know of any in this church.

He raised some uncomfortable issues in sermons by joking about them. He talked about the importance of showing affection to children, since children in the United States are raised without much support from extended-family members. In Kerala, when mothers are busy, grandparents will rock babies to sleep or play with them. He noted that when talking about child care in the United States, he was not talking about mothers, since "we all know who takes care of kids in the United States." There was collective laughter at this statement — the tension-filled laughter of a community trying to deal with its contradictions.

He attempted to introduce new roles for women and girls in the congregation by increasing their opportunities for participation. For instance, he invited both young boys and girls to read parts of the scripture each Sunday during the service. There was strong resistance to this practice, which people viewed as "unorthodox," but the priest was able to restrain the zealous defenders of tradition with the moral authority of his position and his gentle personality. While his attempts at change did not go unopposed, his official voice from the pulpit both highlighted issues of gender inequality and created some space for the introduction of change.

It was this very space that the second generation of young women at St. George's seized when they expressed an interest in caroling with their fathers.[20] For most of the girls, it was a chance to get out of the house at night, stay out late with friends, and go to the homes of friends from other churches in the community.

Because many members of the adult generation consistently expressed concern about increasing their children's level of participation in church activities, the second generation's desire to go caroling, especially in their native language, ought to have been a welcome prospect for their parents.

Additionally, because in Kerala there are apparently no religious restrictions or rigid conventions that prohibit young people from participating in caroling, the resistance expressed by St. George's adults appeared anomalous and required explanation.

It appears that the impetus to preserve and expand male participation in the communal sphere of the church is at odds with the aims to transmit Indian culture and retain the second generation in the church. That people are particularly threatened that it is their daughters, and not their sons, who want to participate points to the gendered and generational nature of the conflict.

While second-generation young women may be more likely than their mothers to voice their dissatisfaction with the status quo, there is also a lot of pressure on them, more than on their male siblings, to conform to cultural norms. This was especially evident in the concern over appropriate clothing for young girls and the patrolling done by their mothers to ensure the enforcement of such norms in communal settings. Despite the relative success in the reproduction of female roles and the extension of male participation in the immigrant congregation, there is a paradoxical loss of status for the men most active in church affairs.

The Paradox of the "Men Who Play"

Tossed around in the ebb and the flow of an unstable U.S. economy, the immigrant men were often unable to hold down steady jobs. Consequently, both at work and at home, they lost a central part of their identity as providers. Given the lack of sufficient space for civic participation by immigrant racial minorities in the wider U.S. society, they looked mostly to the immigrant congregation for opportunities to gain back a sense of belonging and importance.

Ironically, the male attempt to reclaim status in the community turns out to be self-defeating. If splitting opens up new positions in the church hierarchy, at the same time — by making these positions more common, ephemeral, and mundane — it also devalues them and, thus, the men who occupy them. Their increased participation only attracts the resentment and disdain of displaced onlookers, who speak of them as children "playing" in the church.

Mr. Mathen, a member of St. George's who distanced himself from church leadership, characterized the importance of church roles for the husbands of nurses:

Nurses over here make good bucks, and the men go for a clerical job — whatever — and the women make more money. Women have this thing [feeling] that "I am the breadwinner, or I make more money." This is not just my opinion. Several people, even the husbands of nurses, who are my friends — this is their opinion too. Now in the house, there is nothing [for the men]. Husbands don't have the feeling that "I make more money than you." In the house, the husband does not have his proper status. In the society, you are an Indian — what status do you have? For men — where are they going to show their "macho" nature? That's why they play in the church. This is what is going on in our churches, and I am not just talking about St. George's.

Using the metaphor of "playing," Mr. Mathen distanced himself from these men by likening them to little children acting up in church. For Mr. Mathen, they were behaving like children because life after immigration did not allow them the opportunity to be men with "proper status."

In my observation, men's downward economic mobility and their loss of status in the domestic sphere were connected to a more active participation in the church. Consequently, men from the nontraditional households were the most active in church activities and administration. Almost all the men in the nontraditional households were actively involved in the managing committee, in teaching Sunday school, and in serving as acolytes, musicians, and carolers. Not surprisingly, men from traditional households participated the least in the immigrant congregation compared to all other types of households. In fact only one man from a traditional household actively participated in the church administration, and he seemed to have business reasons for his participation.

Men from traditional households distanced themselves from church administration and from the men involved in it. Furthermore, a number of the traditional householders made disparaging comments about men who did involve themselves. They characterized the latter as emasculated, lower-class men without education. Nursing as a marker of gender and class stigma was used by traditional householders to undermine the newly achieved status of the husbands of nurses. The shift in power in the domestic sphere came back to haunt the men in the communal sphere, where their connection to nurses became the most salient feature of their identities.

DEVIANT NURSES AND EMASCULATED NURSE-HUSBANDS

The husbands of nurses, who usually followed their wives to the United States, partly lost their individual identities in the secondary roles they played in the immigration process. One man, himself the husband of a nurse, told me that the new immigrant men were literally identified by their wives' first names upon arrival in the United States: for example, "Annie's husband" or "Molly's husband." Given that the women had arrived first, it was often through them that the men made their social contacts. Dr. Stephen pointed out the contrast between the success of the women in the economic and social realms and the men's seeming failure:

> Almost a 100 percent of the women in churches — not only our church but any church you go to — are nurses. . . . And these nurses, they have their workplace; their life is their workplace. Outside of their workplace, they are struggling to raise their children somehow, instill some of the values in their children. Early in the morning on Sundays, they still manage to gather all their children and bring them to Sunday school. I think that it's really their initiative, they are the ones — the women are the ones who are doing that. For instance, during the women's group meetings which we conduct, they are a little more open and receptive to ideas, especially more than men. The men, they just come and hang around and then go.

Although Dr. Stephen was sympathetic to the nurses, others among traditional householders tended to stereotype them as controlling. Mrs. Itoop, who was not a nurse, voiced a common theme when she told me of some sayings in the community that identify nurse's husbands as frustrated men: for example, "Nurses are the bosses" and "It is the men who are not allowed to say anything at home or at work who come and shout at church." Her husband echoed this sentiment when he said that you could tell by the faces of some of the men at church that they were unhappy at home. Mr. Itoop elaborated: "There [in the church] the wife will not say anything. At home she might, but not in church. . . . It is considered very bad to be a controlling wife back home [in India], because men are the bosses. If it is the opposite, it is a very bad thing. . . . The wives won't try to control openly. His masculinity is shown inside the church; the idea is to show the wife and others. He may be able to get rid of what is inside: 'Even though I am insignificant, I am not bad' — he wants to show that to others." Thus, the deviant femininity attributed to the controlling wife found a parallel in the emasculated stereotype of the "nurse-husband" who was forced to put on a show in church.

And according to Mr. Mathen, even the husbands of the nurses recognized that their greater participation in the church might be compensation for the loss of status in the domestic sphere. He posited that the immigrant congregation's committee membership could be directly correlated to their being the husbands of nurses:

> You take any church, when you go to California, Washington, New York — you take anywhere, that is a fact. I will tell you right now, in our church, the trustee Mr. Varkey — his wife is a nurse. The secretary Mr. Paul — his wife is a nurse. [He goes on to name all of St. George's committee members.] . . . See where it stands — eight of them already, out of ten. There are two more.
>
> It is not my point. Even Varkey, Patrose, Paul — they all say the same thing. Oh, I am not saying behind their backs or anything. This is the fact. . . . Not that there is trouble in their homes. They say that the men are showing off in the church. I am not saying these men have problems in the homes. They are all happily married, and they are my friends too. If you take a church, this is what you see. Kunju — his wife is not a nurse. He was never on a committee.

Yet in the church environment, these men were judged for their inability to meet the norms of the traditional division of labor. They were stigmatized as emasculated because they were forced to participate in household work and were economically dependent on their wives, signifying a loss of patriarchal control over them. The upper class, often professional and educated men and women from Kerala, became the source of such gender stigmatization. In comparing his own situation to that of the husbands of nurses, Mr. Mathen said, "I don't need to show off anything anywhere. If I say something to my wife, I know that she will do it. I don't have to go to church and say, 'You should do as I say.' I don't have to do that." For Mr. Mathen, the critical difference between himself and the husband of a nurse was the patriarchal control he could assume over his wife.

While the husbands of nurses might not have problems in their marriages, they did experience a nontraditional division of labor, which became the basis for their purported emasculation. Men and women of nontraditional households had to struggle and come to terms with the impossibility of maintaining the traditional division of labor in the post-immigration set-up. In most cases, they had to rethink their domestic division of labor.

NOUVEAUX RICHE NURSES AND LOWER-CLASS NURSE-HUSBANDS

Interestingly, not only the gender status of the men but also their class status was questioned as a result of their connection to nurses. Unlike in Kerala, the concentration of nurses in the immigrant community made nursing and the money that nurses earn highly visible. In the absence of the class markers that operated in Kerala, nursing was transformed into an explicit marker of class in the United States that tied the husbands of nurses to the alleged preimmigration lower-class origins of their wives.

In a society where caste, class, and religion are all important indicators of identity, Keralite Christians are themselves separated into different denominations, castes, and classes. Most Keralite Syrian Christians choose to separate themselves from the "lower castes" by claiming that they are directly descended from the Brahmin caste, although Christian theology does not allow for internal caste differentiation. And while Syrian Christian churches began accepting lower-caste converts in the late nineteenth century, almost all the churches maintain separate places of worship, separate congregations, and separate cemeteries for the few lower-caste converts in the churches. Keralite Syrian Christians are a strictly endogamous pseudo-caste group, in that marriages and other affiliations are usually limited to their own group. Class differences within this group are an important means of social differentiation. Although marriages take place among members of different Syrian Christian denominations, such as between Catholics and the orthodox, class differences operate to regulate these alliances.[21]

In Central City, material wealth, family name, and community leadership — three important markers of class in Kerala — recede in importance and in some cases disappear altogether. For most families, immigration and the resulting enrichment homogenizes consumption patterns, rendering differences in material wealth less visible. Whereas only the rich own large homes or cars in India, almost all in the community in the United States are able to afford these items, especially given the availability of credit. Mr. Cherian, whose wife was not a nurse, explained how "nurse money" made it difficult to distinguish between the rich and the poor. When asked if it was still possible to recognize who is rich or poor, he said, "Here the difference between the rich and the poor is much less. In India, you can differentiate the rich and the poor much quicker." Then he added, "No, here you can't tell. Nurses make good money so they can buy the stuff to look rich. So you can't tell who is rich. In India, the rich have good education — you know, doctors, engineers, and lawyers. They don't marry nurses; they marry from good families, only the educated. . . . That is what we see in our church at least. Do you see any doctors working in our kitchen?" According to Mr. Cherian, "nurse money" allowed immigrants to "buy the stuff to look rich." Although he posited that one could not tell the rich from the poor in the United States, he observed that one could tell who was married to a nurse. In his view, men from wealthy "good families" would not marry nurses and would not be working in the church kitchen. Thus, in Mr. Cherian's eyes, despite the nice cars and nice houses, immigrant men's marital affiliation with nurses linked them to a lower-class background.

Viviana Zelizer (1989), in an intriguing argument, posits that money can be seen as having other than simply market value. She proposes a model of "special monies" that can incorporate the social and symbolic significance of money. For example, in the United States, she suggests, domestic money is one example of special money. Historically, when it was money earned by the married woman, it was systematically trivialized as money for trinkets. Similarly, "nurse money" in the Keralite Christian immigrant community carries social and symbolic significance through negative gendered and class-based connotations and becomes a short-form indicator of social status.

Family name, another demarcation of social class, is not always recognized in the United States, since the members of the immigrant community are not from the same parts of Kerala. The importance of family name seemed to be an issue for some of the men I interviewed, who identified themselves as coming from important families. For example, Mr. Lukos talked about how he "knew all the top people in the community, because I come from one of the top families in the area. You ask anyone if they know this family, and they should know us." Mr. Varkey, who claimed that his family was one of the original Brahmin families to be converted to Christianity by St. Thomas about two thousand years ago, talked about the "good recognition" that he had in his village because he was a member of this family. When he was studying at the engineering school in Kerala, the people in his village referred to him as "the engineer from 'so and so' family." In the United States, it is less likely that Mr. Lukos or Mr. Varkey would get the type of "recognition" to which they are accustomed in Kerala, since the immigrant community members have diverse origins in Kerala. Since family name does not function as a means of identifying good families, nursing, again, serves as a stamp of class origins.

Both the husbands and the children of nurses were tied to the class origins of their wives or mothers. This was evident in a comment made by Mr. Lukos: "Some people in our church are class conscious. They think they are something above others. In South India, people only know people of their own status. . . . So many of my cousins — they are all trying to find a proper match for their boys, and they all tell me that they do not want the marriage if there is a nurse in that family. That is what is called class consciousness. They said, 'Can you find a match for my son? He is a doctor so we are looking for a doctor, and her parents should not be nurses for any reason.'" That the cousins of Mr. Lukos did not want nurses' children for marital affiliations, even if the children themselves were doctors in the United States, shows that the Keralite bias against nursing still operated in the immigrant community and could affect even those who were merely related to nurses. The requirement that "her parents should not be nurses for any reason" suggests such an extreme stigma against nursing that even extenuating circumstances could not be taken into account.

Given that he had a nurse for a wife, I asked Mr. Lukos if his children would have qualified as marital options for people like the cousins in Kerala whom he described. He responded, "Then again, they are all rich, and they are all well placed in society; and because I was the oldest, I married a nurse. I am very inferior to them: one, because I married a nurse and two of my sisters are nurses. The feelings are still there."

Despite his good family background, Mr. Lukos was not sure that his children could claim his original class status, given that their mother and aunts were nurses. By requiring that the prospective bride not be the child of a nurse, Mr. Lukos's cousins employed a class control measure, monitoring postimmigration class status in the face of seeming homogeneity brought on by rapid economic mobility in the immigrant community. That these cousins lived in Kerala showed that, in the immigrant community, connections to Kerala contributed to the reconstruction of old patterns of class domination.

Finally, leadership positions in the church and community represented another marker of class status, one that, in Kerala, was reserved for male members of upper-class families. With the concentration of nurses in the United States, the immigrant community institutions had a different class base as a source of leadership. Men from upper-class families here may have felt displaced, may have been indifferent to politics of the immigrant congregation, or may have chosen to distance themselves. Mr. Cherian explained, "Here people who are well off do not do church politics. Look at all the committee members, they are all nurses' husbands. Professionals do not get involved. In India, it is the opposite."

Furthermore, upper-class immigrants, including some of the upper-class bishops and priests, associated the immigrant church's volatile politics with the lower-class origins of the husbands of nurses. According to Mr. Cherian, even the bishops acknowledged this when "they say that all the churches [in the United States] are filled with nurse-husbands. They don't know what's going on, and that these men need to be more educated." Dr. Stephen, the female physician from a well-to-do background, expressed a similar sentiment:

> It's hard to relate to some people. Their philosophy and my philosophy are very different. They are not very reasonable. . . . They just don't understand a lot of things. I don't mean to criticize our men in any way, but I think that a lot of them are not very well educated. People who are educated, you can communicate with them and they understand. These people, they don't have any idea; they don't have a basic knowledge about how to conduct finances. Most of them are just walking around, lifting their hands and legs and jumping around. Only very few people have a real concept about how to do things. And those people don't tend to participate in the church — the ones who have an idea about what is going on. They don't participate because they know that these people [the uneducated men] outnumber them. In my opinion the people who have a real concept about what is going on, they are very few.

In Kerala, material wealth, family name, and community leadership are all explicit markers of class status. In the Keralite immigrant community, it is difficult to tell the difference between the rich and the poor. Family names do not elicit the same recognition. Leadership in the church is no longer the purview of the upper class. Traditional householders from high-status backgrounds in Kerala — the people who "have a real concept about how to do things" — feel outnumbered and displaced by the husbands of nurses.

Early Keralite Christian immigrants in Central City initially formed cultural organizations that cut across regional and religious differences, but these were made up of people from the same class base, since the early immigrant cohort was composed of mostly doctors and scientists. Later, people of different class backgrounds and professions started to come into the immigrant community, and there was a greater awareness of class differences.[22] Within this context, nursing became the telltale signifier that undermined the efforts and aspirations of the husbands of nurses to gain status in the community.

Conclusion

The gendered nature of immigration is partly responsible for the fact that immigrant congregations, such as St. George's, are almost exclusively male run. The increased male need for participation may explain both the prevalence of schisms leading to split-off congregations and the creation and redefinition of male roles within the congregation, which in turn have led to the reassertion of male prerogative. Furthermore, despite some public challenges to the gender order from upper-class women, progressive priests, and second-generation young women, the wider church hierarchy is able to ensure the reproduction of traditional female roles in the immigrant congregation. Ironically, in asserting their male privilege within the church, the husbands of nurses are stigmatized as emasculated, lower-class men because of their connection to nurses.

How do we make sense of this irony? R. W. Connell's understanding of the relationship between gendered spheres (1987) indicates that the gender relations in the spheres of family, work, and community at first seem to be complementary, balancing each other to help maintain equilibrium in gender relations for the Keralite immigrants. It appears that the church sphere is a space where the men successfully compensate for their diminished status at work and at home. For the nurses, increased professional status and economic upward mobility seem to offer greater power in the household as these women maintain the norms of proper femininity in the church. However, paradoxically, the gender relations in these spheres undermine each other. For the men, their lowly positions in the labor market, along with their association with their nurse spouses, return to haunt them as they assert male domination in the church. Similarly, despite their attempts to police themselves in the church, the nurses are equally haunted, but by their elevated positions in the work and family spheres. In other words, both men's and women's attempts to compensate are markedly constrained by the influence across spheres.

In taking over the leadership of immigrant congregations, the husbands of nurses displace men whose families had higher status in Kerala, and who see these leadership positions as their customary right. The presence of the nurses' husbands in traditionally established positions of communal power emphasizes the extraordinary class mobility of nurses and their families, which upsets traditional class and status hierarchies. Furthermore, the nontraditional tendency in the households of nurses is probably cause for disparagement because it underlines the larger threat that the relatively liberal American society poses for the traditional householders. These factors may shape the reaction of the families of higher status, who disparage the nurses and their husbands as deviant women and emasculated men.

Finally, connections to Kerala re-create the old oppressive gender and class relations in new ways in the immigrant community. Mrs. Mathai's experience of being treated as a morally "lost" nurse in Kerala prompted her to guard her reputation even in the United States. And the transnational marriage market in Kerala prompted Mr. Lukos to feel that his high-class cousins in India would exclude his children from marriage alliances in their circles because their mother and aunts were nurses. In the U.S. immigrant community, the meanings of nursing that originate in Kerala act as an ever-present backdrop, informing the ongoing negotiations of gender and class relations within and among different spheres.

CHAPTER 5

Transnational Connections

The Janus-Faced Production of an Immigrant Community

The Malayalam movie titled *Dollar* opens with a woman in her sixties—Annamma—in Kerala receiving a letter from her son in the United States asking her to come and visit. Her brother, her son Kuttapai, and her son's wife are all present to hear the news. As Annamma reads the letter aloud, we find out that one of her two daughters-in-law in the United States is pregnant. Kuttapai opines that his brother is asking Annamma to visit only because he will need help with child care. Annamma disregards this comment and observes that she is glad his two brothers married nurses working in America, despite Kuttapai's lack of enthusiasm about their profession. Annamma's brother warns her that she had better not treat her daughters-in-law in the United States the way she treats Kuttapai's wife in Kerala. He reminds Annamma that her daughters-in-law are nurses, and that earning women will not put up with her.

This movie is one among several Malayalam movies produced in Kerala and available in video and DVD format to the approximately 2 million Keralites who live outside India (Williams 1996). Like Annamma, many family members living in Kerala keep in touch with their relatives around the world. Besides the movie industry and other media, churches, political and civic organizations, and the state are all involved in helping the immigrants maintain connections with their homeland. The existence of such organizations as the World Malayalee Council—which was conceived in New Jersey in 1995 and is headquartered in Kerala, and which has thirty-three regional offices throughout the world, a monthly journal, and a Website to counsel the second-generation immigrants — underlines the far-reaching transnational connections of this community.

The existence of such strong transnational ties contradicts the traditional American story of immigrants uprooting themselves from their homelands and assimilating in the American melting pot of the United States. However, the sociologist Peggy Levitt argues that transnationalism and assimilation are not incompatible, when she asserts that transnational migrants "do not shift their loyalties and participatory energies from one country to another. Instead they are integrated, to varying degrees, into the countries that receive them, at the same time that they remain connected to the countries they leave behind. . . . New forms of representation and participation are emerging that do not require full membership or residence. . . . States play a major role, along with other civic, religious and political institutions, in creating and reinforcing lasting transnational involvements" (2001: 5).

While most recent immigrants participate in at least some transnational practices, one longtime expert on Indian immigration argues that Indian immigrant communities, both in their behavior and attitudes, are among the most consistently transnational communities in the United States (Lessinger 1995). One reason for this distinction is the relative affluence of the community as a whole, which supports an infrastructure (such as information about transnational opportunities, and a plethora of transnational travel, media, communication, and financial service brokers and institutions, etc.) that allows even the less affluent members to engage in transnational practices.

Just as Levitt makes a point about the emergence of new forms of representation and participation, Johanna Lessinger argues that increasing transnational ties challenge conventional notions of "ethnic identity" and "ethnic ties" (1995: 88). Lessinger goes a step further to conclude that it is no longer possible to analytically separate Indian immigrant communities abroad from India. I do not agree with Lessinger's conclusion, since this view does not take seriously the very real differences in political, economic, and social contexts. Rather, Indian immigrant communities and sending communities in India are part of a transnational social field, and we can no longer make sense of one without looking at the other.

On one hand, transnational connections can be critical in sustaining immigrant life, since they can enable immigrants to resist the general race and class oppression experienced in the host society (Rouse 1992; Glick-Schiller et al. 1992; Alicea 1997). On the other hand, they can promote a type of nostalgia about the social relations found at home that can be oppressive for some members of the community. For example, connections between the U.S. immigrant community and Kerala end up reproducing certain discourses and practices in the spheres of home, work, and church that sustain gender meanings that originate in Kerala.

In this chapter, I argue that transnational connections to Kerala are essential in sustaining the immigrant community in the United States as an enclave, despite its tendency toward self-erosion caused by its failure to actively incorporate the second generation and the community's internal class-status differences. The connections include visits to Kerala by immigrants and extended stays by visitors from Kerala, and the transfer of resources and of discourses in both directions. Furthermore, within each sphere I look at the nature of the connections between Kerala and the United States and the effect of these connections on gender relations relative to that sphere. While immigration affects both receiving and sending communities, here I focus only on the implications of the connections on gender relations and on community maintenance in the U.S. immigrant community.

Kerala is considered a front-ranking state among Indian states in international migration, along with Punjab and Goa. It is one of the smallest and most densely populated states in India, occupying 1.2 percent of the land while accommodating 3.4 percent of India's population. Having the smallest industrial base in India, Kerala deals with a significantly large unemployment problem. An estimated 18 percent of the 9.15 million people who make up the workforce in Kerala are unemployed. Of the unemployed, 91 percent are estimated to be literate and two-thirds have studied beyond the primary school level (Department of Economics and Statistics, Government of Kerala 1988).

The combination of overcrowding and lack of economic opportunities in Kerala for a highly literate workforce results in many Keralites seeking employment opportunities all over India and the world. Both India and the state of Kerala are extremely sensitive to supporting the Keralite nonresident Indians (NRIs) because of the importance of their financial remittances. The term *nonresident Indian* is itself symbolic of the Indian state's attempt to welcome Indian emigrants and their children, who may even have citizenship elsewhere, and give them a sense of belonging in India. Remittances from Keralite NRIs are estimated to be one-tenth of India's foreign exchange, and volatility in the rate of these remittances appears to have played an important role in the Indian fiscal crisis of the early 1990s (Isaac 1997). Consequently, the Keralite state took leadership in establishing a governmental agency, the first of its kind in India, to examine the problems specific to NRIs and to help resolve them.

During the six months I spent in Kerala, I was able to see the effect of immigration in the highly visible displays of affluence in daily life. Construction is booming as new, modern-looking homes replace the traditional tile-roof homes.[1] Many of the Keralite families of my U.S. study participants lived in such homes, with accompanying amenities such as refrigerators, television sets, and most important, telephones. I attended weddings and funerals that were grand affairs, with photographers, videographers, and caterers. Such events function as social indicators of status, especially for those with "foreign" money. Some funeral processions are led by hundred-member brass bands and end with a meal for all those invited. The videotaping of these events is especially important for NRI family members unable to attend.

Kerala is an immigration-sensitive society that caters to the needs of NRIs. Consequently, its service sector flourishes. For example, it boasts videography services with the latest equipment, international delivery services, marriage brokers that serve the transnational marriage markets, and real estate and investment services. In the town of Kumbanadu in central Travencore — a heavily Christian region — I counted thirteen different banks in a one-mile strip. The many new two-story houses with big gates, which included the home of a family I interviewed, confirmed the affluence of the town.

While in Kerala, I visited the families of twenty of the immigrants I had interviewed in the United States. I conducted in-depth interviews with multiple family members on the subject of the transnational links between them and their relatives in the United States. I also explored the work-sphere connections between Kerala and the United States, specifically those related to nursing. And I interviewed retired nursing professors and deans and conducted focus group interviews with nurses — including some return migrants — working in two different hospitals in Kerala. Finally, I participated in and observed gender relations in an Orthodox Church in Kerala to gain a basis of comparison for my study of the immigrant Orthodox Church in the United States. I visited the Orthodox seminary in Kerala and interviewed a number of its clerical professors about how transnational links in the church are created and maintained.

Home

In the home sphere, the most obvious connections to Kerala are family members' numerous visits back and forth. Given that many of the immigrants maintain transnational households—which include parents or children in India—financial assistance tends to flow from the United States to Kerala. These visits facilitate the exchange of resources as visitors from the United States take gifts, medical supplies, and money to family members in Kerala. In return, Keralite family members send hard-to-find food items, specialized cooking utensils, and spices to their relatives in the United States.

Connections are especially important in the care and socialization of the second generation. Grandparents visit the United States for short periods and help during the birth of a baby. Extended kin in Kerala are often involved in the upbringing of their American relatives' children, either because children are left in Kerala or because Keralite family members are sponsored as emigrants to the United States, where they live with their sponsoring relatives.

Finally, single immigrants as well as parents of the second generation turn to the transnational marriage market for the arrangement of marriages with prospective Keralites living all over the world. These ties serve not only to reinforce existing gender relations in the immigrant home but also to socialize the second generation and maintain the community's reference point in Kerala.

VISITS AND OBLIGATIONS

Vacations for most immigrants center exclusively on trips back to Kerala, typically for family functions such as weddings, baptisms, and funerals. Immigrants make the approximately eighteen-hour plane journey home to Kerala carrying suitcases filled with gifts not only for their own extended family, friends, and neighbors but also for those of friends in the United States. Thus new networks and ties are created by such deliveries.

Frequently on these trips home, people perform ritual obligations as well as meet more urgent family needs. One man told me that he had to make multiple journeys to Kerala to fulfill his promise to have all three of his children baptized at his natal parish in Kerala. During the delivery of her premature child, one woman promised that, if her child survived, she would go on a pilgrimage to an important shrine in Kerala and dedicate the child to the patron saint there. Her husband, independently of her, made the same promise. Almost all the immigrants I interviewed knew that they would have to make the long and dreaded plane ride home for the funeral of a loved one, or worse still, that they would not be able to attend such a funeral because of work or financial obstacles.

Family obligations, especially for the men, include taking care of parents and widowed and unmarried sisters. For a number of elderly parents, life is difficult despite their having large modern homes built by their emigrant children. Several parents of immigrants I interviewed in Kerala told me that they were lonely because all their children were in either the United States or the Persian Gulf. Traditionally, the youngest son inherits the family home and subsequently becomes responsible for taking care of the parents. Immigrants like Mr. George, who was the youngest in his family, had to become innovative in fulfilling his obligation to take care of his widowed mother. He decided to kill two birds with one stone: he sent his wife and their three daughters back to Kerala to live with his mother, so that the girls would be exposed to Keralite culture and the grandmother would not be alone.

Whereas responsibility for family obligations typically falls to the sons, both immigrant sons and daughters talked about helping family members in times of crisis. Many of the women made the trip back in cases of parental illness and took an active role in helping siblings deal with financial crises; they also contributed to their natal households. However, for the immigrant couples it was in the contact with family members back in Kerala that traditional gendered expectations were often reaffirmed and, in some cases, renegotiated.

For example, Mrs. Patrose's brother, Mr. Thomas, whom I interviewed in Kerala, told me about the typical visits made by his sister and her family: "When they do come back, they tend to stay in his house in Kottayam. They usually come for about a month and stay with us for two or three days. That's all we see them. The reason may be that he thinks that this is the wife's house. Perhaps they stay here for such a short time because he thinks like this." When asked whether he stayed at his wife's house, he answered, "Even if I go there, I will stay there for one or two days. To go and stay there for longer is not right. That is what they have said traditionally." Mr. Thomas understands why his vacationing sister and her family do not stay for more than a couple of days in his house, since he also does not stay long at his wife's house. Even if his sister had wanted to stay in her own natal home for more than a couple of days, it is unlikely that her brother would have supported this.

Yet vacations are also occasions for renegotiation of gender practices, as is evident in the following observations of Mr. Elias, an immigrant whom I interviewed in the United States. He told me about how vacation patterns work for his family:

> In that aspect, like deciding when to go home [to Kerala], we are equal. I want to see my father, and she wants to see hers. That is fine. Even if we go together, I will take her to her house and let her spend time with her father and enjoy. Here we spend all the time together. If not for that, why should we spend money to go home? Not [for her] to take care of me. Not at all. When we go home, I let her stay with her father. Once in a while, we see each other. We go from here together. Here we stay together, don't we? What is the point of going home and fighting? She is going there to spend time with her dad. That is how we do it. We usually go for four weeks. Is it better to stay with me those four weeks or stay with her family and friends? So that is what I do.

Despite Mr. Elias's rhetoric that he "let" his wife spend time with her father, his attempt to avoid fighting about it with his wife shows that the latter had a strong say in the matter. Nevertheless, in Kerala Mrs. Elias's ability to stay with her father, and not take care of her husband, most likely was attributed to her husband's generosity, reinforcing patriarchal gender norms.

Return migration is another area where gendered expectations have to be periodically renegotiated. Many immigrants, especially men, dream about returning to and settling in Kerala. Most Keralite immigrants start out thinking about immigration as a temporary phenomenon. Both men and women expect to be in the United States to work hard and make some money, and to return to India. However, over the years, many immigrants find that mortgages and loan payments, along with the ups and downs of the economy, make it hard to save enough to go back. Furthermore their American-born children are firmly embedded in educational and career tracks in the United States, which makes their parents reluctant to go back to Kerala. While many immigrants may talk about their extensive plans to return, for some this remains a dream and is characterized in the literature as the "myth of return" (Gardner 1993). Others realize this dream by investing in property and constructing homes where they will settle after retirement.

For many families, the desire to return is divided along gender lines, with women wanting to stay on in the United States. Much of the literature to date supports this finding (Grasmuck and Pessar 1991; Hondagneu-Sotelo 1994; Mahler 1999). Sherri Grasmuck and Patricia Pessar point out that men—in this case, the Dominican immigrants they studied—who lost status in the migration process both at work and at home tend to pursue return migration as strategy of coping with their loss. Grasmuck and Pessar, along with Hondagneu-Sotelo, hold that women experience greater freedom in the United States, and that, as a result, fewer of them want to permanently return to India. Based on her research on Puerto

Rican migration to the United States, Marixsa Alicea (1997) argues against binary conceptualizations of the host society as the locus of greater freedom from the backward patriarchal oppressions of home. She found that the women in her study desired the security and stability of their natal home but also acknowledged the oppression present there.

In interviews with Keralite immigrants, I found that men tended to favor returning home, and both men and women expressed some ambivalence regarding permanent return. The difficulty of leaving behind their children, the fact of having lost track of their contemporaries in Kerala, and the problems inherent in establishing themselves in Kerala were reasons they gave for their ambivalence. A number of immigrants I interviewed spoke of exploring real estate investments and buying plots of land for construction of retirement homes in Kerala. One man in Kerala told me about his cousin in the United States who was coming back to Kerala because her daughters were both the independent type and could not be relied upon to take care of their mother in her old age. While most immigrants spoke about returning, few had reached the retirement age. Of those who had retired, few returned permanently to Kerala. Those who did return tended to divide their time between the United States and Kerala, traveling often to visit their children in the United States. But preparing for full or partial return required many visits and the help of relatives in Kerala, resulting in strengthened ties.

The Lukoses typify the gendered divergence in postretirement hopes. Mr. Lukos told me that he would like to go back to live in Kerala and to be buried with his father. His wife, on the other hand, told me that she had no particular attachment to any place and would like to stay in the United States with her children. However, return migration would be feasible only with the help of Keralite relatives willing to help with the resettlement process. This was pointed out by Mr. Lukos's cousin in Kerala, Mr. Mathews, who told me that Mr. Lukos and his wife had talked about buying a flat in Kerala so that they could come back and settle down. Mr. Mathews noted, "Nobody encouraged him, because there has to be somebody here to be there to collect rent and take possession. Nobody encouraged him." The Lukoses' postretirement plans remained up in the air, but their indecision highlights the gendered divergence as well as the need for strong ties to help in the return-migration process.

CHILD CARE AND SOCIALIZATION

In the home sphere, connections to Kerala are eminently apparent in the processes of caring for and socializing immigrant children. Family members I interviewed in Kerala, especially parents, had spent up to several years in the United States specifically to help with child care. They made multiple trips, ranging from short visits in the warmer summer months to extended periods of stay. For Keralite grandparents, these visits involved helping their immigrant children with child care as well as procuring citizenship in order to sponsor their other children living in Kerala.

Often grandparents came to help with baby-sitting, as did Annamma, the heroine of the movie *Dollar*. One such visitor to the United States was Mrs. George's mother, who came in 1987 when her son asked her to help with child care. In our interview in Kerala, she recalled a lighthearted exchange between herself and her son on the topic. As she put it, "He told me that I could make a lot of money being a baby-sitter. I told him that I didn't want to clean the shit of any more children." Nevertheless, she stayed in the United States for several years, until she was diagnosed with diabetes and had to return to Kerala, where she could afford health care.

In some cases immigrant siblings competed among themselves for parental help. Mr. Thambi's parents told me about their visit to the United States upon their children's invitation. While they were at the home of one son, the other was constantly asking them to stay with him. They finally relented because he had two small children and needed their help. But once they got there, their son would not let them leave, even though the parents were homesick.

Because life in tropical Kerala, with its easy access to neighbors and relatives, is a far cry from being cooped up in a suburban house in subzero weather caring for children, many grandparents find such trips extremely difficult. Yet they are motivated by love for their children — both those who are settled in the United States and those still in Kerala. By emigrating to the United States and gaining citizenship, they, as parents, are able to sponsor children remaining in Kerala much more quickly than can immigrant brothers or sisters.[2]

While some immigrants bring parents to the United States, others leave their children in Kerala with relatives who provide necessary child care and socialization. According to research conducted on immigrant communities in the United States, this is a common solution to the need for child care (Levitt 2001; Alicea 1997; Hondagneu-Sotelo and Avila 1997; Lessinger 1995; Williams 1996; Ho, 1993; Soto 1987; Cohen 1977). Soto refers to this practice as "child fostering" and argues that it is a key aspect of the exchange of resources between migrants and kin back home, ultimately resulting in wealth redistribution across international boundaries: "As adults circulate between home and host societies, channeling their resources from one to the other, children provide the link in the exchange systems between the mobile adults and the more stationary ones left at home. For all the individuals involved, this exchange is an investment. For all the participating adults, fostering opens up a wide spectrum of active social ties across which goods flow and commitments are sustained" (1987: 133).

Not only are the costs of reproduction cheaper in Kerala, but also immigrant parents can rest easy about the quality of child care. With the money their immigrant children send them, caretaker grandparents can hire live-in help or recruit other relatives to help with child care. Consequently, parents leave their children in the care of relatives in Kerala during various stages of their growth, strengthening connections between Kerala and the United States.

Some immigrant parents choose to leave their children in Kerala when they make their initial journey to the United States. This allows them to get oriented and save enough money to eventually bring the children over. Some enroll older children in boarding schools, but most leave them with close relatives such as grandparents or siblings.

The sociologists Hondagneu-Sotelo and Avila argue that men and women experience this process differently. Based on their reading of feminist geography, these scholars point out that women generally tend to find jobs closer to home in order to be more available to their children, but that some immigrant women leave their children behind and cross international boundaries in search of employment. Consequently, the Mexican transnational mothers in their study, much like the nurses in my study, "radically break with deeply gendered spatial and temporal boundaries of family and work" (1997: 551). If men leave their children behind, they are seen as fulfilling their obligation as breadwinner to provide for their families, but female migrants who leave their families and children behind go against the grain of cultural expectations.

Such decisions result in guilt, criticism, and stigma for women. For example, even after twenty years, Mrs. Simon, an immigrant woman I interviewed in the United States, shed tears about the guilt and pain of her initial separation from her children: "My daughter knew that I was her mother, but my son was only two when I left, and so he had started calling my sister 'Mummy,' since that's what her children called her. [Here she was visibly moved and her voice broke.] When he got here, whichever lady he saw, he started calling her Mummy. In the beginning he didn't want to sleep with me, but finally, after a lot of talking to him, he started to be with me."

Children born in the United States were often sent to live with grandparents in Kerala and brought back when old enough to attend school. In some cases, women who had to study for their nursing board examinations deposited their young children with their grandparents in Kerala until they passed their exams. For Mrs. Kurien, it was fear for her infant's safety that finally convinced her to take her to Kerala. As she put it, "We never even gave our kids to the baby-sitter, not even for one hour, but we had to send them back home to our parents for a couple of years. Once, when I was working nights and he was working days, one morning I came back from work and he left, and I was feeding my daughter. I was sitting on the couch and I fell asleep, and the bottle fell one way and the baby fell another way. So that's how we decided to send the baby to Kerala."

Other children are taken back to Kerala when they reach junior high school age to expose them to the culture and language and to protect them from the terrors of American teenage freedoms. This was especially true for girls, as was the case for Mrs. George's three daughters. Mrs. George's sister-in-law, with whom I spoke in Kerala, observed, "Many people bring their daughters to Kerala to expose them to Keralite culture. They have to be brought here at a young age to help them compare and appreciate the differences between life there versus here." An increasing number of young people go to India to bypass four years of college and join medical schools right out of high school, after paying hefty donations for admission.

The ties to parents and extended-family members in Kerala greatly influence gender relations among immigrants. The domestic help given by visitors from Kerala, especially child care, reduces some of the pressure of gender role negotiation for the couple. The traditional division of labor is challenged less often in periods when there are relatives around. More important, visitors from Kerala and visits to Kerala are a means of reinforcing traditional patriarchal hierarchies and notions about child rearing. Grandparents and other relatives in the household challenge American notions of child rearing and clarify the boundaries, pushing for the maintenance of Keralite norms and the gendered division of labor.

In the eyes of the cinematic heroine Annamma, the immigrant households of her two sons appear shockingly disordered. Her daughters-in-law do not have time to serve dinner to their husbands. They spoil their children by not spanking the younger ones and not inquiring about the whereabouts of the older ones. In one late-night incident, the two teenage children of her older son — Tony and Tina — both come home very late. Tony is visibly inebriated. Annamma awakens her son and daughter on the spot and warns them that their children are going astray. She is especially upset that her teenage granddaughter is allowed to stay out late. Her daughter-in-law retorts that girls in America are independent and can stand on their own two feet. In a moment of foreshadowing, Annamma warns her that, although American-bred girls may be able to stand on their own two feet, they can nevertheless slip and fall.

Like Annamma, many of the Keralite family members that I spoke with criticized the changes in gendered roles in the immigrant household and the handling of undisciplined children. Mrs. John's parents are a case in point. Mrs. John's mother had been to the United States four times, and her father had visited twice. The trips were usually for periods of several years, which allowed them to form some lasting impressions about life for immigrant families in the United States. Both parents criticized the seeming breakdown of the patriarchal hierarchy and what they saw as the resulting male powerlessness in immigrant homes:

Father: Husbands and wives fight, and if the children make trouble, the parents can't do anything about it.

Mother: As I see it, it's the women that rule everything there. If the husbands say anything, the wives will immediately call the police. I'm not saying that my children did this or it happened this way in my house. I have heard people talking about this. Or if you discipline a child, they can call the police on you. That's why the children are not obedient. In my time, if you told a child to come here he would immediately be there.

Father: Women call the police complaining that their husbands hit them. The children are the same way. Then there are the husbands — they can't call the police.

Mother: Of course, this is only in some homes. Whether in Kerala or the United States, the good ones are always good. Those who have *tandaedum* [chutzpah] will have it everywhere.

When asked if it was bad for women to have *tandaedum,* Mrs. John's mother replied, "It's not good to have that kind of *tandaedum.* They should live under the rule of men. That is the right way to live in this world. Otherwise the man has no peace of mind." In her opinion, not only was any demonstration of *tandaedum* that undermined the authority of men morally bad, but also it resulted in a lack of discipline in the lives of the children.[3]

THE TRANSNATIONAL MARRIAGE MARKET

The transnational marriage market is another site of connection between Kerala and the United States that has implications for the reproduction of family and community ties. Given that marriages are usually arranged, unmarried immigrants and the parents of the second generation who come of age tend to look for marriage partners by means of their connections to Kerala. Primarily, suitable partners are found by word of mouth. Parents often let relatives and friends know that they are seeking a spouse for their son or daughter (Dugger 1998). Other immigrants advertise in the matrimonial sections of Malayalee newspapers based in Kerala and the United States, often using family members in Kerala as their contact people (Luthra 1989). Finally, some immigrants use marriage brokers in Kerala who act as matchmakers for a fee. Immigrants and their children use one or all of these avenues to search for prospective partners not only in Kerala or India but also in the United States and other parts of the world.

During my stay in Kerala, I observed that many people there were aware of the rules and requirements of participating in the transnational marriage market. Kerala has a surplus educated labor force, and emigration is the main way out for this labor force. While some people can count on brothers and sisters to sponsor them, a lot of people have no one in their immediate family to do so. Consequently, for such people who want to emigrate, their only hope may be to marry somebody from the United States or one of the Gulf countries.

I found that many Keralites were well informed about the pros and cons of these different immigration options. Gulf immigrants tend to be temporary workers who usually come back and settle in Kerala. Emigrants to North America and Europe tend to leave the country permanently. Many people in Kerala are aware of these different outcomes, and so craft their children's education to make them appealing as potential grooms or brides in the right markets. For instance, immigrants who return from the United States tend to look for prospective spouses with training in a medical field. Nurses are more attractive if they have at least a bachelor's degree and have passed their exams administered by the Commission on Graduates of Foreign Nursing Schools.[4] Those from the Gulf countries seem open to a wider range of professionals, since they are able to find jobs more easily in these countries. Having citizenship or permanent residence in the United States makes prospective brides and grooms extremely desirable in the transnational marriage market. Consequently, immigrant families gain greater status, enter a higher class, and are able to move up the social ladder back in Kerala by marrying their children into families with higher social rankings and desirable professional backgrounds, all because they offer the prospect of immigration.

Typically, the Keralite family members of immigrants look for prospective partners using their own personal networks. Sometimes immigrants put advertisements in newspapers or register with marriage brokers and ask a relative in Kerala to be the contact person and conduct the preliminary screening of respondents. Because immigrants are typically home for short vacations, this help from relatives facilitates quick marriage decisions. Such dependence on relatives also strengthens the transnational ties to Kerala.

A number of the people I interviewed in Kerala told me about immigrant relatives who had asked them to help find spouses for their children. Mrs. Paul's sister was one such person, and she told me that she was not in favor of using newspaper advertisements or brokers because they have higher rates of failure. According to this woman:

> What they do is that they are coming for a short vacation. Their families can't quickly find them a mate in such a short time. so they put an advertisement in a newspaper. Many letters come. and they read them in one day and select a few. They go and see those people; and if they happened to know anyone else in the area, they inquire about the prospective bride or groom. And they quickly fix the marriage in a week. But for the people who live in Kerala, they can take their time and look around and decide on a marriage more leisurely. Marriages take place after five or six months of inquiry. They inquire about the boy and they inquire about the girl, and it is the relatives that do most of the inquiring. Usually problems don't arise with these marriages, because it is our own relatives that do the searching, and they are more accountable.

Mrs. John's mother illustrated the potential unreliability of impersonal marriage arrangements when she told me about what happened in her own family. Her son had come back to Kerala three times with the express purpose of getting married. The family had placed advertisements in newspapers, and yet it had been difficult to find him a wife. So when they found a woman he liked on his third trip, he decided to marry her. His mother complained that he had not received any dowry because the woman claimed to be a nurse with a bachelor's degree. However, his mother doubts that her daughter-in-law has the education she claims to have, since she was unable to pass the licensing exam in the United States. His mother thought they were tricked into this marriage because her son was in a hurry to get married.

The transnational marriage market meets a need within the immigrant community and helps maintain strong ties back to Kerala. However, the presence of this institution, and participation in it, reinforces certain gendered practices and expectations in the immigrant community. The dowry — typically large amounts of money or property — is still an expectation in Kerala and one that, for the most part, survives in the transnational marriage market.

In the United States, many immigrant families of prospective brides can afford the higher rates of dowry associated with marriage with a Keralite groom from a family of higher class or status. There is room for negotiation on the matter of dowry because of the immigration prospects that come with such a bride. In a similar vein, the United States–based groom has tremendous market appeal, which allows him the option of receiving a large dowry. Not surprisingly, more second-generation men than women appear to seek partners in the transnational marriage market (Dasgupta and Dasgupta 1996; Williams 1996; Lessinger 1995).

Participation in the transnational marriage market produces a gendered double standard that prejudices Keralites against prospective American-born brides. For example, Mr. Elias's uncle told me that young women from the United States had a reputation for being outspoken and causing difficulties in marriages, which then ended in divorce. Mrs. Patrose's brother told me that both he and his sister had been invited by Mrs. Patrose to emigrate to the United States, but that they were not interested. They felt that the United States would not be the right environment in which to raise teenage daughters. He told me that the general impression of the United States was that it was an unsafe place for teenage daughters.

For the second-generation prospective bride from the United States to have success in the marriage market, she must be represented as "homely" and as having been taught Indian culture and linguistic skills. In this context, "homely" means homebound (Luthra 1989). She must not have left home for college or lived without parental supervision at any time. Given that American-born women are assumed to have boyfriends, being "homely" connotes parental control over female sexuality. Moreover, since women are expected to adapt to the norms of the husband and his family, it is especially important for the bride to have been trained to fulfill this cultural expectation. Perhaps this explains why some immigrants bring their daughters back to Kerala for schooling: to expose them to Keralite culture and the expectation of "homeliness." That these standards do not apply to prospective second-generation bridegrooms points to the fact that asymmetric gender norms are reproduced in the immigrant community, which prescribes limitations on independence for women but not for men.

Beyond the reproduction of patriarchal traditional Indian culture, these asymmetric gender norms are also a response to the conditions that Indian immigrants find in the United States. Recent scholarship on South Asians in the United States has highlighted the role that second-generation women play as symbols of the public face and integrity of "a model minority" community (Dasgupta and Dasgupta 1996 and 1998; Bhattacharjee 1992). The control of women's sexuality becomes linked to notions of nationalism and the upholding of religion, tradition, and Indian culture. As Dasgupta and Dasgupta point out, the "bad immigrant daughter" who has not met such expectations is not only a "whore" but also the "betrayer of the community." Consequently, there is much pressure on the daughters of the community, but not the sons, to maintain "homeliness" (1998: 124). In contrast, because second-generation males, like other Asian American men, tend to be emasculated in the wider American society, they have greater incentive to remain endogamous and to seek both assurances of male privilege in the immigrant community and the gender specific benefits inherent in the transnational marriage arrangement.

In conclusion, in the home sphere, connections to Kerala are cultivated mainly to meet the concrete needs of the family, particularly in fulfilling the obligations to kin and in the reproduction of the next generation. The ties to Kerala not only act as a channel through which gendered notions about filial obligations, child care, and socialization make their way to the immigrant community but also firmly orient the immigrant community's identity in Kerala. It is partially through these same channels that discourses about the meaning of work make their way from Kerala to the U.S. immigrant community.

Work

Whereas the connections in the home sphere are concretely based in family relationships, the connections in the work sphere — particularly related to nursing — are more widely dispersed in society. The discourses and practices related to nursing and nurses in Kerala arrive in the U.S. immigrant community via many different channels, such as the media, film, and the transnational marriage market. Immigrants who return to Kerala for visits also encounter them in their social interactions. Although nurses are respected professionals in the United States, the connections to the sending community reinforce the negative discourses and practices imported from Kerala to the immigrant community. Consequently these discourses and practices powerfully shape gender relations between the nurses and their families in the immigrant community.

To understand the continuing negative evaluations of nurses, it is important to get a sense of how social relations between the sexes are structured in present-day Kerala. During my stay there, I was able to observe how social space is gendered and strictly demarcated. Not only do men and women leave a very respectable physical space between themselves, but also they are careful about laughing too much or displaying any intimacy in public. Conversations are formal, and even relatives have to observe some decorum to avoid rumors.

The importance of the physical separation of the sexes is evident in public buses, where women have a section in the front and men have a section in the back of the bus.[5] In fact, women tend to use the front door of the bus, and men tend to use the back door. Even if there are extra seats in either section, a member of the opposite sex will stand in his or her allotted section rather than sit down in the wrong section.

I had a number of experiences where the importance of maintaining physical space became clear to me, especially when I broke the rules without meaning to do so. One example is the auto-rickshaw incident mentioned earlier, when I tapped the driver on his back to get his attention and my aunt reacted strongly to my touching a male stranger.

Keralite society is set up with clearly gendered demarcations of public and private spheres. Ideally, men interact with the world outside, while women are in charge of the domestic realm. Despite the fact that many middle-class women work outside the home, for most official, bureaucratic ventures or substantial business transactions it is assumed that a male relative must accompany women. Because I traveled around Kerala by myself, I often found it difficult to maneuver around these expectations. I resorted to hiring a male assistant—whom I called my "cousin"—to accompany me on research expeditions and to the occasional movie, since movie theaters are particularly difficult places for the solitary woman.

Given the strict demarcations of gendered space and mobility in the late 1990s, it is not surprising that thirty years ago society unequivocally frowned upon the nursing profession, in which women had to cross all the social boundaries of gendered interactions. Nurses clearly are valued in present-day Kerala for their ability to immigrate easily and find jobs. Yet this valuation is an ambivalent one, because it operates in a society where male-female interaction in public is rigidly curtailed and monitored.

Ambivalence toward Nurses in Kerala

In Kerala, nursing education has undergone extended institutionalization: there is an increasing number of nursing schools, and standards of admission and accreditation requirements are now relatively higher. Nursing is one of the few professions in Kerala with the guarantee of a job upon graduation and opportunities to make money abroad.

The number of applications to nursing programs is now so great that, much as with engineering and medical school admission, the prospective applicant has to pay a capitation fee of thousands of rupees, as opposed to receiving a stipend to attend as in the past. The four-year bachelor's of science degree and the master of science degree in nursing are widely available in India, and applicants need high marks in science subjects to qualify for admission.

The increased professionalization of nursing in Kerala today attracts women to the profession from a wider base of social origins. As one woman in Kerala described the changes, "In those days . . . only those people with financial difficulties would send their daughters for this job. Nowadays, [it is] those who want to go to America, the financially well off and even the Muslims [a community considered more conservative than Christians or Hindus in Kerala]. After you study nursing, you can get a job right away."

The earning power of nurses is more clearly negotiated in Kerala today. For instance, nurses have more bargaining power in the transnational marriage market, where it is known that men who marry nurses cannot expect a dowry. Since nurses are in great demand in most places, it is understood that their earning potential and job security will more than make up for the unpaid dowry. In fact, nurses with degrees and a good family background are so in demand that they get "booked up" (betrothed) while still in school.

Nonetheless, the ambivalence toward nurses and their profession remains palpably present in Kerala. In focus group interviews that I conducted with nurses currently working there, the consensus was that nurses were treated much worse in Kerala than anywhere else — both inside and outside India. The negative attitudes toward nurses were the result of gender- and class-based stigmas, which were buttressed by social and institutional structures and practices. When the positive market value of nurses is combined with the negative attitudes, the resulting contradiction creates a profound ambivalence toward nurses in Kerala. This ambivalence is most clearly apparent in the behavior of nurses who return and settle down in Kerala but distance themselves from their former profession.

Much as in the past, the gendered stigma faced by nurses in Kerala arises from their being seen as sexually loose or bossy and too independent. One nurse with a lot of work experience outside Kerala explained: "Here, if a nurse speaks to a patient too much, they say that they are having an affair. Outside Kerala, they would think that it is a friendship. . . . Even now it is just like it was in the fifties. There is not much change." Mr. Babu, the brother of a U.S. immigrant, remarked on what he felt was the general attitude in Kerala toward nurses: "It is a sexual kind of thinking. You can get them for anything. They are loose. Maybe one or two people may see this as a profession not worthy of respect. But can a whole society put on an act? . . . This is the general talk in our society. 'Oh, she is nurse from the Gulf—that is how she got her money.' That's how they say it—contemptuously. I don't feel that way, because my sister and sister-in-law are both nurses."

Additionally, a number of people I interviewed in Kerala felt that nurses tended to be too independent. One man told me that his son, who is in the United States, refused to marry a nurse because nurses are "proud, willful, and disobedient." One nurse told me that her husband confessed to her after their arranged marriage in 1996 that he and all his friends had discussed their aversion to marrying nurses. He chose to marry her only because of what he perceived to be divine guidance that overruled his personal convictions.

Similarly, some Keralites expressed negative opinions about nursing as low-status work. Mrs. Paul's sister explained why she did not want her daughter to be a nurse despite the increased demand:

> In the olden days it was the people who failed in tenth who went for nursing. Now there is a great demand; you have to have high marks and a focus in science subjects in order to get admission. But still we don't like to send our daughter for nursing, and she doesn't like it either. When all her cousins are going for medicine or engineering, we want her to have an equal status with them. So she is studying for engineering. But they are all in such high positions; we don't want to have the feeling that only our daughter is a nurse. If the people in our family were the type to send their children for nursing, then we would not feel so bad.

Mrs. Paul and others like her recognize the attractions of the nursing profession, but her social status does not allow her or her daughter to make such a choice.

Despite the upward mobility of many nurses and their families, some Keralites, with presumably older money, characterized nurses with their new wealth as uncultured and ostentatious. Mr. Mathen's sister, Susan Mathews, who is herself a former immigrant from a Persian Gulf country and permanently settled in Kerala, told me that she could always spot a nurse because their "way is different." The following is an exchange between Mathews (SM) and me (SG):

SG: When you say "the nurse's way," what exactly do you mean? What behaviors have you noticed that are different among nurses?

SM: They are just different. [She falters as she tries to find a way to describe the difference.] What should I say? [She gives an embarrassed laugh.] The nurses' way is different. They are not like me — I don't have a profession. I am at home. They are different, because you know a nurse when you see one.

SG: How do you know?

SM: You can tell who is a nurse by their hairstyle, their fashion, their walk, and their way of talking — they use some English.

SG: You know the nurses by their English?

SM: It's not that they speak English, but it's a special way of talking. But you can tell when you see a nurse. The way they wear their saris and other clothes. Their walk and talk. How should I explain it? I told you, it is things like their hairstyle.

SG: How is their hairstyle different?

SM: [She laughs.] You can tell when you see it. The hair is tied up very high, and it is cut in the front.

SG: With their hair cut and everything, is it a modern look?

SM: It's not modern, it is awkward.

SG: So they really don't have style?

SM: Yes, they don't have it.

SG: And their saris are too showy?

SM: Yes, they wear those saris with a lot of glitter and gold — very showy. I don't know. I am not finding fault with them. I am not the only one with this opinion. All our friends say this.

SG: When you say that theirs is a different way, do you mean anything besides their appearance? For example, do you see a difference in their family life?

SM: Yes, there is a difference in their family life as well. They will have more — it is probably in "the care of" the nurse that most of these men have gone abroad. Their husbands have gone there in this manner. The nurses will go there first and then bring their husbands. So this is a different way of life — the way they treat their husbands. You could recognize the difference when you see it. Then the way they talk too much about their children. It's all there.

For Susan Mathews, the ostentatious and "awkward" style that she saw in nurses all added up to a different way of life. She described nurses as if they were people with a different culture — as often Keralites describe people from a different linguistic region or religion. In her eyes, their profession had turned them into a distinct type of people with "a different way of life" that even affected their family life.

I also heard expressions of class-based resentment toward nurses, perhaps because of the mobility achieved by many nurses and their families. For example, this resentment became clear in the conversation I had with Susan Mathews after the taped interview. She told me about a nurse who was the daughter of a servant who had worked for her natal family. This daughter was able to go to the United States, sponsor the rest of her siblings, and build a new home for her parents that was bigger than Susan's natal home. Susan told me that her family always said the servant's family was able to build their big house and become rich by "eating our [Susan's family's] rice." This is a colloquial way of saying that the servant's family was dependent on them for an income, and that their new wealth and big house did not alter their status as servants.

While many individuals I encountered in Kerala conveyed both personal and societal negative evaluations of nursing, some nurses and nursing administrators working in Kerala told me about the institutional structures and practices they experienced in their day-to-day professional lives that bolstered these attitudes. For example, Dr. Mary Varghese, a retired professor of nursing who was a former immigrant, told me that the nurse's professional independence in Kerala is compromised by the very structure of the administration in both nursing schools and hospitals. The nursing school is under the authority of the medical college, and the nursing superintendent in a hospital is under the medical superintendent in the administrative hierarchy. Consequently, nurses and their supervisors have to defer to doctors.

Nurses working in Kerala told me that the treatment of nurses there was unique compared to the rest of India. One nurse who had studied and worked at the Christian Medical Center in Vellore — one of the premier institutions in India that trains both doctors and nurses — complained about the differential treatment of nurses and doctors in Keralite hospitals: "There [in Vellore] we consider the doctors the same as the nurses. They do their job and we do ours. In Kerala, they [the doctors] consider themselves as superiors, and they will consider us as subordinates. That is not the correct way. We are just colleagues. . . . In Kerala as a whole, it is this way. Even salarywise: they get paid much more than us. Here doctors get four or five times as much. There, there wasn't such a gap."

Aleyamma Kuruvilla, who served as dean of the nursing school in the Christian Medical College at Vellore for eighteen years, had returned to Kerala for her retirement, and she helped out as the superintendent of nursing in a small hospital in Kerala. She told me about a number of incidents at her hospital that confirmed that nurses were on the bottom of the professional totem pole in medical institutions in Kerala. She expressed her frustration with the situation, saying, "The doctors think they have a right over the nurses, and the nurses take it lying down. That is what I don't understand. These nurses who have been working outside Kerala with equal status, they come back here and say yes to whatever the doctor says." Adding to her frustration, Ms. Kuruvilla finds that the general public in Kerala also sees nurses as being subordinate to the doctors.

Given the hierarchy of doctors over nurses, the low salaries, and the negative social stigma, many nurses look for every opportunity to migrate rather than resort to collective action like other workers in Kerala. And those who return to settle down after retirement come back to a Kerala that has changed its evaluation of nursing only to the extent that nurses are desirable for their ability to emigrate. Consequently, Kerala's ambivalence toward nurses is most clearly discernable in these return migrants' disassociation with their profession. For example, Dr. Mary Varghese told me that she is personally acquainted with many former nurses who will not admit to anyone that they used to be nurses. Such ambivalence about nurses and nursing in Kerala is transferred to the U.S. immigrant community through transnational connections.

REINFORCING STIGMA THROUGH CONNECTIONS

The discourses and practices related to nursing and nurses in Kerala travel to the U.S. immigrant community through channels such as film and the transnational marriage market. Immigrants who return for visits and who host visitors from Kerala also encounter them in their social interactions. Given the sensitivity of the topic, in the immigrant community the stigma against nurses is not widely discussed or easily detectable. However, it is apparent that the stigmatizing discourses and practices originate in Kerala and inform the undercurrent of communal life among immigrants.

Movies in the mother tongue are important cultural products that help immigrants connect to the homeland. The Indian film industry is one of the largest in the world and produces a huge number of films every year in different languages. The Keralite film industry ranges near the top in the number of films produced annually. The overwhelming majority of the films — regardless of quality — circulate among the global colonies of immigrant Keralites hungry for images of home. The movie *Dollar,* dealing with immigrant life in the United States, is one such film. It provides an excellent example of how the negative discourses about nurses travel to immigrant communities through the transnational film circuit.

In the opening scene of the movie, as Annamma shares with family and friends the news of her imminent trip to the United States, there are portents that all may not go well. Her son suggests that his brothers want her to visit only to use her for child care purposes. She gets a dire warning from her brother that she should be careful about how she treats her nurse daughters-in-law, who may not be as pliant as women in Kerala.

As the film unfolds, the two daughters-in-law are portrayed as domineering and disrespectful women who abuse the poor mother-in-law, and whose sole focus in life is making more money. They are petty, competitive women and jealous of each other's success, which leads to family disharmony. Furthermore, their husbands are depicted as emasculated men who have no say in decision making in the home. When Annamma first gets there, each daughter-in-law tells her privately, in an attempt to win favor, about the hidden and disreputable lower-class origins of the other. From Annamma's perspective, they do not take proper care of their husbands or children. For instance, the older daughter-in-law does not serve her husband his meals, and neither woman disciplines her children enough.

The purported greed of the nurses for the "almighty dollar" becomes the basis for the unraveling of each woman's life. Both have to learn their lessons, and not without tragic consequences. Only when her husband physically abuses her and threatens to leave her does the younger daughter-in-law become the obedient wife. Tony, the son of the elder daughter-in-law, is killed in a fight when he tries to forcibly separate his sister Tina from her American boyfriend. Tina loses her mental stability after her brother's death. The movie ends with both women brought low by the circumstances of life.

The primary message in the movie is that the dollar corrupts, that it becomes more important than kinship obligations — and that nurses are especially susceptible to its corrupting influence. When nurses do not fulfill their duties as good wives and mothers, the whole family is in trouble. Men are the unequivocal victims in this scenario. Their loss of patriarchal power over their wives and kids leaves them emasculated and helpless to intervene. Things begin to improve only when the younger son stands up against his wife and regains his manhood.

In this film, Kerala is always the reference point, and American immigrant life is seen from the eyes of the visiting grandmother. The negative caricature of immigrant nurses as bossy, greedy, disrespectful, low-class women clearly originates in Kerala. Changes in the relationships between nurses and their families in the United States are measured against the traditional order in Kerala, where wives obey husbands and children obey parents. In the end, the movie blames the daughters-in-law for the loss of harmony in Annamma's family. Movies such as *Dollar* transmit attitudes about nursing from Kerala to the United States that inevitably affect gender relations in the immigrant community.

The transnational marriage market is another site of connections that transmits and reinforces the stigma against nursing. When immigrants go back to Kerala to find spouses for themselves, their children, or their siblings, their inquiries about prospective marriage partners include an extensive investigation of family background. They scrutinize not only the prospective bride or groom but also the professional and personal backgrounds of parents and siblings. Because immigration has brought a lot of class mobility in Kerala, it has become even more important to check the preimmigration class background of the prospective spouse and in-laws — and here the stigma against nursing rears its ugly head. Mrs. Lukos's sister, the dean of a nursing school in Kerala, explained to me that the children of a teacher have greater value in the transnational marriage market than the children of a nurse like herself. As she put it, "If there are two boys — a nursery teacher's son and a nursing superintendent's son — the teacher's son will have more demand. . . . For instance, my son just passed his MBA. If I were a bank official or my husband was a bank official, we would have had a marriage proposal from a very high-standard family. When they come now, they will ask my son, 'What was your mother's job?' and when he says, 'A nurse,' then we see a superiority complex there."

The experiences of nurses in the marriage market reveal the contradictions of their existence in Kerala. Even though some people told me that nurses are "booked up" for marriage even before they graduate, others told me that nurses had difficulty getting married. Ms. Kuruvilla, the retired dean from Christian Medical College in Vellore, gave me some insight into the paradox: "But you know, this is all in Kerala. We have had several people, where one brother was doing medicine and one sister was doing nursing, or one sister was doing medicine and one sister was doing nursing. In Vellore, we don't think of these two as different at all. Come to Kerala, and we say, 'Why is she doing nursing?' And that nurse has trouble getting married." When asked if this was true even now, given how easily nurses get jobs, she replied, "That's right. The high-status people will not marry her. She may get a person who is lower in status socially and financially." Ms. Kuruvilla provided an illustration: "I had a nursing student and her sister was doing physiotherapy. . . . When they finished, the physiotherapy girl got married the year after she finished, and the other girl had to wait three years before she got married. From the same family, identical twins — just because she did nursing." Given the identical family background and looks of the two young women, it does seem as though the professional difference critically hampered the marital chances of the nurse. Ms. Kuruvilla's point that the nurse had trouble finding a social and financial equal explained the paradox. Nurses may have many prospective suitors, but it is more difficult for them to find a suitable groom who shares their class background and status. Consequently, they may have to marry someone from a lower class or with less status.

Through their interactions in the transnational marriage market, immigrant nurses and their families discover the limits of their post-immigration class mobility. While immigration allows them to enter into a higher class bracket, high-status prospective suitors in Kerala identify them as new money and therefore unsuitable. Nursing functions as a class-control measure, monitoring for preimmigration class status in the face of rapid economic mobility in Kerala.

A number of people I interviewed in Kerala told me about family members or friends who rejected marriage proposals from places like the United States because the mother was a nurse. Mrs. Paul's sister told me about such a case in her immediate family: "When they were looking for a wife for my husband's nephew, they didn't want the daughter of a nurse. There was one proposal where the mother was a nurse and the family was outside India — very wealthy — and offered a lot of money as dowry. The girl was very well educated, but they said no because she was a nurse's daughter. And so there are still some people who don't like nurses." Immigrants who enter the space of the transnational marriage market become reexposed to such attitudes, reinforcing the stigma.

Mrs. Elias, an immigrant nurse in the United States, told me about an encounter which shows that stigma is not limited only to those in the marriage market. It can touch those who provide information anywhere along the grapevine. One of her acquaintances in the United States inquired about a prospective bridegroom for the daughter of a friend. In describing the boy, Mrs. Elias mentioned that his mother was a nurse. The acquaintance responded that the girl's high-status parents would not consider the son of a nurse. Mrs. Elias told me that this made her feel bad, especially because the acquaintance with whom she was discussing the matter was also a nurse.

The stigma attached to nursing also arises during immigrants' visits to Kerala and in their interactions with visitors from Kerala. Because this is a delicate issue, people do not openly talk about the negative attitudes concerning nurses, as I discovered during a personal encounter while doing fieldwork in Kerala. As I walked to a bus stop, a man working in front of his house stopped me to ask if I were going to nursing school. I was caught off guard, not because he had asked me a question but because of the specificity of his question. In Kerala, it is common even for people who do not know each other to ask where one is headed—it is a way of saying hello. But this man had specifically brought up the subject of nursing, as if I had given some clue in my appearance or carriage. So even though I missed my bus, I stopped to talk to him.

When he discovered where I was staying, he asked me how I was related to the people living there (my grandparents) and told me some stories about my grandfather's generosity to his family. I asked him why he had thought I was going to nursing school. He said there was no particular reason and quickly changed the subject to ask me about my mother's whereabouts. I persisted and asked again about the nursing question. He became a little defensive and told me that nursing was a good profession. Especially in Malaysia, he said, nurses can make a lot of money, and that, in fact, they are like computer professionals these days. He said that he was not sure how much money nurses made in the United States. I did not get much farther with him, since he brushed me off by saying that I had better go and catch the next bus.

In reflecting on this incident, I realized he had been defensive because he thought he had offended me by suggesting that I might be studying nursing. Whereas I persisted in asking him about his question due to academic interest, he interpreted my persistence as a reflection of the degree to which I had taken offense. That he was not willing to talk about it any further demonstrates the sensitivity around the topic of nursing.

For many nurses who visit Kerala, such awkward moments occur even when nothing explicit is said about nursing. In our conversations about the status of nursing, Dr. Maria Koshy, a former immigrant who had lived in Canada and returned to Kerala, told me that she felt slighted all the time by the responses of people in Kerala when they found out she had a degree in nursing. People at first were impressed when she introduced herself as Dr. Koshy. But once they found out that her specialty was nursing, she could see that she lost esteem in their eyes.

She told me about a incident that revealed how her own extended family felt about nursing. Her brother, who lived in Canada, had married an immigrant woman from Kerala who did not meet the family's approval. Not only was she a few years older than her brother, but also she was a nurse. When the extended family was looking for a bride for one of her cousins, Maria's uncle had decided that it was best not to involve Maria's sister-in-law in the search. He told Maria, "She's a nurse and has some money with which she shows off. Who knows how she made it?" This comment implied that her money was not earned by nursing alone, alluding to the claims that some nurses are also prostitutes. Although Maria protested that she too was a nurse, her uncle merely said that she was different — not really a nurse but a professor of nursing. Maria knew that, because she had a doctorate to bolster her status, she was spared the disrespect aimed at her sister-in-law.

In some cases, immigrant nurses who visit Kerala find that they customarily behave differently than the women around them. Mrs. Thomas had had such an experience and concluded that her well-educated Keralite sister-in-law attributed her different behavior to the professional influences of nursing. It was at an informal tea party in the United States with four other immigrant nurses and myself that Mrs. Thomas brought up the incident. After being in the United States for over fifteen years, she had been traveling by train with her children and her sister-in-law in Kerala. When they got on the train, there were a couple of seats available adjacent to some men. Mrs. Thomas recalled that she sat down in one of the available seats and then realized that her sister-in-law did not do the same. Eventually, her sister-in-law took one of the children and sat down with the child between herself and a man. Mrs. Thomas reflected that her sister-in-law, who had a doctorate, must have thought she (Mrs. Thomas) was after all only a "dirty nurse" because she sat next to a man. When I asked her why she thought that, the four other immigrant nurses listening to this conversation all proceeded to tell me how nurses were seen back home as having low morals.

The existence of the discourse from Kerala that equates nursing with sexual looseness in the immigrant community is evidenced by the reaction of the nurses at the tea party to Mrs. Thomas's comment about being seen as a "dirty nurse." The immigrant nurse friends of Mrs. Thomas did not need an explanation as to why Mrs. Thomas would assume she knew what her well-educated sister-in-law thought about her in this case. In fact, they were quick to tell me more about such negative assumptions about nurses in Kerala. On trips back to Kerala, women like Mrs. Thomas are likely to be reminded of these discourses.

In conclusion, immigrants maintain connections that link the work sphere — particularly nursing — to Kerala. These links include transnational film circuits, marriage markets, and visits back and forth. The connections reinforce the cohesion of the immigrant community and provide channels of valuable service and support for both immigrants and the sending community. At the same time, these links transmit Kerala's profound ambivalence about nursing to the immigrant community and help reinforce the gender- and class-based stigmas against nurses. Despite nurses' newfound sense of professional respectability outside Kerala, the negative discourses around nursing that originate in Kerala affect not only the nurses but also their husbands and children and shape gender relations in the immigrant community.

Church

The institution of the church plays a key role in the formation and development of the immigrant community. Connections back to Kerala in this sphere happen at both the individual and institutional levels. Individuals are tied to Keralite churches by their financial contributions and pilgrimages. At the institutional level, the immigrant congregation is a part of the larger church in Kerala and looks to it for guidance in spiritual and administrative issues. Frequent letters from the patriarch of the church in Kerala are read to the whole congregation. There is a constant flow of ecclesiastical visitors from Kerala making fund-raising visits and personal visits.

The importance of the transnational connections to the Keralite church became evident in my conversations with priests, seminary professors, and churchgoers in Kerala. Primarily, the church depends on the congregations outside Kerala, particularly those in the United States and the Persian Gulf countries, for a disproportionally significant percentage of its funding. The importance of this connection is depicted in the movie *Dollar*, as Annamma goes to church in Kerala before her journey to the United States. The priest announces Annamma's imminent departure and adds that her visit will benefit not only her family but also the church. She has already promised that she will ask her children to send donations back to the parish in Kerala.

The transnational connections in the church sphere affect gender relations in the immigrant community by reinforcing male headship in families and in the congregation. Despite the marked changes in discourse and practice concerning women's participation in society, particularly in churches in Kerala, these changes are not evident in the immigrant congregations. It appears that a selective transfer of those discourses and practices reinforces the chosen parameters of the immigrant community, whose main focus is the re-creation of an imagined homeland in the United States. Consequently, the gender norms of an imagined Kerala are reinforced in the United States in the communal sphere of the immigrant congregation, even as the society and the church in Kerala are changing.

INDIVIDUAL CONNECTIONS AND MALE HEADSHIP

For most immigrants, connections to the church in Kerala at the individual level occur in the context of ritual occasions, the need for official documentation, and financial contributions. Orthodox Christians also have, in addition to baptism, wedding, and funeral ceremonies, memorial services for the departed and housewarmings, all of which require the prayers and blessings of a priest. Consequently, for Keralite Christians the church is thoroughly integrated into many aspects of life. Immigrants from the United States go back to Kerala not only to participate in ritual occasions but also to fulfill promises to visit holy sites on pilgrimages. A number of the people I interviewed in the United States talked about fulfilling promises to visit a particular shrine in Kerala if they were granted a prayer request.

Individual immigrants are solicited for contributions through many different channels. In addition to fund-raising visits from bishops and priests, they receive letters from diverse church-based organizations. While visiting their natal homes, priests and other administrators of their home parishes approach them for funds for special projects. Such requests are hard for immigrants to turn down, since the contributions become a matter of pride not only for them but also for their extended-family members. It is typically the men who gain status from such contributions, since wives are considered to be a part of their husbands' families and would not make donations to their natal churches in their own family's name.

The brand new parish hall of the church I attended in Kerala had a number of portraits, varying in size, displayed on its freshly painted walls. Father Mathews told me that the hall had been built by immigrant money, and that the portraits were typically of the deceased parents of the donors. He humorously observed that the size of the portrait was proportionately equivalent to the size of the donation. Another church member told me that immigrants who donate furniture and other fixtures to the church have their names inscribed on the items for all to see.

Similarly a number of the people I interviewed in Kerala told me about the tangible immigrant presence in their parishes. For instance, Mrs. Papi's brother told me that a priest from his parish was able to collect money from immigrants to build a home for the elderly, which ultimately became useful for the immigrants whose parents needed such assistance. In his observation, the priest and committee members in his parish expected twice as much from those who migrated to the United States as they did from anyone else. Mr. Babu, the brother of a U.S. immigrant, explained such expectations to me: "It is our church's Sunday school centenary. We are expecting to collect fifteen lakhs. Ten of those fifteen lakhs we plan to get from those NRIs who grew up in this church." When asked how they would collect this money, he responded:

> We will get their addresses and contact them by letter. Because they have studied in this Sunday school, they are alumni. Last week, somebody came here from the States. I went to sing at his son's wedding. We told him about this fund-raising effort. He said to the priest, "Father, how much should I give?" I suggested, "Why don't you donate the money to build a room in the new building?" He said he could not do that right now, but would five thousand rupees be all right? In reality, we only expected five thousand rupees from him. However, when he asked if five thousand was okay, we realized that we could get more. So the priest suggested that he reconsider. He immediately volunteered ten thousand rupees. He increased his original amount by another five thousand rupees. The average person in Kerala can only afford to give five hundred rupees. But this man doubled his original amount. Then he added, "I'm leaving on the twenty-ninth. I will give you a check for this amount before I leave. If you need more money, I will send it to you after I get back to the States." So I said all this to make the point that immigration is a gain as far as the church is concerned. In a humorous vein, one might say that it is better for more people to go to the United States and the Gulf than stay in Kerala.

Immigrants and those they sponsor also come to the church for official documentation, such as baptism and marriage certificates. This can become a problem for the church, according to Father Mathews, the priest of the congregation that I attended while in Kerala. After the service one Sunday, Father Mathews announced that he was feeling harassed by people who needed church documents for immigration. He brought up a recent encounter with a man attempting to go to the United States who had needed the church to give him a certificate of baptism as an official document for his visa application. The problem was that the spelling of his name in the church document did not match that in his high school certificate, another official document that he had to submit. He wanted the priest to change the spelling on the church document to match the school document. The priest explained to the congregation that he is unable to make such changes on official documents. Rather, anyone with a similar problem must make a petition to the bishop, who would evaluate each one on a case-by-case basis.

Father Mathews later told me in an interview that this type of harassment by immigrants was on the rise. He pointed out that immigrants are an extremely important financial resource in Kerala, and NRI money has corrupted the church, which breaks all kinds of rules and traditions to accommodate immigrants. Priests and bishops feel personally obligated to the NRIs who have donated money for their pet projects. Consequently, when such people come back to Kerala and need to bend the rules, most of the priests and bishops comply. He also commented that the American consulate is more likely to accept an immigration document as valid if it is from the records of the local government rather than from the church, because of the known corruption at the church level.

Such changes in the religious institutions of the sending community are not unique to Kerala. Peggy Levitt (2001), in her work on transnationalism between the United States and the Dominican Republic, reports similar changes. She found that parishioners who wanted counterfeit documents such as birth and baptismal certificates in order to obtain visas put the church in the Dominican Republic under pressure. The church had to create a new office to cope with the increase in paperwork, and the relationship between parishioners and priests took on an increasingly utilitarian tone as priests were asked to conduct "sacraments for visas."

The transnational church is responsible for many of the connections between U.S. immigrants and the homeland. Exerting influence on church officials and gaining status by making large contributions to their natal parishes are typically in the domain of male immigrants. Consequently, such interactions with the church in Kerala strengthen their positions as male representative of the household.

INSTITUTIONAL CONNECTIONS: FINANCIAL AND ADMINISTRATIVE LINKS AND MALE HEADSHIP

At the institutional level, immigrant U.S. congregations are inherently linked to the mother church in Kerala in many ways. Particularly, the administrative and financial links play a large role in shaping the nature of the relationship. Furthermore, these institutional links, too, allow male immigrants greater participation and strengthen their position as male representatives of the household.

The American Diocese of the Indian Orthodox Syrian Christian Church is composed of fifty-six immigrant congregations. These congregations not only make an annual contribution to the diocesan bishop but also send money to India by means of five churchwide collections during the year. Furthermore, each congregation can support separate charities in India. For instance, the women's group at St. George's supported a charity in Kerala that provided dowry for poor women whose parents could not afford it.[6] Immigrant congregations receive a steady flow of additional requests, often personally conveyed by distinguished officials of the church. The Keralite church is not unusual in its financial reliance on its U.S. members. Even though there are no reliable estimates of the total remittances, one expert holds that immigrant participants in the United States and the Gulf nations function as the primary source of external income for all religious organizations throughout India (Williams 1996).

Bishops and priests tour congregations in the United States with the express purpose of raising funds for a particular charity or project in their diocese. Because there is no central coordination of such visits, these fund-raising efforts tend to occur haphazardly. As one clerical observer, Father Kuriakose, put it, "In fact there is a kind of competition developing among the bishops. There is no general prioritizing of projects. The first step is that the bishop will go there with his personal charisma and the value of the project. When he gets to a particular parish, he will find some people from his original diocese. They will organize a campaign for him. . . . When I was in the United States recently, I was told that certain people are very active when a particular bishop comes and not so active when other bishops come."

Visits from bishops or priests not only provide a channel for money for the church but also strengthen individual members' connections back to Kerala by inspiring people to organize fund-raising campaigns for their original dioceses in Kerala. By staying at the homes of congregational members, these visiting church dignitaries confer status on their hosts. Father Mathai, who served as a priest in the United States before going back to teach in Kerala, explained why this is so:

> Many of these people come from backgrounds where, in the church's structure, they could only see bishops from far off. They wouldn't have the social standing

or the economic position to have a bishop come to their house. In Kerala, the bishops have their own homes, and few of them ever have to stay in somebody's house. In America, what has happened is that, because we do not have a center, most of the bishops stay with families; and there the question is, how much of your influence can you use to get the bishops to stay over? As the upward mobility of the family increased, these were some of the signs by which you established the fact that you had come of reckoning and you needed to be taken into consideration in the social set-up of the parish. That was the only place where Malayalees can expect that social standing, because in the society at large, you would be just one among the larger group. But in the social structure of the Malayalee Christian community, this was certainly a major achievement, and it became one of the standards by which you were measured—your close proximity and contact, and obviously the fact that you can influence the bishop with decisions. You can speak to him regarding various issues and get him to agree on this or that.

As Father Mathai pointed out, the church is one of the few spaces where Keralite immigrants can expect to have a social standing. Connections to Kerala—particularly through the visits of bishops—reinvest the immigrant congregation with class and status meanings that come from Kerala. The connections also engage individual male immigrants in the transnational political field of the church by permitting them to gain the attention of church leaders.[7]

In addition to maintaining financial links, the immigrant congregation also looks to the mother church in Kerala for spiritual and administrative guidance. Priests trained in Kerala serve the U.S. congregations, since there is no seminary or training center in the United States. However, the administrative issue is more significant for the church, both in Kerala and the United States. The nature of the difficulties that the American diocese faces testifies to the challenges of transnational administration. (See fig. 3, in appendix 3, for an organizational diagram outlining the transnational administrative structure of the church and for short descriptions of the leadership positions of the church hierarchy.)

Established in 1977, the American diocese of the Indian Orthodox Church was the first one of its kind among Asian-Indian Christian groups (Williams 1996). Bishop Thomas Mar Makarios was the metropolitan in charge of the diocese until 1993, when he resigned because of growing dissatisfaction with his vision of how the diocese should develop. In addition to being accused of moral and political corruption, he was judged to be too Americanized in his emphasis on adapting liturgy and church practices to fit the needs of the second generation.

The mother church appointed Mathew Mar Barnabas, a bishop from Kerala, as a replacement, which led to the intensification of disunity in the American diocese. Some congregations support Mar Makarios and resist the authority of Mar Barnabas.

It is clear that a large part of the conflict can be attributed to the uncertainty over the future course of the church — whether it will continue as one more diocese within the Keralite church or evolve into its own autonomous entity. As one outside observer and scholar describes it:

> Thus, two metropolitans [bishops] stand poles apart as symbols of potentials in the future of the church for becoming too American or too Indian. . . . One future involves a strategy of rapid Americanization of the liturgical, administrative and social aspects of the Church's life. The cry here is, "The church in America cannot be a carbon copy of the church in Kottayam." . . . A second potential future involves a strategy of Indianization, at least stressing the strong ethnic and religious ties to Kerala. . . . The appeal has more emotional power with members of the first generation than with youth of the second generation. (Williams 1996: 125–27)

Each of the groups supporting the respective bishops takes its grievances to Kerala, resulting in transnational propaganda campaigns. In addition to the designated elected representatives from the American diocese who go to Kerala for the annual managing-committee meetings of the church, interested individuals spend their own time and money to go and influence decisions. Consequently, the conflict in the American diocese has received disproportionate attention in the church in Kerala. Father Mathai told me that representatives from both sides come with documented evidence, using money from the United States to fund public propaganda campaigns and promote their own perspectives.

Furthermore, when the church synod in Kerala makes decisions that are unpopular in America, the American diocese makes its disapproval felt. Father Mathai explained how this works: "If you are a person who contributed significantly to the church, then you are given more of a hearing. Priests [from the United States] are given a little bit more hearing, since they are in charge of a congregation and these congregations contribute to the pool, such as the Catholicate Day collection or whatever. If there is a negative reaction to some decision that is taken here, one of the ways that it is communicated is by the decreased amounts given to the Catholicate Day collection or something like that. People make their disapproval felt." To the comment that the church is very sensitive to how people in the United States may respond, he laughed and replied, "Oh

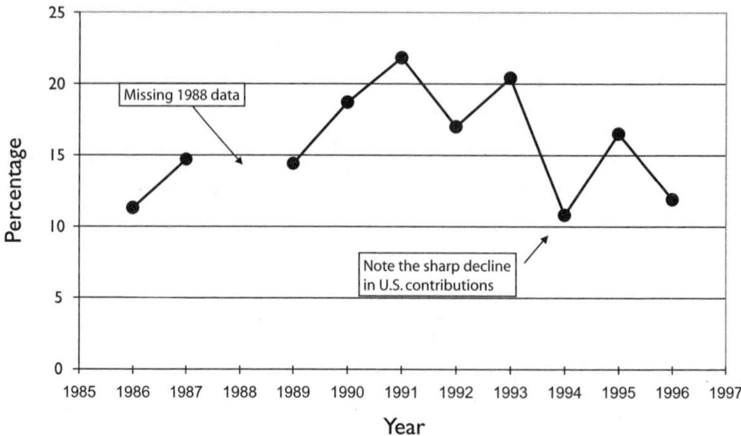

FIGURE 2. Catholicate Day collection: financial contributions from the United States Diocese as a percentage of worldwide church donations.

yes, sensitive; or rather, they have been sensitized to the issues over there." That the American diocese makes its displeasure felt through the reduction of contributions is apparent from an analysis of the Catholicate Day funds collected from the American diocese.[8] As fig. 2 demonstrates, there was a sharp decrease — by 45 percent — in donations in 1994 from the American diocese.

This decrease can be explained by the political upheaval of the previous year, when Bishop Mar Makarios resigned. The congregations in the diocese were extremely polarized over this issue, and many individuals were unhappy with Kerala's handling of the situation. Partly because of such tangible financial consequences, the Keralite church administration is sensitive to the problems of the American diocese and open to the individuals who desire to represent their particular positions.

The institutional connections of the immigrant congregation to the church in India firmly embed the immigrant community in Kerala. The fund-raising and administrative visits strengthen regional alliances with Kerala and cultivate the immigrant community's roots in India. Furthermore, all these connections critically affect gender relations within the immigrant community by reinforcing the understanding that the male is head and representative of the family unit, and by keeping shut most avenues of participation for women. But these connections fail to reflect some of the changes that are going on in Kerala in the arena of gender relations both in church and society.

CHANGES IN THE GENDERED SOCIAL RELATIONS IN THE CHURCH IN KERALA

With significant increases in female literacy and the decrease in female infant death rates, Kerala is hailed as one of the more progressive states in India for women. Kerala has recently increased female participation in politics with the help of an affirmative action policy to encourage women in politics. A certain number of legislative assembly seats are reserved for women in every election. In a landmark case decided in 1986, the Supreme Court of India abolished the 1916 Bill of Christian Inheritance Law that allowed daughters to claim only one-fourth of the share that sons got in the absence of a written will.[9]

The Orthodox Church in Kerala is also going through some changes as it is being pushed by external forces to permit greater participation by its female members. The wider Indian society is becoming more open to women in public offices, and the Indian Supreme Court has stipulated that the Orthodox Church must increase opportunities for women's participation and leadership in the church. According to Father Mathai, "There seems to be strong talk going around that the Supreme Court would now ask for representation on the diocesan and parish level irrespective of whether it is a woman or a man." This, he noted, was "not something the church has done. It always has to be prodded. That has always been the characteristic of the Orthodox Church. Very, very conservative body, so that any changes have taken a lot of prodding and pushing." Furthermore, international organizations such as the World Council of Churches (WCC) have also exerted pressure on the church to increase opportunities for women. For instance, the WCC requires that a certain percentage of the representatives attending international conferences be female.

In fact, there is a public discourse in Kerala that includes a critique of church and state regarding the issue of participation by women in these institutional settings. The Women's Association of Kerala convened a conference at St. Mary's College in Trichur, Kerala, in the late spring of 1998, titled "Women's Social Status and Related Problems." The conference brought home the conclusion that justice had been denied to women in the Christian churches in Kerala.

Dissatisfaction with women's level of participation is not limited to the political and public intellectual arenas. I observed the rumblings at the Orthodox Church where I engaged in participant observation while in Kerala. In one of the women's group meetings I attended at the church, the vicar—the official president of the women's group—proceeded to sermonize on the topic of the power of the clergy to forgive sins. He explained that one of the key beliefs of the Orthodox Church is that the clergy do have this power. He complained that several women in the parish appear to have eschewed this belief, given their involvement with charismatic prayer groups from other denominations who do not believe in this special role for the clergy.

In an interview after this meeting, he told me that he was concerned about women in the church who were organizing prayer groups independently and inviting their own unauthorized speakers to lead them in prayer. He had tried to intervene a few times, but to no avail. As he put it,

> These "weak" women have been misguided by the wolves that are out there in sheep's clothing, who distract them away from the true faith. In their homes, we can surmise that the men are not in charge as the heads of the household. That is why these women behave in these ways. For example, in a typical Pentecostal convention, 90 percent of the members are women, and the 10 percent men are only there because the women have beaten them into submission. However, this is not the case in Orthodox churches, where there are plenty of men around who are the heads of households. So just as men are in charge in the homes, priests also are in charge of forgiving sins.

The involvement of some women in prayer groups outside the aegis of the Orthodox Church is threatening to the church hierarchy. That the priest attributes the root of the problem to cuckolded husbands shows how important it is to the church for the hierarchy in the home to be maintained in order to support other hierarchies, such as the one in the church.

I asked him if it were possible that women in the church were dissatisfied with the present opportunities for participation open to them. He agreed that this was indeed the case. In his own parish, women complained about their lack of roles. He personally advocated expanding women's roles, since he believed that the church could never progress without the fuller participation of women, who are the spiritual backbone of the church.

That the women in Kerala are resisting pressure by the church and forming renegade prayer groups indicates radical change. And the church in Kerala has to acquiesce to such social pressures by allowing women's greater participation. However, renegade prayer groups and the attendant discourses about extending participation for women are not evident in the immigrant congregation. And this highlights the fact that the immigrant community does not adopt all practices and discourses found in Kerala. Rather, it selects discourses and practices that bolster the hierarchies that invest men in individual households, and priests and bishops in the community, with leadership and higher status.

Conclusion

Whereas some scholars of transnationalism paint an image of deterritorialized migrants existing in a third space outside the boundaries of the nation-state, Keralite immigrants necessarily remain bound to their native shores while simultaneously making a home for themselves in the United States. Both immigrant and sending communities are firmly tied to each other for myriad reasons. Most important are the transnational connections that provide invaluable assistance and resources to immigrants and those they leave behind. That the assistance goes in both directions is clear from the analysis of each of the three spheres.

In the home sphere, the immigrant is often the embodiment of an entire family's dreams and efforts to get someone "on the other side." Consequently, many strands of obligations can tie migrants to the sending community, as illustrated by the family members in Kerala who expect sponsorship for their own immigration. The immigrants, in turn, depend on family members in Kerala for assistance and support, particularly with child care and the socialization of the second generation. In the work sphere, nursing networks provide an example of how immigrant nurses assist those remaining in India. In the community sphere, the relationship between the immigrant congregation and the mother church in Kerala exemplifies the symbiotic relationship that ties immigrants to the sending community. The immigrant congregation looks to the mother church for guidance and support, and the mother church relies on immigrant congregations to share their prosperity with it.

While transnational connections tie immigrants to the sending community through mutual assistance, they also serve to reproduce the immigrant community, despite its tendencies toward dissolution through generational and class conflict. The case of the aspiring teenage carolers illustrates gendered and generational conflict. The transnational behavioral prescriptions for a "homely" girl from the likes of the cinematic grandmother Annamma tempered the revolutionary urges of young Anna at St. George's. The political conflict in the American diocese provides another example of the effects of transnational connections. The mother church in

Kerala takes the threat of dissolution very seriously as it faces the crisis of the renegade bishop who allegedly wants to break away from the Keralite church. As it resorts to the transnational administration of the American diocese, the Keralite church hierarchy encourages and welcomes interactions with the American lay membership. This interaction results not only in strengthened ties between the mother church and the diocese but also in the reproduction of the immigrant community, with its identity based firmly in Kerala.

However, the reproduction of the community is Janus faced. Whereas the scholarly trend is to identify transnational connections as spaces of resistance, I found both liberatory and repressive moments in the interplay of transnational connections that contribute to the reproduction of the community. In the liberatory moment, transnational connections allow for the creation of new space for those traditionally excluded or restricted by social norms. For example, the transnational marriage market models potential institutional space for class mobility, since migrants and their children can leverage their immigrant status to move up the social ladder. Nurses are not expected to pay dowries if they participate in the transnational marriage market. Similarly, the transnational institution of the church allows men who were excluded from top leadership positions before migration to use their NRI influence—to "have some pull."

Yet these same institutions can also give rise to repressive moments that result in the reproduction of oppressive social hierarchies. In the transnational marriage market, nursing becomes a marker of premigration status, helping reproduce gender- and class-based stigmas. This institution also supports the reproduction of asymmetric gender norms that require second-generation girls to be "homely," unlike their male counterparts. Likewise, the transnational church, while allowing some space for male mobility, staunchly supports the reproduction of oppressive gender norms through the selective transfer of discourses.

CHAPTER 6

Conclusions

Most scholars agree that social relations undergo continuous yet incremental changes over time. Given that such changes are almost imperceptible to the actors involved, actors experience these social structures as immutable and permanent. The immigration process interrupts this perception, as individuals and communities are placed in extraordinary circumstances. Such dramatic changes to the status quo are particularly useful to scholarly research, because they provide rare glimpses into how individuals and communities go about reestablishing social equilibrium.

In this book, I examine the effects of such an extraordinary circumstance on a community from Kerala, India. More specifically, I explore how gender relations change when women take the uncommon step of migrating before their husbands and families and, as primary breadwinners, become economically dominant in their homes and community. I look specifically at gender relations within and across three spheres—work, home, and community—focusing on the different experiences of women and men. Finally, I explore the role of transnational connections in producing a little Kerala in the United States, and in creating some opportunities for new gender and class relations but limiting other possibilities for change. What broader implications—for the study of migration, gender, and transnationalism—emerge from this project?

Implications for the Study of Migration

PROFESSIONAL IMMIGRANT WOMEN

In the large body of literature on gender and migration produced during the last two decades, one major focus has been working-class immigrant women and their experiences in the migration and settlement processes. Little has been written about women from other social strata. My examination of immigrant nurses from Kerala suggests a number of ways in which the experiences of professional immigrant women differ considerably from those of working-class immigrant women. These variations in experiences and their consequent effect on gender relations are evident not only in the various stages of migration and settlement but also in the different spheres of work, home, and community.

As discussed in chapter 2, migration clearly magnifies the already contrasting experiences of working-class and professional women. In the case of the Keralite nurses, not only were they actively recruited by hospitals in host countries, but also their migration process and entry into the workforce were institutionalized and regulated by a licensing process that gave them some measure of security as they contemplated and completed immigration. For working-class immigrant women, whose primary occupational options are limited to the service industry—such as domestic work or factory work—migration is a more haphazard process in which their lives are more often subject to chance.

The findings of this study point to networks as another factor that differentiates the migration and settlement experiences of working-class and professional immigrant women. It is instructive to compare the experiences of professional Indian nurses with the experiences of Mexican and Central American working-class women in their use of migration networks (Kossoudji and Ranney 1984; Hondagneu-Sotelo 1994).[1] Professional Indian nurses are like the Latina working-class immigrants not only because they depend on mostly female networks but also because these networks determine their final migration destinations and the type of jobs they secure.

The differences between these two groups stem from the type and quality of the networks available. Whereas Latina immigrant working-class women tend to depend on family, kin, and local networks, the Indian professional women also use their professional nursing networks from India. Nursing students meet women from all over Kerala and India—in nursing schools and hospitals where they train in North India—women whom they would not otherwise meet. Consequently, they receive specific help from their predecessors and peers with both migration and settlement processes.

Professional networks not only widen their potential contacts but also are richer in social capital, because members of such networks, on the whole, are not living in conditions as highly constrained as those of the members of working-class networks. For example, the typical Latina working-class immigrant needing help must ask for help from other migrants already stretched thin by such challenges as extreme poverty, unstable employment, lack of documentation, and overcrowded living conditions (Menjivar 2000). The relative fragility of this working-class network can make assistance at best limited and at worst unavailable. The relative strength in the structure of opportunities available within professional networks is far greater and contributes to significantly different experiences for the Keralite nurses.

The avenues of immigration available to the Keralite nurses afford them greater control over the migration and settlement process. They have more choices regarding where they will settle and when they will bring their families over. Because their professional credentials allow them to be primary migrants, they are typically the first ones in their family to become conversant with the ways of the host society. Consequently, their husbands and other relatives depend on them considerably in the settlement process. In contrast, working-class women who are dependent on kin, particularly husbands, in the immigration process must also depend on them in the settlement process.

The differences between working-class and professional immigrant women remain distinct when considering gender relations in the work sphere. For example, Indian immigrant nurses in the United States have access to better technology and an improved work process that allows them to apply their skills more efficiently and to feel more professional. They also enter a labor market that has consistently experienced a shortage of workers over the last few decades. Despite the racism that immigrant nurses can face on the hospital ward floors, their vocational self-esteem increases as the result of a relatively consistent demand for nurses and a more meritorious evaluation of the nursing profession by the U.S. host society as compared to Kerala. The work experiences of working-class immigrant women are markedly less positive. Because they are treated as unskilled and often unwanted workers, their reception and experiences in workplaces leave them more insecure, both economically and socially.

When professional immigrant women, such as the Keralite nurses, become the primary breadwinners after immigration, they have a greater ability to shape gender relations in the home and community spheres. Working-class women, even when they are the primary breadwinners, are less able to do so largely because their typically unstable and often dependent economic status does not require a restructuring of conventional gender relations. It is not economically reductionist to observe that, especially among immigrant households, which are often trying to establish or better themselves financially, the economic status of women plays a defining role in the ensuing gender relations after immigration.

In future studies, it would be worthwhile to juxtapose the experiences of the Indian nurses with Filipina and Korean nurses in the United States in order to compare the experiences of professional women in the same occupation across cultural backgrounds. Additionally, the findings of my study merit a comparison across professions to see how other professionals, such as female doctors and computer scientists, in the context of their families and communities, experience the migration and settlement process.

VARIATIONS IN THE EXPERIENCES OF MEN

An understanding of immigrant gender relations is incomplete without knowledge of what men encounter in the process of migration and settlement. In much of the migration and gender literature, men are treated as a monolithic category with uniform motivations guided by their desire to preserve male privilege. Their presence is studied only to the extent that they either hinder or help immigrant women gain social power. My findings indicate that it is also important to look at men as agentic beings whose experiences differ according to factors such as the gender order of migration, intracommunal class relations, and postimmigration social status in the host society.

Historically, men have migrated first, and, given this strong male-first pattern, most students of migration have paid little attention to the gender order of migration. Currently, there are increasing opportunities for women to migrate before men. As my study shows, the order of arrival profoundly affects who gets established first economically and socially and who is able to sponsor family members based on length of stay and consequent length of time to obtain citizenship. The experiences of the men from the traditional households described in chapters 3 and 4 differed from those of the other men in my sample not only because they maintained breadwinner status after migration but also because they arrived first and became established first in the United States.

Second, my findings point to the importance of examining intracommunal class relations, particularly as these affect men and the construction of different types of masculinity. We must pay particular attention to how immigrant communities operate within culturally specific social hierarchies based on class, religion, caste, and other relevant social differences. Such hierarchies "form the structural and cultural contexts in which gender is enacted in everyday life, thereby fragmenting gender into multiple masculinities and femininities" (Pyke 1996: 531). Thus, men of the traditional households come from a higher-class background and embody a hegemonic masculinity from Kerala that is associated with household headship and church leadership. These traditional householders disassociate themselves from the husbands of nurses, whom they characterize as not being heads of their own households and as just "playing around" in the church. Consequently, not only do their relationships with their wives shape their postimmigration gender relations, but so does their perceived social standing relative to other men in the community.

Finally, my study highlights the importance of examining how men's experiences may differ based on their level of economic and social integration into the host society. Are upwardly mobile men with influence and lucrative jobs less likely to maintain traditional markers of status in their homes or communities? For the majority of the men in my sample, migration marginalized men in relation to both their wives and the wider American society. Like Korean immigrant men, they sought to compensate for their losses in the communal arena of the immigrant congregation (Shin and Park 1988; Hurh and Kim 1990).

Given the variations in men's experiences, it is important to move beyond an unvarying notion of the patriarchal male immigrant. We must examine more closely men's experiences in relation to women's experiences and relative to other men's experiences. How do men in other immigrant communities deal with such social losses? In which arenas besides the immigrant religious congregation do they have opportunities for participation?

Implications for the Study of Gender

GENDERED SPHERES

Most scholarship on gender relations examines the effects of gender on individual lives or within particular institutions such as the family or the workplace. This is also true of the existing literature on gender and immigration, where the unit of analysis is typically the immigrant woman or the immigrant household in relationship to the host or sending societies. When considering gender relations, we must look at the specificities and balances of gender relations within and across social spheres.

I used R. W. Connell's framework of gender relations to study gendered spheres. Connell argues that gender relations are organized by gender structures (I focus on the gender structures of labor and power) that situationally constrain the play of practices in different spheres (I focus on work, home, and community). Although he identifies three different types of relations between gendered spheres — complementary, conflictive, and parallel — he does not explain how these relations emerge and are reproduced. Focusing on the work sphere as the site of primary change and of greatest effect, I asked whether gender relations in the other spheres were complementary, conflictive, or parallel when immigrant women gained primary status with respect to work.

I found that each sphere had its own assortment of conditions that shaped gender relations. Despite the variation in household types — from traditional to female-led households — gender relations were necessarily refashioned in the domestic sphere by women's work requirements. While the shift in women's status in the work sphere also affected gender relations in the communal sphere, the consequences were quite different. Conventional patriarchal gender relations were reinforced as men who lost status in the immigration process sought to compensate for it in the immigrant congregation and as the nurses maintained the proper norms of femininity. Looking at this in terms of Connell's framework, there is a balance in gender relations among the three spheres of work, home, and community.

However, this seeming equilibrium is not stable. Gender relations in these spheres ultimately undermine each other. Despite men's position as church leaders, their attempt to assert themselves in the church is weakened by their connection to nurses. Similarly, despite the nurses' efforts to abide by the stringent norms of appropriate feminine behavior, their economic and social successes in the work and family spheres are still held against them. Although men and women seem to have a complementary set of gender relations, a closer look reveals that their attempts to compensate for men's lost status are constrained by the influence across spheres.

This study shows the importance of examining different social spheres when studying gender relations, whether one focuses on immigrants or any subcategory of the native born. Only by concurrently studying multiple spheres was I able to see how gender relations emerged in each sphere and, in turn, interacted with the gendered outcomes in other spheres to produce a comprehensive set of gender relations for this particular immigrant community.

PATRIARCHY: NEGOTIATED RESILIENCE IN MULTIPLE SPHERES

I posited in the introduction that this instance, where women immigrated first and men were dependent on them, offers a test case for the durability of patriarchy. That is, I ask what happens to the taken-for-granted model of patriarchal gender relations when the material bases for male privilege are eroded. The sociologist Manuel Castells answers this question with a picture of the dissolution of patriarchy. Referring to "all contemporary societies," Castells argues that, as women enter the labor market and acquire a feminist consciousness, there is an "undoing of the patriarchal family." Consequently, men lose privilege in the family because they are no longer the traditional breadwinners and must contend with wives made more aware of their rights. Castells holds that "men's anger—both individual and collective—in losing power results in widespread interpersonal violence" (1997: 136).

This breakdown of patriarchy and the violent expression of male frustration form the backdrop to the stereotype of widespread domestic violence among immigrants. For example, in the concluding essay of an edited volume titled *Gender and Immigration,* Gregory Kelson explains the cause for domestic violence among immigrant couples as follows: "The man will want to continue being the breadwinner for the family and want his wife to stay home and take care of the home and kids. The wife on the other hand, embracing Western and feminist ideals, will want more independence and the ability to make her own decisions. The male spouse will usually lose control and resort to domestic violence to keep everything under the status quo in his opinion" (Kelson and DeLaet 1999: 214). Both Castells's "contemporary" man and Kelson's non-Western immigrant man respond violently to a world filled with feminist ideals, where patriarchy has broken down.

A competing viewpoint represented by neo-Marxist feminist scholars is that patriarchy has not gone anywhere (Hartman 1979; Mies 1986; Walby 1990). Despite extended debates about the nature of the relationship of patriarchy to capitalism, these feminists agree that the dual exploitation of women in the household and the labor market supported by patriarchal ideology is extremely beneficial to the capitalist system. Whether patriarchy is seen as a by-product of class relations (the Orthodox Marxist feminist view) or as an independent system of oppression that works in cooperation with capitalism (the Socialist feminist position), it is nevertheless seen as a necessary component of capitalist societies. In the face of crises such as the one painted by Castells, these feminists argue, there is a successful reproduction of patriarchy despite the changes in society.

For instance, in *Theorizing Patriarchy,* Sylvia Walby holds that changes in British society have led to modifications in some aspects of gender relations, such as a slight reduction in the male-female wage gap (1990). However, Walby points out that the more significant change has been a shift from a private to a public form of patriarchy. That is, the primary site of women's oppression has moved from the private space of the household to more public forms, such as in employment and in relations to the state, constituting the continuing reproduction of patriarchy.

Both the dissolution and reproduction arguments present only partial pictures. Those who argue that patriarchy in immigrant communities has ended fail to notice that patriarchal relations are unevenly present in different gendered spheres. Those who argue that patriarchy is reproduced would benefit by looking at the intertwining of gender with other sources of social oppression to see how this reproduction is limited. Rather than a complete dissolution of or a perfect reproduction of patriarchy, I found a negotiated reconfiguration of patriarchy in the Keralite immigrant community.

What is missing in the argument of dissolution is a more nuanced understanding of patriarchy as a set of social relations negotiated within and across different gendered spheres. For example, an inclusion of the analysis of different gendered spheres in Castells's formulation of the dissolution of patriarchy might reveal that there are alternatives to interpersonal violence available to frustrated men facing significant social and economic changes. Immigration scholars such as Kelson may find that immigrant men may avail themselves of options other than "usually los[ing] control and resort[ing] to violence."

This is not to say that domestic violence is not present in this community as in the rest of society. I am aware of the social conditions that lead to domestic abuse and the reasons for women's reluctance to report such abuse. Several feminist academics and activists not only have highlighted the presence of domestic violence in the Indian immigrant community but also have led efforts to create organizations and safe havens to support victims of domestic abuse (Bhattacharjee 1992; Abraham 1995; Dasgupta and Dasgupta 1996; Shukla 1997; Krishnan et al. 1998; Nankani 2000). I believe that such activist efforts are important and necessary steps in publicizing and politicizing violence against women.

However, I also agree with the sociologist Aparna Rayaprol (1997), who cautions against the trend toward victimologies in feminist research, where the focus is on violent forms of patriarchy and a tendency to underestimate women's agency and their ability to resist patriarchy. Such an overemphasis on the victimization of immigrant women in the feminist literature contributes to the general perception that domestic violence is rampant in Indian immigrant communities. Thus, I was asked by my scholarly interrogator why, in my sample, I had not found that domestic violence exists, given that "all the feminists say so" (see the introduction).

Analytically, we must move beyond only pointing out that domestic violence is present and hidden in immigrant communities. Instead of focusing exclusively on the experiences of women, we must understand the changes that occur with immigration and settlement and how they affect the gendered interactions of both men and women in a relational way. The postimmigration absence of domestic help, which is a staple of middle-class South Asian family life in India, can add great stress to the immigrant conjugal relationship. The decrease or lack of immediate familial support and intervention when problems arise also affects how couples resolve those problems. Furthermore, immigrants find themselves in a society with a different sociolegal system, one that has a distinctive ethos concerning individual rights. That is, the relationship of the individual to the state and the potential intervening role of the state in domestic affairs can be confusing for immigrant families.[2] How do these factors affect gender relations among immigrants in the United States? What role do community spaces and religious leaders (such as priests) have in shaping these relations?

To combat the ubiquitous stereotype that domestic abuse is synonymous with non-Western immigrant communities, whose men automatically resort to patriarchally inspired violence, we must understand what options men have besides resorting to violence to compensate for any losses in status. For instance, how does the balancing of gender relations in different spheres play a part in providing opportunities for "reactive compensation" to men?

By examining different spheres, I was able to see how the men I studied took an active role in creating an alternate space that provided them with support and status when they encountered social and economic marginalization in the wider host society. They utilized the immigrant congregation because it was inherently supportive of patriarchal privilege. They broadened opportunities for male participation—through the propagation, creation, and redefinition of existing opportunities—to make up for the losses they suffered. Their female partners asserted themselves in some spheres, were denied the opportunity to do so in some spheres, and consciously chose to retreat in others. Nevertheless, I observed men and women attempting to maintain a balance of sorts, both as couples and as a community, through a strategy of complementary gender relations in the different spheres.

Ironically, the men were not fully successful in their compensation efforts. Their alleged premigration class background—marked by their connection to wives who are nurses—limited not only their attempt to regain status but also the scope of the reproduction of patriarchal relations. It is here that we see that the reproduction of patriarchal relations is a negotiated process, and gender and class relations are inextricably tied together in this instance. Neither the dissolution camp nor the reproduction camp is sensitive to the ways in which gender and patriarchal relations always exist in tandem with other social relations and systems of oppression.

The feminist scholars Inderpal Grewal and Caren Kaplan underline the importance of deconstructing monolithic categories such as patriarchy to make them more useful. They prescribe transnational feminist practices "to compare multiple, overlapping and discrete oppressions rather than to construct a theory of hegemonic oppression under a unified category of gender" (1994: 17). The resilience of patriarchy is limited by the resilience of class and status configurations, which are themselves reproduced via transnational ties. My case study of Keralite immigrants not only demonstrates the importance of studying such overlapping oppressions but also points to the increasing importance of transnational ties in a global context that can help sustain or challenge what Grewal and Kaplan call "scattered hegemonies."

Transnationalism and Its Future

In the classic model of immigration, immigrant communities shed old national identities in the American melting pot and adopt a new American identity. While immigrant racial minorities were never successful at achieving this goal, it was still assumed that the American-born generations that followed would eventually lose all concrete ties with their ancestors' native lands. With the new conditions that allow for the maintenance of global ties, there is a new model of the transnational migrant who "forge[s] and sustain[s] simultaneous multi-stranded social relations that link together societies of origin and settlement" (Glick-Schiller et al. 1995: 48). Are transnational relations so powerful that they constitute a whole new way of reproducing communities and cultures? If so, what does this mean for the future of immigrant and sending communities and the institutions and individuals within them?

It is impossible to definitively answer these questions based on this single case. However, my study does suggest important possibilities for transnationalism, both in the near and distant futures. In the short term, access to resources may be what keeps the immigrant and second generations tied to Kerala. In the long term, an expanded mix of elements may determine how much future generations will depend on transnational ties for their identity. These elements include the level of racism and anti-immigrant tendencies in the host society, coupled with the level of support from the sending state and the strength of immigrant institutions.

For the first-generation immigrant, the relationship to the homeland is complex and can be full of contradictions, as described in chapter 5. Most important, transnational ties provide access to crucial resources in the initial years of settlement and child rearing. Transnational ties also link immigrants to a community of meaning, a community based on shared histories and worldviews that spans both the sending and immigrant populations. In the face of dynamic changes brought about by immigration and settlement, the transnational community of meaning becomes the point of reference for most immigrants, where they gauge the extent of their progress and make status claims that can be understood by peers.

Furthermore, as the first generation ages, they are faced with the dilemma of where to retire. On one hand, many immigrants desire to fulfill the cherished dream of going back to settle on their native soil, a dream that sustained them through the initial years of hardship. On the other hand, they also want to be with their children and grandchildren in their waning years. But with most of the second-generation firmly embedded in two-job families, the old-timers cannot rely on familial care. Fearing the specter of the American nursing home as their inevitable last resort, many of the immigrant generation plan to retire in Kerala, where they can more easily hire people to care for them in their own homes. The economic, political, and civic participation of return migrants in their community of origin can lead to denser ties and help sustain transnational connections with the settlement community. The state as well as transnational institutions like the church can play an important role in facilitating the return of migrants and the establishment of continuing ties between sending and immigrant communities.

The state of Kerala, like other sending communities, welcomes return migrants, giving financial incentives to nonresident Indians (NRIs) who return to settle. The state can play an important role in facilitating the participation of NRIs in their communities of origin by providing economic incentive programs and special tax breaks for investments and the opportunity to maintain dual citizenship, which allows for active political participation in the communities of origin. As mentioned earlier, Kerala is one of the few states in India to have established a special governmental agency that focuses on the political and legal problems encountered by Keralites abroad. Such welcoming gestures on the part of the state can solidify transnational ties past the first generation.

Transnational institutions such as the church also play a part in maintaining transnational ties for the first generation. First-generation immigrants, particularly men, continue to be involved in the church in Kerala (see chapter 5). Alumni institutions of colleges, universities, seminaries, nursing schools, medical schools, and even Sunday schools look to alumni abroad as a wealthy resource for operating funds. From churches to charity and alumni organizations, institutions are becoming increasingly transnational and are adjusting their organizational structures and administrative strategies to the new reality of their own global potential. Some have been successful in this; others, like the Orthodox Church in Kerala, are still struggling with the difficulty of transnational administration and the divergent goals of its various constituencies. For example, the Orthodox immigrant faithful in the United States complain that the mother church should not expect the same level of financial contribution from them as from immigrant churches in the Persian Gulf. They argue that, since most immigrant churches in the Persian Gulf are not able to establish permanent religious institutions in their respective countries, they do not carry as great a financial burden as the American immigrant churches (Williams 1996: 223). As churches, alumni organizations, and other such institutions become more adept at dealing with the needs of their varying global sectors, they contribute to the conditions for the continuing maintenance of transnational ties.

For the second generation, the sending community is not the main community of meaning. Kerala is mostly a place where their parents came from and to which they were possibly taken a handful of times in their lives. Interestingly, while many of the second-generation Keralite Christians may not have a strong sense of connection to Kerala, they seem to relate to a larger, pan-Indian identity that appears to be present particularly on college and university campuses. Shared pan-Indian parental expectations regarding career and spouse selection play a part in uniting many young South Asians of diverse language, regional, and religious backgrounds to form pan-ethnic South Asian cultural organizations in higher educational institutions. I met several young Keralite Christians who were trying to learn Hindi rather than Malayalam so they could better understand Bollywood movies and music, which is the lingua franca of the pan-ethnic South Asian community of mainstream second-generation youth.

As their parents begin retiring and returning to their homeland, children and grandchildren are sure to be linked to Kerala. Additionally, Kerala still offers some resources to members of the second generation who need child care for their own families. Cases such as that of Sunil Eapen, a second-generation Keralite Christian whose child was allegedly killed by a negligent English nanny (Louise Woodward), has motivated several second-generation parents to find alternate sources of child care within the community. While second-generation parents are less likely than their parents to send their children to Kerala, they may chose to bring child-care workers from Kerala to the United States. This recent trend is an attractive option for busy second-generation parents not only because of the reliability of in-house child care but also because it ensures the transfer of culture and language to their children in their early formative years. Such connections can continue to maintain strong ties between the two communities.

It is not clear what will happen in the long term, beyond the second generation. The current ease of travel and communication makes India much more accessible to immigrants and their children than it was for earlier immigrants. The continuing presence of transnational institutions such as the church and the marriage market, along with the replenishment of the community with new immigrants, will allow future generations the choice of maintaining their ethnic ties to India. Yet to the extent that these institutions reproduce oppressive hierarchies of gender and class, future generations will distance themselves from them and from their ethnic identities.

Their choices will also depend on the level of goodwill toward racial minorities in the United States. In the context of the post-2001 homeland security regime and increasing xenophobia sparked by fears of terrorism, anyone in the United States with discernible loyalties to another nation can become suspect. Consequently, transnational migrants will have to be more cautious about their connection to their homelands. Politically, they may have fewer opportunities to take advantage of the new forms of participatory opportunities discussed by scholars of transnationalism. Economically, they will be less adventurous when international conditions appear unstable. In light of these emerging factors, it is difficult to determine what will become of transnational ties.

Given that the racial minority populations in the United States, especially in states like California, are steadily increasing, future generations may have much less incentive to identify with the nation of their ancestors. Perhaps Indian immigrants will turn to a pan-ethnic form of identity, such as Asian American or South Asian, that is more clearly based in the United States. But as the historian Arif Dirlik points out, "Asian America is no longer just a location in the United States, but is at the same time a location on a metaphorical rim constituted by diasporas and motions of individuals" (1996: 13).

A *New York Times* article dated February 10, 2003, mentioned Annamma George, a nurse living and working in Bangalore, India, who was preparing to take exams that would allow her the opportunity to come to the United States (Rai 2003). The article noted that, after not having taken an exam for fifteen years, she pored over books alongside her ten-year-old son. It mentioned the increasing number of Indian nurses coming to the United States to meet its demand for new nurses. According to the article, the Health Resources and Services Administration has projected that the demand will rise from the current need for 110,000 new nurses to a number exceeding 700,000 by 2020. While the article discussed the recruitment process and the immigration hurdles that nurses faced, it did not refer again to Annamma George or her ten-year-old son, who had already served their purpose as the human-interest element introducing the piece.

However, as I read the article I was transported back some twenty-five years, to another Annamma George, my mother, who was also a nurse working in Bangalore, India. In 1977, that Annamma George too was studying for exams after many years of not having taken an exam, alongside her then-ten-year-old daughter. I wondered how things would be different for the young Annamma George of 2003, her son, and her family. As long as there is a continuing demand for nurses that attracts more

Annamma Georges to the United States, transnational ties will continue to exist for the new immigrants. As for the Annamma George of 2003, she will probably leave her ten-year-old son behind and undergo a journey similar to my mother's. However, for the younger Annamma George, a more developed transnational infrastructure will perhaps make her stay apart from her family easier and the settlement process for her family less difficult.

APPENDIX I

Interview Participants by Household Type

TABLE 3. Interview Participants in Traditional Households

Pseudonym	Year of Migration from Kerala	Reason for Migration from Kerala	Intermediate Residency	Year of Arrival in the United States	Sponsor	Occupation	Initiator of Migration to United States
Mrs. Abraham	1972	Higher studies in North India	North India	1980	Husband	M.S. degree/teacher	Husband
Mr. Abraham	1963	Veterinarian school in Madras	None	1980	Student visa	Veterinarian	Self
Mrs. Cherian	Born and raised in Madras	Never lived in Kerala	None	1973	Husband	M.S. degree/ post office employee	Husband
Mr. Cherian	1967	Higher studies in the United States	None	1967	Brother	M.S. degree/teacher	His family
Mrs. Itoop	1972	Joined husband	None	1972	Husband	Data entry	Husband
Mr. Itoop	1970	Higher studies in the United States	None	1970	Student visa	Administrator of nursing home	Self
Mrs. Mathai	1964	Nursing education	North India	1982	Husband's friend	Nurse's aide	Husband
Mr. Mathai	1962	Education	North India	1982	His friend	Screen printer	Self
Mrs. Mathen	After high school*	Joined her family	None	1978	Sibling	Homemaker/ recent worker	Her family
Mr. Mathen	1972	Higher studies in the United States	Delhi	1974	Neighbor	M.B.A.	His family
Mrs. Paul	1979	Nursing education	Delhi, Saudi Arabia	1986	Husband's family	RN/ full-time homemaker	Husband
Mr. Paul	1975	Employment in Saudi Arabia	Saudi Arabia	1986	His family	Insurance agency owner	Self
Mrs. Zachariah	1963	Nursing education	Germany	1971	Hospital	RN/works part-time	Self
Mr. Zachariah	1974	Joined wife	None	1974	Wife	Engineer/M.S. degree	Wife

* The interview subject either did not remember the exact year when he or she left Kerala and said it was after high school, or failed to mention the year in the course of the interview.

TABLE 4. Interview Participants in Forced-Participation Households

Pseudonym	Year of Migration from Kerala	Reason for Migration from Kerala	Intermediate Residency	Year of Arrival in the United States	Sponsor	Occupation	Initiator of Migration to United States
Mrs. Elias	1967	Nursing education	North India	1976	Husband's brother	LPN	Husband
Mr. Elias	1975	Joined wife	None	1976	Wife	Furniture store owner	Self
Mrs. George	1967	Nursing education	North India	1973	Brother	RN	Brother
Mr. George	1977	Joined wife	None	1977	Wife	Clerical worker	Wife
Mrs. Joseph	1969	Nursing education	Delhi	1975	Friend from nursing network	RN	Self
Mr. Joseph	After high school	Navy training	Delhi	1978	Wife	Electronics technician	Wife
Mrs. Papi	1966	Nursing education	North India	1980	Cousin	Ex-nurse, technician	Self
Mr. Papi	1965	Employment	All over India	1981	Wife	Unemployed technician	Wife
Mrs. Patrose	After high school	Nursing education	Delhi	1976	Husband's cousin	RN	Self
Mr. Patrose	After high school	Army training	Delhi	1977	Cousin	Clerical worker	Wife
Mrs. Peter	1969	Nursing education	North India	1976	Sister	RN	Self
Mr. Peter	1956	Education	North India	1979	Wife	Office manager	Wife
Mrs. Thambi	1967	Nursing education	North India and Dubai	1975	Father's friend	RN	Her father
Mr. Thambi	1972	Education	North India and Dubai	1977	Wife	Computer operator	Wife

TABLE 5. Interview Participants in Female-Led Households

Pseudonym	Year of Migration from Kerala	Reason for Migration from Kerala	Intermediate Residency	Year of Arrival in the United States	Sponsor	Occupation	Initiator of Migration to United States
Mrs. Jacob	1968	Nursing education	Kuwait	1974	Connection from nursing network	RN	Self
Mr. Jacob (deceased)	—	—	—	—	—	—	—
Mrs. John	1971	Nursing education	None	1975	Aunt	RN	Self
Mr. John	1965	Technical training	Muscat	1976	Wife	Unemployed	Wife and self
Mrs. Kurien	1966	Nursing education	North India	1976	Husband's friend	RN	Self
Mr. Kurien	After high school	Employment	North India	1976	His friend	LPN (after immigration)	Wife
Mrs. Mathew	1991	Joined husband	None	1991	Husband	RN	Husband and self
Mr. Mathew	1984	Employment	None	1984	Sister	Nurse's aide	Sister
Mrs. Simon	1963	Nursing education	Madras	1976	Husband's cousin	RN	Self
Mr. Simon (no interview)	?*	Employment	Madras	1970	Wife	Manual laborer	Wife

* The interview subject either did not remember the exact year when he or she left Kerala and said it was after high school, or failed to mention the year in the course of the interview.

TABLE 6. Interview Participants in Partnership Households

Pseudonym	Year of Migration from Kerala	Reason for Migration from Kerala	Intermediate Residency	Year of Arrival in the United States	Sponsor	Occupation	Initiator of Migration to United States
Mrs. Eapen	1969	Nursing education	North India	1976	Cousin	RN	Self
Mr. Eapen	1979	Joined wife	None	1979	Wife	Respiratory therapist	Wife
Mrs. Lukos	After high school	Nursing education	Delhi	1974	Self	RN/Master's in Public Health	Self
Mr. Lukos	Born and raised in Madras	Education	Delhi	1974	Wife	Bookkeeper	Wife
Mrs. Markos	1969	Nursing education	Delhi	1976	Hospital	RN	Self and father
Mr. Markos	After high school	Navy training	Bombay	1977	Wife	Electronics technician	Wife
Mrs. Philip	1962	Nursing education	North India	1977	Nursing coworker	RN	Self
Mr. Philip	After high school	Education	North India	1978	Wife	Engineer	Wife
Mrs. Punoose	1963	Nursing education	North India	1977	Friend from nursing network	RN	Self
Mr. Punoose	1962	Employment	North India	1977	Wife	Bus conductor	Wife
Mrs. Samuel	1965	Nursing education	North India, Zambia	1976	Cousin	RN	Self
Mr. Samuel	1970	Employment	North India	1976	Wife	Clerical assistant	Wife and self
Mrs. Thomas	After high school	Nursing education	North India, Iran	1979	Friend from nursing network	RN	Self
Mr. Thomas	1966	Technical training	None	1979	Wife	Machine operator	Wife
Mrs. Varghese	1971	Nursing education	North India	1977	Distant relative	RN/disabled/ store owner	Self
Mr. Varghese	1977	Employment	None	1977	Sister	Machine operator/ electrician	Self

APPENDIX 2

Types of Nursing Jobs

Nursing Aides, or Nursing Assistants

Nursing aides, also known as nursing assistants, geriatric aides, unlicensed assistive personnel, or hospital attendants, perform routine tasks under the supervision of nursing and medical staff. They answer patients' call bells, deliver messages, serve meals, make beds, and help patients eat, dress, and bathe. In many cases, neither a high school diploma nor previous work experience is necessary for a job as a nursing aide. Hospitals may require experience as a nursing aide or home health aide. Nursing homes often hire inexperienced workers who must complete a minimum of seventy-five hours of mandatory training and pass a competency evaluation program within four months of employment. Aides who complete the program are certified and placed on the state registry of nursing aides.

Licensed Vocational Nurses, or Licensed Practical Nurses

Licensed practical nurses (LPNs), or licensed vocational nurses (LVNs) as they are called in Texas and California, care for the sick, injured, convalescent, and disabled under the direction of physicians and registered

The information in this appendix is from the U.S. Department of Labor, Bureau of Labor Statistics, Occupational Outlook Handbook, found at www.bls.gov/oco/home.htm, accessed in August 2003.

nurses. Most LPNs provide basic bedside care. They take vital signs such as temperature, blood pressure, pulse, and respiration. They also treat bedsores, prepare and give injections and enemas, apply dressings, give alcohol rubs and massages, apply ice packs and hot water bottles, and monitor catheters. All states and the District of Columbia require that LPNs pass a licensing examination after completing a state-approved practical nursing program. A high school diploma, or equivalent, is usually required for entry. Most practical nursing programs last about one year and include both classroom study and supervised clinical practice (patient care).

Registered Nurses

In addition to providing direct patient care, registered nurses also act as advocates for and educators of patients and their families and assist physicians in the process of examination and treatment. In all states and the District of Columbia, students must graduate from an approved nursing program and pass a national licensing examination to obtain a nursing license. Nurses may be licensed in more than one state, either by examination, by endorsement of a license issued by another state, or through a multistate licensing agreement. All states require periodic license renewal, which may involve continuing education.

APPENDIX 3

Transnational Organizational Structure of the Indian Orthodox Church

Hierarchy of the Indian Orthodox Church

CATHOLICOS, OR PATRIARCH

At the top of the church hierarchy is the Catholicos of the East, who holds the title of Patriarch of the Church. He is chosen through an electoral process conducted by the church's Episcopal Synod. The Catholicos presides over the Episcopal Synod and declares and implements its decisions in both spiritual and administrative matters. He also serves as president of the Church Association Managing Committee, the democratically elected representative body of the church. Although the Catholicos may travel occasionally, he typically conducts his activities from Kerala.

EPISCOPAL SYNOD

Supporting the Catholicos is the Episcopal Synod. The synod is a governing body whose membership includes all the bishops of the church. The synod elects the Catholicos and has authority over disciplinary issues in the church and matters concerning faith. The synod meets regularly in Kerala, but the bishops themselves are distributed worldwide in service of their respective dioceses.

CHURCH ASSOCIATION

The Episcopal Synod and Catholicos constitute a leadership group that is restricted to the clergy of the church. In order to include the

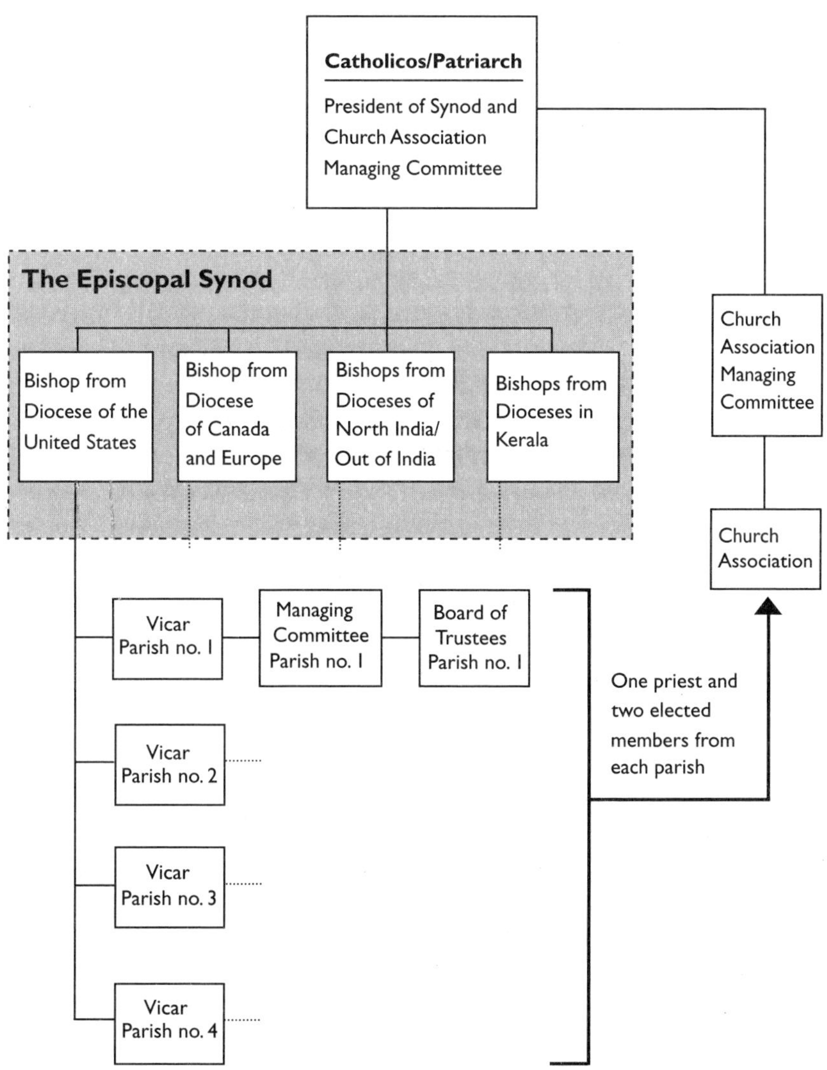

FIGURE 3. The Indian Orthodox Church.

church laity in governance, the church makes use of the Church Association. This association is composed of priests and laymen elected to their positions by the diocesan membership. Members of the association are responsible not only for representing the needs of their dioceses regarding proposals for new policies or activities but also for electing the bishops. Like the synod, the Church Association meets in Kerala at least annually.

CHURCH ASSOCIATION MANAGING COMMITTEE

Within the Church Association is the Church Association Managing Committee. This committee is composed of elected and nominated members from each diocese, and it has the administrative responsibility to oversee decisions of the association and to represent them to the synod. The committee meets during assemblies of the Church Association in Kerala.

DIOCESE

The dioceses are distributed around the globe, including in Europe, the Middle East, and the Unites States, among other places. As defined by the church, a diocese is a collection of parishes in a geographical location, and it is headed by an elected diocesan bishop known as the metropolitan.

PARISH

The local institution of the church is the parish, the group of church members who meet regularly to worship, manage local affairs, and promote intrachurch fellowship. The leader of the parish is the vicar, who is appointed to his post by the diocesan bishop. The vicar, beyond his spiritual duties, is also president of all organizations within the parish.

PARISH MANAGING COMMITTEE

The parish laity participates in local management along with the vicar. The primary vehicle for this management is the Managing Committee, which is composed of church members elected by the general parish membership. The committee typically manages budgetary and administrative matters for the parish. The general body of the parish, which meets on a regular basis, elects the Managing Committee. Only dues-paying men over the age of twenty-one are allowed to vote in this body.

PARISH BOARD OF TRUSTEES (ONLY IN THE UNITED STATES)

Each parish in the United States also has a board of trustees, which holds legal authority over congregational property. The board exists, to a large extent, to satisfy legal requirements concerning not-for-profit organizations in the United States, and it takes financial responsibility for mortgage payments on behalf of the parish.

MARTHA MARIA SAMAJAM (THE WOMEN'S GROUP)

Beyond worship, there are few opportunities for women to actively participate in the church, as most positions are reserved for male parishioners or the clergy. One exception is the Martha Maria Samajam, a women's prayer and service group.

SUNDAY SCHOOL AND THE YOUTH LEAGUE

The primary outlets for youth participation in the church, aside from worship, are Sunday school and the Youth League. The Sunday school provides religious education classes to children throughout the high school years. The Youth League is a social organization that focuses on transmitting religious and social values to young adults.

Notes

Introduction

1. For an in-depth description of the history and organization of various Christian groups in Kerala, as well as the immigrant congregations in the United States, see Williams 1996.

2. While I make the distinction between the parish in India and the congregation in the United States — since the former tends to be ascriptively organized around geographical divisions, whereas the latter is formed on the basis of convenience and political splits — I use them somewhat interchangeably when describing St. George's.

3. See George (1998) for an extensive account of this incident.

4. While I use the term *insider* here, I recognize that it is problematic to adopt a dichotomized view of the ethnographer as either insider or outsider, native or other. I, along with anthropologist Kirin Narayan, believe that it is more useful to look at the fieldworker in terms of "shifting identifications amid a field of interpenetrating communities and power relations" (1993: 671).

5. I address the issue of the portrayal of domestic abuse in the South Asian immigrant community at greater length in chapter 6.

Chapter 1. Contradictions of Gender When Women Immigrate First

1. After the great famine in the mid-1800s, the proportion of women emigrating from Ireland steadily rose until, by the 1950s, 57 percent of the emigrants from Ireland were women (Jackson 1984). However, it is not clear what percentage of the women were primary immigrants or breadwinners for the family.

2. Because much of the early literature on women and migration was a

response to the exclusion of women, the focus was on "adding in" women's experiences and emphasizing the female perspective. As a result, the analysis of gender was often limited to women's experiences.

3. While Connell discusses a third structure of gender called cathexis, which has to do with emotions and sexuality, it is difficult to sort out what he means by this or to identify how it constrains practices. Therefore I do not use this structure in my analysis.

4. Because religion is a fundamental basis of identity in India, participating in the religious congregation allows immigrants to maintain continuity with their homeland and to transmit this identity to the second generation. Furthermore, in the United States, as Raymond Williams argues, establishing a distinct identity based on religion is more acceptable than on ethnic or political identities (1988: 3). I found that the immigrants in Central City participated more actively and frequently in religious organizations than in cultural ones.

5. I follow Pessar (1999) in using this concept.

6. My use of *cultural capital* here follows Ann Swidler's concept of a "cultural tool kit" (1986: 273) and does not indicate a means by which dominant classes impose and institutionalize specific cultural norms as superior while concealing the power relations behind their legitimacy.

7. An individual's social capital is determined by the size of that person's relationship network, the sum of its cumulated resources (both cultural and economic), and how successfully the individual sets them in motion. According to Pierre Bourdieu and Loic Wacquant, social networks must be continuously maintained and fostered over time in order for them to be utilized efficiently (Bourdieu and Wacquant 1992).

8. In my article titled "Caroling with the Keralites: The Negotiation of Gendered Space in an Indian Immigrant Congregation" (1998), I discuss my findings about the male use of congregational space to regain status lost in the immigration process. The sociologists Helen Rose Ebaugh and Janet Chafetz Saltzman have since come to similar conclusions regarding immigrant gender relations in their comparative ethnographic studies of thirteen religious institutions. As they put it, "The extent of women's access to formal congregational roles is significantly an inverse function of the strength of men's desires to fill them, which, in turn, reflects the extent to which men have suffered social status loss in the migration process" (1999: 585).

Chapter 2. Work

1. While the majority of the immigrants came here as nurses or the spouses of nurses, the earliest immigrants were male students who came before 1965 for higher education and who usually settled here with their families. More recently, there is a new wave of immigration resulting from the family reunification clause of the Immigration and Nationality Act of 1965, which allows earlier immigrants to sponsor immediate family members.

2. I am grateful to Louise Lamphere for pointing me to the scholarship of Suad Joseph.

3. The historian C. B. Firth reports that, around the period of the Second World War, 90 percent of all Indian nurses were Christian, and 80 percent of Christian Indian nurses were trained in mission hospitals (1960: 202).

4. Although the Indian government in 1961 officially banned the practice of dowry giving and receiving, it is still widely practiced in Kerala and among immigrants in the United States.

5. There is a long tradition of conceptualizing migration and women's entry into wage labor as a family strategy, and this literature has been soundly critiqued for the assumption that the household is a monolithic unit in which all members are motivated by rational economic behavior. Several scholars have convincingly argued that households are divided by gender and generational differences (Hondagneu-Sotelo 1994; Kibria 1993; Grasmuck and Pessar 1991). For example, the anthropologist Diane Wolf finds that, whereas the literature had depicted the entrance of young, rural Javanese women into factory work as a household strategy, her qualitative data showed that often young women decided to take factory work despite parental opposition. Wolf makes the interesting point that household strategies can be retrospectively imputed to individual decisions even though, in lived experience, especially with the newness of a situation like factory employment (or nursing, as in this case), people are not necessarily strategizing. However, she does concede that a coherent set of practices emerges at least temporarily that benefits most members of the household (1992).

6. While bringing back gifts for one's family is not an uncommon motivation for migration (Small 1997), Katy Gardner argues that the "imagined destinations" play an important part in the motivation to migrate. She contrasts the "imagined homelands" common to migrants to the "imagined destinations" common to those left behind, the latter of which are typically associated with material bounty and economic transformation where "local desire has become centered on travel abroad as the only route to material prosperity " (1993: 1).

7. It is possible that some of the mothers may have participated in an informal economy by raising hens and cows in order to sell eggs and milk for a small profit.

8. In her study of rural Javanese women who undertook paid work, Diane Wolf (1992) found that parents were not pushing single daughters into marriage, since there were economic benefits to be gained from having single daughters. The new earning power for women probably represented a quandary for parents, who had the responsibility to marry off their daughters before they got too old and yet needed their daughters' help for economic survival.

9. Questioning women's morality when they step outside the domestic sphere does not appear to be unusual within rural, patriarchal societies, particularly when they are experiencing social change from such processes as migration or reorganization of work. Eugenia Georges's study of a transnational community in the Dominican Republic highlights the contradictions of social change

resulting in the distinction between "serious women" and women of the street (1992). Diane Wolf similarly found that the prevailing stereotype of women who entered factory work held that they were loose women because they joked and talked with the truck drivers who passed by on the roads (1992).

10. Indian hospitals rely on the compulsory period of labor set up by nursing schools as part of their requirement for nursing graduates. In this system, newly graduated nurses have to serve for up to three years in the particular hospital designated by the nursing school.

11. Shockley's study prescribes three methods of recruitment: (1) The hospital can conduct an advertisement campaign and recruit nurses on its own, (2) contract with a recruitment agency, or (3) send representatives to work with recruitment agencies in foreign countries (1989).

12. Elinor Kelly, in her research on migrants from Gujarat, India, to Lancashire, England, had a moment of discovery about the transcontinental nature of her informants, similar to my own discovery that nurses were part of a step-migration process. As she put it, "Gradually, as they told me stories and discussed the pros and cons of the different countries where they worked, I realised that Britain was not the centre of their world and that my country was only one of a number of options which they would consider in order to earn the cash which should flow as remittances into their village" (1990: 251).

13. While there is a global demand for health professionals, the global distribution of nurses to meet the demand is far from equitable. In a study conducted for the World Health Organization, Mejia and colleagues report that, of 3.6 million nurses worldwide, 3.1 million (85 percent) work in developed countries, which contain only a third of the world's population. Furthermore, developed countries continue to receive 92 percent of migrant nurses (1979).

14. Explanations for the discrepancy between social and economic development in Kerala vary. While most point to the unusual level of political mobilization in the state as a causal factor, whether it is characterized as the empowerment of the working classes or their growing militancy depends on political perspective. The sociologist Patrick Heller, who falls into the former camp, recognizes the more conservative position when he observes, "Social expenditures, labor legislation, union controlled labor markets and high wages, it is argued, have fettered productive economic activity and driven away investors" (1994: 2). But Heller argues that the state's substantial investments in social overhead and class mobilization are key to necessary institutional development and structural transformations that will most likely lead to economic development in the future.

15. Williams (1996) found that, whereas higher incomes and not having to pay taxes made employment in the Gulf states a lucrative option for the nurses, their sense of insecurity resulting from fixed-term contracts and the unavailability of citizenship or permanent resident options ultimately led them to emigrate to the United States.

16. There is a large literature on social networks and their role in immigration. See chapter 1 of Menjivar (2000) for a useful discussion that traces the

development of the concept of social networks particularly as it is used in contemporary immigration studies.

17. The literature on female migration networks supports my findings. For example, Kossoudji and Ranney (1984) found that mature migration networks and the contacts they provide have a strong influence on the wage-earning potential of female migrants.

18. Raymond Williams also found that, in response to American hospital recruitment, nearly half of some graduating classes in the 1970s left almost immediately for the United States (1996: 17).

19. Sponsors must be permanent residents or naturalized citizens who can petition for the admission of would-be emigrants to the United States. They must also undertake various actions to substantiate the application, including showing that, if necessary, they are financially capable of supporting those they sponsor.

20. See also Benjamin Davis and Paul Winters, 2000, *Gender, Networks, and Mexico–U.S. Migration,* Working Paper Series in Agricultural and Resource Economics no. 2000–7 (May), University of New England Graduate School of Agricultural and Resource Economics and School of Economic Studies, www.une.edu.au/febl/GSARE/AREwp00–7.pdf; accessed on November 10, 2004.

21. The sociologist Mary Waters (1999) discusses the issue of accents in her study of English-speaking Caribbean immigrants. She found that Caribbean immigrants utilize accents to differentiate themselves from African Americans. Whereas upper-class South Asian immigrants may rely on their British-inflected English accents in the context of American Anglophilia to garner greater status, most middle- and working-class South Asian immigrants, with their regional accents, cannot exercise the same option.

22. I am referring only to the experiences of registered nurses, who made up the overwhelming majority of women I interviewed. Some women in the community who work as licensed vocational nurses and nurses' aides gain less autonomy and empowerment through their work experiences. See appendix 2.

23. The Comprehensive Employment and Training Act was established in 1973 and phased out in the early 1980s. Under this act, state and local organizations contracted with public agencies and industries to provide subsidized jobs and job training.

Chapter 3. Home

1. See Shelton and John's 1996 review of the literature on household division of labor for a full discussion of the dominant theoretical explanations in this field.

2. I relied mostly on my interviews with these couples, although I did try to elicit information to compare what people said with what they did. I asked subjects how often they did the concrete tasks that constitute the labor of a household. I also stayed overnight whenever possible so that I could observe who did what.

3. While I am aware that household work also involves "invisible" work, done most often by women, which is not accounted for in easily identifiable categories such as cooking or cleaning, I do not deal with the subtleties of invisible work in this project. For more on this, see DeVault 1994.

4. As already mentioned, I conducted interviews separately with men and women, recruiting my subjects using convenience sampling. The tables listing the interviewed couples by household type in appendix 1 show that the men and women I interviewed are part of a cohort of individuals who immigrated mostly in the 1970s. Because it would have been inappropriate for me to ask them their ages, I did not do so. However, the overwhelming majority of my subjects appeared to be in their early forties to early fifties. I conducted the interviews in Malayalam or English or a mixture of both, following the lead of the person I interviewed. Consequently, some interviews were not only transcribed but also translated.

5. Time of arrival may have a secondary effect on gender relations within each of these household types. However, it would be difficult to isolate this effect, given the small number of families in each household type.

6. Research on gender relations in immigrant communities reveals that it is not uncommon for women to compensate for male loss of status. For example, Cecilia Menjivar (1999a) observes that, among Central American immigrants, when women were the sole earners they did all the housework and made conscious efforts to avoid making the men feel inadequate. Similarly, Kudat (1982) discusses the balancing act of Turkish immigrant women, and Pessar (1995) talks about women compensating because they needed the financial help of their husbands. In yet another instance, Kibria (1993) writes that immigrant Vietnamese women chose to work in informal sectors of the economy and prop up rituals and symbols of male domination in order to maximize both class position and influence within the family and over the second generation.

7. In their study of fathering among Indian immigrants in the United States, Jain and Belsky report that men belonging to the least acculturated families were the least involved in fathering, and that the most acculturated men were the most involved in fathering. While Jain and Belsky describe "modernity (in attitudes and behavior) as central to the acculturation process" and therefore to the level of engagement in fathering activities (1997: 876), my study points to ideological factors and structural factors—such as immigration patterns, relationship to the labor market, and options for child care—as having a critical effect.

8. In her study of Mexican immigrants in the United States, Hondagneu-Sotelo also found that men who arrived first in a family-stage-migration process were more proficient in domestic work, which was forced upon them by living in "bachelor communities" without their wives present (1994: 104). Consequently, these men were more willing to participate in household work upon reunification with their families.

9. It is interesting that seemingly insignificant everyday consumer items can play a motivating role in migration decisions. The anthropologist Diane Wolf, in her research on female factory workers in Java, found that young women in

rural Java were inspired to enter factory work because of their desire for consumer items such as scented soap. As Wolf puts it, "Whereas most villagers purchased blocks of soap which they used for bathing, washing dishes and clothes, factory workers bought bars of scented soap for which they paid half a day's wages. Buying their own bar of soap signified their independence and higher status" (1992: 174). Similarly, "sweet-smelling soap" became symbolic to Mrs. Jacob in her quest for independence and a life different from what her village offered.

Chapter 4. Community

1. I analyze this incident at length in "Caroling with the Keralites: The Negotiation of Gendered Space in an Indian Immigrant Congregation" (1998).

2. At the 1995 national Indian Orthodox Church family conference that I attended, a main topic of discussion was the retention of young people in the church. At the conference's concluding session, in response to a young college graduate who expressed interest in the ministry, a spontaneous collection was taken up for his financial support, and the priest at St. George's offered free room and board to the young man in return for working with the young people at St. George's. This example illustrates the urgent need felt by the church members to increase the participation of young people and to better retain them.

3. I am aware of the feminist critique of the conceptual use of "sex roles" because of the functionalist assumptions inherent in the language of roles (see Thorne and Yalom, 1982; Connell 1987). As my analysis shows, I am cognizant of the power differences between men and women and the conflict that can result from such differences. I do not use roles here as descriptive of social reality but as indicators of social expectations — similar to social scripts.

4. I analyze this phenomenon at greater length in the article titled "Why Can't They Just Get Along? An Analysis of Schisms in an Indian Immigrant Church" (2003).

5. Schisms are also prevalent in Korean immigrant churches (Shin and Park 1988; Hurh and Kim 1990; Min 1992). For example, Eui Hang Shin and Hyung Park (1988) find that competition for status-enhancing staff positions is one of the major reasons for the prevalence of schisms.

6. Other scholars who study immigrant religious groups have also found that, for the groups they studied, religious organizations become surrogates for the extended family after immigration. Williams (1988) and Ralston (1996a) note that, among South Asian immigrants, religious organizations are not only surrogate extended families but also a complex site for the negotiations between generations and other groups.

7. Williams (1996) notes that the wife of a Indian immigrant pastor reported that four out of five wives of immigrant pastors in the United States were nurses.

8. While he is no longer the diocesan bishop, Bishop Mar Makarios holds the title of senior bishop and is in charge of a group of congregations and priests who refuse the supervision of the new bishop. Since his resignation, Bishop Makarios has annually presided over a competing annual national conference for families that is conducted by his supporters, and that has consistently been scheduled on the same weekend as the official annual family conference of the U.S. diocese.

9. Some of the carols they sing are written by members of the community in the United States to the tunes of film songs from Kerala. Additionally, Christian songs from the growing Christian popular music scene in Kerala are also used. Having the latest tunes with instrumental accompaniment is a matter of pride among the caroling groups from the different congregations as they try to outdo each other in the caroling and annual Christmas ecumenical program. These programs give the Keralite Christian congregations the opportunity to represent their respective singing talents.

10. My source is the untitled year-end financial report for 1994 presented at the general-body meeting.

11. I have received conflicting reports from interview accounts about the gender of those who go caroling in Kerala. Some people report that both boys and girls go, but the majority claim that only young boys do so. But all accounts are consistent on the point that it is not an adult activity, even though there are no official church regulations about who is allowed to go caroling.

12. Indira Gandhi was the first and only female prime minister of India and is a symbol of female leadership in India.

13. Because I speak Malayalam fluently, the adults who were parents often expressed surprise and approval.

14. Williams (1988), Ralston (1996a), and Rayaprol (1997) all make a similar point about ethnoreligious organizations becoming surrogates for the extended family lost in the migration process.

15. In 1987, the church synod revised the constitution to permit girls under the age of five to be brought along with the male children to kiss the altar during baptism ceremony. That the church chose the age of five is not accidental. Females under the age of five are seen as nonsexual.

16. Annual family conferences sponsored by the diocese attract individuals from immigrant congregations all over the United States. These are not only sites for religious education and socialization of the young people but also informal spaces for the exchange of information, such as regarding marriage alliances. These are also spaces where people, often teenagers, collectively make known to the administrative hierarchy their dissatisfaction regarding church practices.

17. While Father Rudolph's interpretation of the Trinitarian order seems unorthodox by most standards, it is still noteworthy that the administrators of the American diocese selected him to deliver the keynote address, emphasizing the importance of hierarchical order at a time when the diocese was dealing with internal dissension.

18. It is interesting to compare women's opportunities for participation in

the immigrant Orthodox Church to those in a Keralite immigrant church with a less explicitly patriarchal ideology. The Marthoma Church is such a Keralite Christian Protestant church; it has a comparable presence in the United States relative to the Orthodox Church and a similar overwhelmingly nursing-based immigrant membership. However, the Marthoma Church has a relatively more egalitarian ideology regarding women's participation in the church. But despite its progressive ideals, Father John Joseph, secretary to the North American diocesan bishop of the Marthoma Church, informed me that, while the constitution allows women to be present in the general-body meetings and to hold administrative leadership positions, the great majority of leadership positions continue to be filled by men. He opined that "women hold themselves back" to explain why there are not more women in these positions. While he blamed their lack of visible leadership roles on the women, I believe it may be better explained by the same gendered immigration and settlement factors that affect women in the Orthodox Church. Even so, the relatively less patriarchal official ideology of the Marthoma church allows women in this church a little more space for challenging the status quo.

19. In this chapter, I focus on the absence of formal, public leadership positions for women in the church partially because I am responding to the literature on immigration that suggests women tend to have greater official roles after immigration (Haddad and Lummis 1987; Min 1992; Warner 1992; Rayaprol 1997). However, I am aware of feminist literature that underlines the importance of leadership contributions made by women while they hold positions that are less formal and public. For instance, in her report on the Civil Rights movement, Bernice Barnett talks about "invisible women leaders" (1993: 162). Belinda Robnett reports on behind-the-scenes "bridge leaders" without official positions who were key to the success of the movement, and whose participation even exceeded that of the men involved (1997: 19). Similarly, Karen Sacks, in her research on women and organizing at Duke Medical Center, found that many women operated as leaders but did not accept the titles, which challenged Sacks's own a priori notions of leadership. Sacks identified them as "Center Women . . . who were key actors in network formation and consciousness shaping" (1988: 121).

20. One reviewer of my manuscript wondered what my influence was in the empowerment of the teenage girls. I believe my initial interaction with Anna regarding caroling was the spark that started conversations among the girls and with the priest. However, the priest galvanized the girls and officially created the space for them to participate.

21. Class differences play a part in potential marital alliances via the different rates of dowry for each class expected from the woman's family.

22. In a study of a South Asian community in Canada, the sociologist Helen Ralston (1996a) talks about how ethnic community organizations cut across class boundaries. One of her interview respondents observed that she mixed with Indians whom she would not have met back home. Ralston concludes that, while friendships and social activities tend to be class-based in India, ethnic

identity–based activities that cut across class lines become necessary in post-immigrant life.

Chapter 5. Transnational Connections

1. The construction of new housing as a result of booms induced by foreign remittances is common in many transnational communities (see Levitt 2001; Gardner 1993). Levitt notes that several halfway completed "dream palaces" were left abandoned in villages in the Dominican Republic because money dried up. Similarly, in Kerala, I saw homes in various stages of construction, occupied by residents who were either waiting for more money from relatives abroad or who otherwise did not have the resources to finish what they had started.

2. Whereas siblings can be sponsored only under numerical quotas with long delays, parents and children of citizens are not restricted by quotas and can immigrate with shorter delays (Williams 1996).

3. Several studies report that immigrant families have to adapt their premigration customs and beliefs to the standards of the different legal system they encounter in the United States. For example, Kibria (1993) reports that wife beating is less common among Vietnamese immigrants in the United States than back home because the immigrants are aware that this is illegal in the United States. Foner (1997) reports that children of Jamaican immigrants sometimes threatened their parents and even called the police to stop physical abuse from their parents. Peggy Levitt (2001) found that the Dominican immigrant families she studied in Boston had to learn about new child abuse laws in the United States. There was a general perception among them that spanking children could lead to arrest, and some children threatened to call the Department of Social Services if their parents touched them, leading to parental feelings of powerlessness.

4. To respond to foreign nurses' dismal failure rates on state board exams, the Commission on Graduates of Foreign Nursing Schools, established in 1978 in the United States, administered screening examinations to aspiring immigrant nurses in their own countries.

5. Government transport buses that travel long distances with few stops do not have separate sections for men and women, but they do have a number of seats designated for women.

6. A bishop reported that marriage assistance schemes for poor women are very popular among women's groups in immigrant congregations (Williams 1996: 241).

7. Williams reports that one layman living in the United States spoke with pride about having received the largest number of votes in an election for an important position on a church council in India, signifying the importance of immigrant church members (1996: 247).

8. Catholicate Day commemorates the establishment of the independent church in India when it broke off ties with the Syrian Antiochian Church in 1912.

One among several annual collections designated by the church for all its parishes, the Catholicate Day collection is mostly used to support the day-to-day administrative functions of the synod, dioceses, and headquarters of the church in India.

9. Mary Roy, mother of Arundhati Roy (winner of England's Booker Prize in 1997), was the main plaintiff who challenged the existing Christian Inheritance Laws in 1982, a suit that she took all the way to a favorable Supreme Court decision.

Chapter 6. Conclusions

1. See also Benjamin Davis and Paul Winters, 2000, *Gender, Networks, and Mexico–U.S. Migration,* Working Paper Series in Agricultural and Resource Economics no. 2000–7 (May), University of New England Graduate School of Agricultural and Resource Economics and School of Economic Studies, www.une.edu.au/febl/GSARE/AREwp00–7.pdf; accessed on November 10, 2004.

2. See chapter 5, n. 3, for examples of the new intervening role of the state in the lives of immigrant groups in the United States.

References

Abraham, Margaret. 1995. "Ethnicity, Gender, and Marital Violence: South Asian Women's Organizations in the United States." *Gender and Society* 9: 450–68.

Abraham, Meera. 1996. *Religion, Caste, and Gender: Missionaries and Nursing History in South India.* Bangalore: B. I. Publications.

Alicea, Marixsa. 1997. "A Chambered Nautilus": The Contradictory Nature of Puerto Rican Women's Roles in the Social Construction of a Transnational Community." *Gender and Society* 11, no. 5 (October): 597–626.

Andrews, Kunnuparampil Punnoose. 1983. *Keralites in America: Community Reference Book.* New York: Literary Market Review.

Anthias, Floya. 1992. *Ethnicity, Class, Gender, and Migration: Greek/Cypriots in Britain.* Brookfield: Avebury Ashgate Publishing.

Appadurai, Arjun. 1990. "Disjuncture and Difference in the Global Cultural Economy." *Theory, Culture, and Society* 7: 295–310.

Barnett, Bernice. 1993. "Invisible Southern Black Women Leaders in the Civil Rights Movement: The Triple Constraints of Gender, Race, and Class." *Gender and Society* 7, no. 2 (June): 162–82.

Basch, Linda, Nina Glick-Schiller, and Cristina Szanton Blanc. 1994. *Nations Unbound: Transnational Projects, Postcolonial Predicaments, and Deterritorialized Nation-States.* Switzerland: Gordeon and Breach.

Berk, Sarah Fenstermaker. 1985. *The Gender Factory: The Apportionment of Work in American Households.* New York: Plenum.

Bhabha, Homi K., ed. 1990. *Nation and Narration.* New York: Routledge.

Bhattacharjee, Anannya. 1992. "The Habit of Ex-Nomination: Nation, Woman, and the Indian Immigrant Bourgeoisie." *Public Culture* 5: 19–44.

Bianchi, Suzanne M., Melissa A. Milkie, Liana C. Sayer, and John P. Robinson. 2000. "Is Anyone Doing the Housework? Trends in the Gender Division of Household Labor." *Social Forces* 79, no. 1 (September): 191–228.

Bott, Elizabeth. 1957. *Family and Social Network: Roles, Norms, and External Relationships in Ordinary Urban Families.* London: Tavistock Publications.

Bourdieu, Pierre, and Loic Wacquant. 1992. *An Invitation to Reflexive Sociology.* Chicago: University of Chicago.

Boyd, Monica. 1989. "Family and Personal Networks in International Migration: Recent Developments and New Agendas." *International Migration Review* 23, no. 3: 638–70.

Brettell, Caroline B., and Rita James Simon. 1986. *International Migration: The Female Experience.* New Jersey: Rowman and Allanheld.

Brines, Julie. 1994. "Economic Dependency, Gender, and the Division of Labor at Home." *American Journal of Sociology* 100, no. 3 (November): 652–88.

Brouwer, Lenie, and Marjike Priester. 1983. "Living in Between: Turkish Women in Their Homelands and in the Netherlands." In *One Way Ticket: Migration and Female Labor,* ed. Annie Phizacklea, pp. 113–29. Boston: Routledge and Kegan Paul.

Burawoy, Michael. 1976. "The Functions and Reproduction of Migrant Labor: Comparative Material from Southern Africa and the United States." *American Journal of Sociology* 81, no. 5: 1050–87.

———. 1991. *Ethnography Unbound: Power and Resistance in the Modern Metropolis.* Berkeley: University of California Press.

———. 1998. "The Extended Case Method." *Sociological Theory* 16, no. 1: 4–33.

Castells, Manuel. 1997. *The Power of Identity.* Malden, MA: Blackwell.

Chai, Karen. 1998. "Competing for the Second Generation: English-Language Ministry at a Korean Protestant Church." In *Gatherings in Diaspora: Religious Communities and the New Immigration,* ed. R. Stephen Warner and Judith G. Wittner, pp. 295–331. Philadelphia: Temple University Press.

Clifford, James. 1992. "Traveling Cultures." In *Cultural Studies,* ed. Lawrence Grossberg, Cary Nelson, and Paula A. Treichler, pp. 96–116. New York: Routledge.

Coffey, Rosanna M., Dean E. Farley, Keith Lind, and Renate Wilson. 1988. "Nursing Shortage in the Hospital Sector, 1982–87." Washington, D.C.: U.S. Department of Health and Human Services, Public Health Service, National Center for Health Services Research and Health Care Technology Assessment.

Cohen, Lucy. 1977. "The Female Factor in Resettlement." *Society* 14, no. 6 (September–October): 27–30.

Connell, John. 1984. "Status or Subjugation? Women, Migration, and Development in the South Pacific." *International Migration Review* 18, no. 4: 964–83.

Connell, R. W. 1987. *Gender and Power: Society, the Person, and Sexual Politics.* Stanford, CA: Stanford University Press.

Coontz, Stephanie, and Maya Parson. 1997. "Complicating the Contested Terrain of Work/Family Intersections." *Signs: Journal of Women in Culture and Society* 22, no. 21: 440–52.

Curran, Connie R., Ann Minnick, and Joan Moss. 1987. "Who Needs Nurses?" *American Journal of Nursing* (April): 444.

Department of Economics and Statistics, Government of Kerala. 1988. *Report of the Survey on the Utilization of Gulf Remittances in Kerala*. Trivandrum, India.

Department of Public Relations, Government of Kerala. 1996. *Responses to the Problems of Non-Resident Keralites*. Trivandrum, India.

———. 1997. *Succor to Non-Resident Keralites*. Trivandrum, India.

Daniels, Roger. 1989. *History of Immigration to the United States: An Interpretive Essay*. New York: Asia Society.

Dasgupta, Sayantani, and Shamita Das Dasgupta. 1996. "Women in Exile: Gender Relations in the Asian Indian Community in the United States." In *Contours of the Heart: South Asians Map North America*, ed. Sunaina Maira and Rajini Srikanth. New York: Asian American Writers' Workshop.

———. 1998. "Sex, Lies, and Women's Lives: An Intergenerational Dialogue." In *A Patchwork Shawl: Chronicles of South Asian Women in America*, ed. Shamita Das Dasgupta, pp. 206–21. New Jersey: Rutgers University Press.

DeVault, Marjorie L. 1994. *Feeding the Family: The Social Organization of Caring as Gendered Work*. Chicago: University of Chicago Press.

Diner, Hasia. 1983. *Erin's Daughters in America: Irish Immigrant Women in the Nineteenth Century*. Baltimore: Johns Hopkins University Press.

Dirlik, Arif. 1996. "Asians on the Rim: Transnational Capital and Local Community in the Making of Contemporary Asian America." *Amerasia Journal* 22, no. 3: 1–24.

Donato, Katharine. 1992. "Understanding U.S. Immigration: Why Some Countries Send Women and Others Send Men." In *Seeking Common Ground: Multidisciplinary Studies of Immigrant Women in the U.S.*, ed. Donna Gabaccia. Westport, CT: Greenwood Press.

Donato, Katharine, and Andrea Tyree. 1986. "Family Reunification, Health Professionals, and the Sex Composition of Immigrants to the United States." *Sociology and Social Research* 70, no. 3: 226–30.

Dugger, Celia W. 1998. "In India, an Arranged Marriage of Two Worlds." *New York Times*, July 20, p. A1.

Dvorak, Eileen McQuaid, and Mark Waymack. 1991. "Is It Ethical to Recruit Foreign Nurses?" *Nursing Outlook* 39, no. 3: 120–23.

Ebaugh, Helen Rose, and Janet Chafetz Saltzman. 1999. "Agents for Cultural Reproduction and Structural Change: The Ironic Role of Women in Immigrant Religious Institutions." *Social Forces* 78, no. 2: 585–612.

Erwin, William. 1993. "American Hospital Association Survey: Nurse Shortage Eases Dramatically." *Hospitals* (February 5): 52.

Espiritu, Yen Le. 1997. *Asian American Women and Men: Labor, Laws, and Love*. Thousand Oaks, CA: Sage Publications.

———. 1999 "Gender and Labor in Asian Immigrant Families." *American Behavioral Scientist* 42, no. 4: 628–47.

———. 2001. "'We Don't Sleep Around Like White Girls Do': Family, Culture, and Gender in Filipina American Lives." *Signs* 26, no. 21: 415–40.

Fernandez-Kelly, Maria Patricia. 1990. "Delicate Transactions: Gender, Home, and Employment among Hispanic Women." In *Uncertain Terms: Negotiating Gender in American Culture,* ed. Faye Ginsburg and Anna Tsing, pp. 183–95. Boston: Beacon Press.

Fernandez-Kelly, Maria Patricia, and Anna Garcia. 1991. "Power Surrendered, Power Restored: The Politics of Home and Work among Hispanic Women in Southern California." In *Women and Politics in America,* ed. Louise Tilly and Patricia Guerin, pp. 130–49. New York: Russell Sage Foundation.

Firth, C. B. 1960. *An Introduction to Indian History.* Bangalore: Christian Literature Society.

Foner, Nancy. 1978. *Jamaican Farewell: Jamaican Migrants in London.* Berkeley: University of California Press.

———. 1997. "The Immigrant Family: Cultural Legacies and Cultural Changes." *International Migration Review* 31, no. 4: 961–75.

Friedman, Emily. 1990. "Nursing: New Power, Old Problems." *Journal of the American Medical Association* 264, no. 23: 2977–82.

Gabaccia, Donna, ed. 1992. *Seeking Common Ground: Multidisciplinary Studies of Immigrant Women in the United States.* Westport, CT: Greenwood Press.

Gardner, Katy. 1993. "Desh-bidesh: Sylheti Images of Home and Away." *Man,* n.s., 28, no. 1 (March): 1–15.

George, Sheba. 1998. "Caroling with the Keralites: The Negotiation of Gendered Space in an Indian Immigration Congregation." In *Gatherings in Diaspora: Religious Communities and the New Immigration,* ed. R. Stephen Warner and Judith G. Wittner, pp. 265–94. Philadelphia: Temple University Press.

———. 1999. "Gendered Ideologies and Strategies: The Negotiation of the Household Division of Labor among Middle-Class South Asian American Families." Working Paper no. 8. Berkeley: Alfred P. Sloan Center for Working Families.

———. 2000. "'Dirty Nurses' and 'Men Who Play': Gender and Class in Transnational Migration." In *Global Ethnographies: Forces, Connections, and Imaginations in a Postmodern World,* ed. Michael Burawoy et al. California: University of California Press.

———. 2001. "When Women Come First: Gender, Class, and Transnational Ties among Indian Immigrants in the United States." Ph.D. diss., University of California, Berkeley.

———. 2003. "Why Can't They Just Get Along? An Analysis of Schisms in an Indian Immigrant Church." In *Revealing the Sacred in Asian and Pacific America,* ed. Jane Naomi Iwamura and Paul Spickard. New York: Routledge.

Georges, Eugenia. 1990. *The Making of a Transnational Community: Migration, Development, and Cultural Change in the Dominican Republic.* New York: Columbia University Press.

———. 1992. "Gender, Class, and Migration in the Dominican Republic: Women's Experiences in a Transnational Community." In *Towards a Transnational Perspective on Migration: Annals of the New York Academy of Sciences.* Vol. 654, ed. Nina Glick-Schiller et al., pp. 81–99. New York: New York Academy of Sciences.

Gilbertson, Grace, and Roger Waldinger. 1994. "Immigrants' Progress: Ethnic and Gender Differences among U.S. Immigrants in the 1980s." *Sociological Perspectives* 3, no. 3: 431–44.

Gilkes, Cheryl. 1985. "'Together in Harness': Women's Traditions in the Sanctified Church." *Signs: Journal of Women in Culture and Society* 10: 678–99.

Glick-Schiller, Nina, Linda Basch, and Cristina Szanton Blanc. 1995. "From Immigrant to Transmigrant: Theorizing Transnational Migration." *Anthropological Quarterly* 68, no. 1: 48–63.

——, eds. 1992. *Towards a Transnational Perspective on Migration: Annals of the New York Academy of Sciences*. Vol. 654. New York: New York Academy of Sciences.

Goldring, Luin. 1998. "The Power of Status in Transnational Social Fields." In *Transnationalism from Below: Comparative Urban and Community Research*. Vol. 6, ed. Michael P. Smith and Luis Eduardo Guarnizo, pp. 165–95. New Brunswick, NJ: Transaction Publishers.

Govindankutty, K. 1990. *Vararuchi's Children: Aspects of Kerala*. Trivandrum, India: Macmillan India.

Grasmuck, Sherri, and Patricia Pessar. 1991. *Between Two Islands: Dominican International Migration*. Berkeley: University of California Press.

Grewal, Inderpal, and Caren Kaplan, eds. 1994. *Scattered Hegemonies: Postmodernity and Transnational Feminist Practices*. Minneapolis: University of Minnesota Press.

Guendelman, Sylvia, and Auristela Perez-Itriago. 1987. "Migration Tradeoffs: Men's Experiences with Seasonal Lifestyles." *International Migration Review* 21, no. 3: 709–27.

Gulati, Leela. 1993. *In the Absence of Their Men: The Impact of Male Migration on Women*. New Delhi: Sage Publications.

——. 1996. *Kerala's Women: A Profile*. Thiruvanthuparam, India: Center for Development Studies.

Haddad, Yvonne, and Adair Lummis. 1987. *Islamic Values in the United States: A Comparative Study*. New York: Oxford University Press.

Hartman, Heidi. 1979. "The Unhappy Marriage of Marxism and Feminism: Towards a More Progressive Union." *Capital and Class* 8: 1–33.

——. 1981. "The Family as the Locus of Gender, Class, and Political Struggle: The Example of Housework." *Signs: Journal of Women in Culture and Society* 6, no. 3: 366–94.

Heller, Patrick. 1994. "The Politics of Redistributive Development: Class and State in Kerala, India." Ph.D. diss., University of California, Berkeley.

Hendricks, Ann M. 1989. "Hospital Wage Gradients within U.S. Urban Areas." *Journal of Health Economics* 8, no. 2: 233–46.

Herberg, Will. 1960. *Protestant-Catholic-Jew: An Essay in American Religious Sociology*. New York: Doubleday.

Hine, Darlene Clark. 1989. *Black Women in White: Racial Conflict and Cooperation in the Nursing Profession, 1890–1950*. Indianapolis: Indiana University Press.

Hirsch, Jennifer S. 1999. "En el Norte la Mujer Manda: Gender, Generation, and Geography in a Mexican Transnational Community." *American Behavioral Scientist* 42, no. 9: 1332–49.

———. 2003. *A Courtship after Marriage: Sexuality and Love in Mexican Transnational Families.* Berkeley: University of California Press.

Ho, Christine. 1993. "The Internationalization of Kinship and the Feminization of Caribbean Migration: The Case of Afro-Trinidadian Immigrants in Los Angeles." *Human Organization* 25, no. 1: 32–40.

Hochschild, Arlie. 1989. *The Second Shift: Working Parents and the Revolution at Home.* New York: Viking.

Hondagneu-Sotelo, Pierrette. 1992. "Overcoming Patriarchal Constraints: The Reconstruction of Gender Relations among Mexican Immigrant Women and Men." *Gender and Society* 6, no. 3 (September): 393–415.

———. 1994. *Gendered Transition: Mexican Experiences of Immigration.* Berkeley: University of California Press.

———. 1999. "Gender and Contemporary U.S. Immigration." *American Behavioral Scientist* 42, no. 4: 565–76.

Hondagneu-Sotelo, Pierrette, and Ernestine Avila. 1997. "'I'm Here, but I'm There': The Meanings of Latina Transnational Motherhood." *Society* 11, no. 5 (October): 548–70.

Houstoun, Marion F., Roger G. Kramer, and Joan Mackin Barrett. 1984. "Female Predominance in Immigration to the United States since 1930: A First Look." *International Migration Review* 18, no. 4: 908–63.

Hurh, Won Moo, and Kwang Chung Kim. 1990. "Religious Participation of Korean Immigrants in the United States." *Journal for the Scientific Study of Religion* 29: 19–34.

Isaac, Thomas T. M. 1997. "Economic Consequences of Gulf Migration." In *Kerala's Demographic Transition: Determinants and Consequences,* ed. K. C. Zachariah and S. Irudaya Rajan, pp. 269–309. New Delhi: Sage Publications India.

Ishi, Tomoji. 1987. "Class Conflict, the State, and Linkage: The International Migration of Nurses from the Philippines." *Berkeley Journal of Sociology* 32: 281–312.

Jackson, Janet, Pamela A. MacFalda, and Kathleen McManus. 1989. "Status of the Nursing Shortage and Projections." In *Managing the Nursing Shortage: A Guide to Recruitment and Retention,* ed. Terence F. Moore and Earl A. Simendinger. Rockville, MD: Aspen Publishers.

Jackson, Pauline. 1984. "Women in Nineteenth Century Irish Emigration." *International Migration Review* 18, no. 4: 1004–20.

Jain, Anju, and Jay Belsky. 1997. "Fathering and Acculturation: Immigrant Indian Families with Young Children." *Journal of Marriage and the Family* 59, no. 4 (November): 873–974.

Jeffrey, Robin. 1992. *Politics, Women, and Well-Being: How Kerala Became "a Model."* London: Macmillan Press.

Joseph, R. 1992. "Perceived Change of Immigrants in the U.S.: A Study of Kerala (Asian Indian) Immigrant Couples in Greater Chicago." Ph.D. diss., Loyola University, Chicago.

Joseph, Suad. 1993. "Connectivity and Patriarchy among Urban Working Class Arab Families in Lebanon." *Ethos* 21, no. 4: 452–84.

——. 1994. "Brother/Sister Relationships: Connectivity, Love, and Power in the Reproduction of Patriarchy in Lebanon." *Journal of the American Ethnological Society* 21, no. 1: 50–73.

——. 1996. "Relationality and Ethnographic Subjectivity: Key Informants and the Construction of Personhood in Fieldwork." In *Feminist Dilemmas in Fieldwork,* ed. Diane L. Wolf. Boulder, CO: Westview Press.

Kanaiaupuni, Shawn Malia. 2000. "Reframing the Migration Question: An Analysis of Men, Women, and Gender in Mexico." *Social Forces* 78, no. 4 (June): 1311–47.

Kandiyoti, Deniz. 1988. "Bargaining with Patriarchy." *Gender and Society* 2: 274–90.

Kearney, Michael. 1991. "Borders and Boundaries of State and Self at the End of Empire." *Journal of Historical Sociology* 4, no. 1 (March): 52–74.

——. 1995. "The Local and the Global: The Anthropology of Globalization and Transnationalism." *Annual Review of Anthropology* 24: 547–65.

Kelly, Elinor. 1990. "Transcontinental Families, Gujarat and Lancashire: A Comparative Study of Social Policy." In *South Asian Overseas: Migration and Ethnicity,* ed. C. Clarke., C. Peach, and S. Vertovec. New York: Cambridge University Press.

Kelson, Gregory, and Debra DeLaet, eds. 1999. *Gender and Immigration.* New York: New York University Press.

Kibria, Nazlia. 1993. *Family Tightrope: The Changing Lives of Vietnamese Americans.* Princeton: Princeton University Press.

Kivisto, Peter. 1993. "Religion and the New Immigrants." In *A Future for Religion? New Paradigms for Social Analysis,* ed. William H. Swatos Jr., pp. 92–108. Newbury Park: Sage Publications.

Kossoudji, Sherrie A., and Susan I. Ranney. 1984. "The Labor Market Experience of Female Migrants: The Case of Temporary Mexican Migration to the United States." *International Migration Review* 18, no. 4: 1120–43.

Krishnan, S., M. Baig-Amin, L. Gilbert, N. El-Bassel, and A. Waters. 1998. "Lifting the Veil of Secrecy: Domestic Violence among South Asian Women in the U.S." In *A Patchwork Shawl: Chronicles of South Asian Women in America,* ed. Shamita Das Gupta, pp. 145–59. New Jersey: Rutgers University Press.

Kudat, Ayse. 1982. "Personal, Familial, and Societal Impacts of Turkish Women's Migration to Europe." In *Living in Two Cultures: The Sociocultural Situation of Migrant Workers and Their Families,* ed. R. G. Parris, pp. 291–305. New York: Gower and UNESCOPRESS.

Kurian, George. 1961. *The Indian Family in Transition.* The Hague: P. H. Klop Printers.

Kurien, Prema. 1998. "Becoming American by Becoming Hindu: Indian Americans Take Their Place at the Multicultural Table." In *Gatherings in Diaspora: Religious Communities and the New Immigration,* ed. R. Stephen Warner and Judith Wittner, pp. 37–70. Philadelphia: Temple University Press.

——. 1999. "Gendered Ethnicity: Creating a Hindu Indian Identity in the United States." *American Behavioral Scientist* 42, no. 4: 648–70.

Lamphere, Louise. 1987. *From Working Daughters to Working Mothers: Immigrant Women in a New England Industrial Community.* Ithaca: Cornell University Press.

Lamphere, Louise, Patricia Zavella, and Felipe Gonzales, with Peter B. Evans. 1993. *Sunbelt Working Mothers: Reconciling Family and Factory.* Ithaca: Cornell University Press.

Leonard, Karen. 1992. *Making Ethnic Choices: California's Punjabi Mexican Americans.* Philadelphia: Temple University Press.

——. 1993. "Ethnic Identity and Gender: South Asians in the United States." In *Ethnicity, Identity, Migration: The South Asian Context,* ed. Milton Israel and N. K. Nagel. Toronto: University of Toronto, Center for South Asian Studies.

Lessinger, Johanna. 1992. "Investing or Going Home? A Transnational Strategy among Indian Immigrants in the United State." In *Towards a Transnational Perspective on Migration: Annals of the New York Academy of Sciences.* Vol. 654, ed. Nina Glick-Schiller et al., pp. 53–80. New York: New York Academy of Sciences.

——. 1995. *From the Ganges to the Hudson: Indian Immigrants in New York.* Boston: Allyn and Bacon.

Levitt, Peggy. 1996. "Assimilation, Pluralism, or Transnationalism? Migration's Transformation of Religious Life in Boston and the Dominican Republic." Paper presented at the American Sociological Association meetings, New York City, August.

——. 1997. "Variations in Transnationalism: Lessons from Organizational Experiences in Boston and the Dominican Republic." Paper presented at the American Sociological Association meetings, Toronto, Canada, August.

——. 2001. *The Transnational Villagers.* Berkeley: University of California Press.

Lim, In-Sook. 1997. "Korean Immigrant Women's Challenge to Gender Inequality at Home: The Interplay of Economic Resources, Gender, and the Family." *Gender and Society* 11, no. 1: 31–51.

Lui, John M., Paul M. Ong, and Carolyn Rosenstein. 1991. "Dual Chain Migration: Post-1965 Filipino Immigration to the United States." *International Migration Review* 25, no. 3: 487–513.

Luthra, Rashmi. 1989. "Matchmaking in the Classifieds of the Immigrant Indian Press." In *Making Waves: An Anthology of Writings by and about Asian American Women,* ed. Asian Women United of California, pp. 337–44. Boston: Beacon Press.

Mahler, Sarah. 1998. "Theoretical and Empirical Contributions toward a Research Agenda for Transnationalism." In *Transnationalism from Below: Comparative Urban and Community Research.* Vol. 6, ed. Michael P. Smith and Luis Eduardo Guarnizo, pp. 64–100. New Brunswick, NJ: Transaction Publishers.

———. 1999. "Engendering Transnational Migration: A Case Study of Salvadoreans." *American Behavioral Scientist* 42, no. 4: 690–719.

Martin, Biddy, and Chandra Talpade Mohanty. 1986. "Feminist Politics: What's Home Got to Do with It?" In *Feminist Studies, Critical Studies,* ed. Teresa de Lauretis, pp. 191–212. Bloomington: Indiana University Press.

Massey, Douglas S., Luin Goldring, and Jorge Durand. 1994. "Continuities in Transnational Migration: An Analysis of Nineteen Mexican Communities." *American Journal of Sociology* 99, no. 6: 1468–533.

Mejia, Alfonso, Helena Pizurki, and Erica Royston. 1979. *Physician and Nurse Migration: Analysis and Policy Implications.* Geneva: World Health Organization.

Menjivar, Cecilia. 1999a. "The Intersection of Work and Gender: Central American Immigrant Women and Employment in California." *American Behavioral Scientist* 42, no. 4: 601–27.

———. 1999b. "Religious Institutions and Transnationalism: A Case Study of Catholic and Evangelical Salvadorean Immigrants." *International Journal of Politics, Culture, and Society* 12, no. 4: 589–612.

———. 2000. *Fragmented Ties: Salvadoran Immigrant Networks in America.* Berkeley: University of California Press.

Mies, Maria. 1986. *Patriarchy and Accumulation on a World Scale: Women in the International Division of Labour.* London: Zed Books.

Min, Pyong Gap. 1992. "The Structures and Social Functions of Korean Immigrant Churches in the United States." *International Migration Review* 26, no. 4: 1370–94.

Morawska, Ewa. 1990. "The Sociology and Historiography of Immigration." In *Immigration Reconsidered: History, Sociology, and Politics,* ed. Virginia Yans-McLaughlin, pp. 187–238. New York: Oxford University Press.

Morokvasic, Mirjana. 1984. "Birds of Passage Are Also Women . . ." *International Migration Review* 18, no. 4: 886–907.

Nakano Glenn, E. 1986. *Issei, Nissei, War Bride: Three Generations of Japanese American Women in Domestic Service.* Philadelphia: Temple University Press.

———. 1992. "From Servitude to Service Work: Historical Continuities in the Racial Division of Paid Reproductive Labor." *Signs: Journal of Women in Culture and Society* 18, no. 1: 1–43.

Nankani, Sandhya, ed. 2000. *Breaking the Silence: Domestic Violence in the South Asian American Community: An Anthology.* Philadelphia: Xlibris Corporation.

Narayan, Kirin. 1993. "How Native Is the 'Native Anthropologist'?" *American Anthropologist* 95, no. 3: 671–86.

Oakley, Ann. 1981. *Subject Women.* Oxford: Martin Robertson.

O'Connor, Mary I. 1990. "Women's Networks and the Social Needs of Mexican Immigrants." *Urban Anthropology* 19, nos. 1–2: 81–98.

Ong, Paul, and Tania Azores. 1994. "The Migration and Incorporation of Filipino Nurses." In *The New Asian Immigration in Los Angeles and Global Restructuring,* ed. Paul Ong, Edna Bonacich, and Lucie Cheng, pp. 164–95. Philadelphia: Temple University Press.

Oommen, T. K. 1978. *Doctors and Nurses: A Study in Occupational Role Structures.* Delhi: Macmillan India.

Park, Kyeyoung. 1989. "Impact of New Productive Activities on the Organization of Domestic Life: A Case Study of the Korean American Community." In *Frontiers of Asian American Studies: Writing, Research, and Commentary,* ed. Gail Nomura et al. Washington: Washington State University Press.

Parrenas, Rhacel. 1998. "The Global Servants: (Im)Migrant Filipina Domestic Workers in Rome and Los Angeles." Ph.D. diss., University of California, Berkeley.

Pedraza-Bailey, Sylvia. 1990. "Immigration Research: A Conceptual Map." *Social Science History* 14: 43–67.

———. 1991. "Women and Migration: The Social Consequences of Gender." *Annual Review of Sociology* 17: 303–25.

Pessar, Patricia R. 1984. "The Linkage between the Household and the Workplace in the Experience of Dominican Women in the U.S." *International Immigration Review* 18: 1188–1212.

———. 1995. "On the Homefront and in the Workplace: Integrating Women into Feminist Discourse." *Anthropological Quarterly* 68, no. 1: 37–47.

———. 1999. "Engendering Migration: The Case of New Immigrants in the United States." *American Behavioral Scientist* 4, no. 4: 577–600.

Phizacklea, A., ed. 1983. *One Way Ticket: Migration and Female Labor.* Boston: Routledge and Kegan Paul.

Portes, Alejandro, Luis E. Guarnizo, and Patricia Landolt. 1999. "The Study of Transnationalism: Pitfalls and Promise of an Emergent Research Field." *Ethnic and Racial Studies* 22, no. 2: 217–37.

Portes, Alejandro, and Ruben Rumbaut. 1990. *Immigrant America: A Portrait.* Berkeley: University of California Press.

"Pre-immigration Tests Start in October for Foreign Graduate Nurses." 1978. *American Journal of Nursing* (March): 359.

Pyke, Karen. 1996. "Class-Based Masculinities: The Interdependence of Gender, Class, and Interpersonal Power." *Gender and Society* 10, no. 5 (October): 527–49.

Quillen, Terrilynn. 1990. "How to Help Foreign Nurses Adapt." *Nursing* (November): 131–33.

Ragavachari, Ranjana. 1990. *Conflicts and Adjustments: Indian Nurses in an Urban Milieu.* Delhi: Academic Foundation.

Rai, Saritha. 2003. "Indian Nurses Sought to Staff U.S. Hospitals." *New York Times,* February 10.

Ralston, Helen. 1996a. *The Lived Experience of South Asian Immigrant Women in Atlantic Canada: The Interconnections of Race, Class, and Gender.* New York: Edwin Mellen Press.

———. 1996b. "'The Temple Is the Last Place I Would Go for Help': The Ambiguous Role of Religious Ideology in Family Life." Paper presented at the Association for the Sociology of Religion meetings, New York, August 15–17.

Ram, Kalpana. 1991. *Mukkuvar Women: Gender, Hegemony, and Capitalist Trans-*

formation in a South Indian Fishing Community. North Sidney: Allen and Unwin.

Rangaswamy, Padma Iyer. 1996. "The Imperative of Choice and Change: Post-1965 Immigrants from India in Metropolitan Chicago." Ph.D. diss., University of Illinois, Chicago.

Rayaprol, Aparna. 1995. "Gender Ideologies and Practices among South Indian Immigrants in Pittsburgh." *Sagar: South Asian Graduate Research Journal* 2, no. 1: 15–38.

———. 1997. *Negotiating Identities: Women in the Indian Diaspora.* Delhi: Oxford University Press.

Repak, Terry. A. 1995. *Waiting on Washington: Central American Workers in the Nation's Capital.* Philadelphia: Temple University Press.

———. 1997. "New Roles in a New Landscape." In *Challenging Fronteras: Structuring Latina and Latino Lives in the U.S.,* ed. Mary Romero et al., pp 247–57. Routledge: New York.

Robnett, Belinda. 1997. *How Long? How Long?: African American Women in the Struggle for Civil Rights.* New York: Oxford University Press.

Rouse, Roger. 1992. "Making Sense of Settlement: Class Transformation, Cultural Struggle, and Transnationalism among Mexican Migrants in the United States." In *Towards a Transnational Perspective on Migration: Annals of the New York Academy of Sciences.* Vol. 654, ed. Nina Glick-Schiller et al., pp. 25–52. New York: New York Academy of Sciences.

———. 1995. "Personhood and Collectivity in Transnational Migration to the United States." *Critique of Anthropology* 15, no. 4: 351–80.

Sacks, Karen. 1988. *Caring by the Hour.* Chicago: University of Illinois Press.

Safa, Helen. 1981. "Runaway Shops and Female Employment: The Search for Cheap Labor." *Signs: Journal of Women in Culture and Society* 7, no. 2: 418–33.

Sassen-Koob, Saskia. 1984. "Notes on the Incorporation of Third World Women into Wage-Labor through Immigration and Off-Shore Production." *International Migration Review* 18: 1144–67.

Segura, Denise. 1991. "Ambivalence or Continuity? Motherhood and Employment among Chicanas and Mexican Immigrant Women Workers." *Aztlan* 20, nos. 1–2: 119–50.

Seller, Maxine Schwartz. 1981. *Immigrant Women.* Philadelphia: Temple University Press.

Shah, Sonia. 1998. "Three Hot Meals and a Full Day of Work: South Asian Women's Labor in the United States." In *A Patchwork Shawl: Chronicles of South Asian Women in America,* ed. Shamita Das Gupta, pp. 206–21. New Jersey: Rutgers University Press.

Shelton, Beth Anne, and Daphne John. 1996. "The Division of Household Labor." *Annual Review of Sociology* 22: 299–322.

Shin, Eui Hang, and Kyung-Sup Chang. 1988. "Peripherization of Immigrant Professionals: Korean Physicians in the United States." *International Migration Review* 22, no. 4: 609–26.

Shin, Eui Hang, and Hyung Park. 1988. "An Analysis of Causes of Schisms in Ethnic Churches: The Case of Korean-American Churches." In *Koreans in*

North America, ed. S. H. Lee and T. Kwak, pp. 231–52. Seoul: Kyungnam University Press.

Shockley, Barbara. 1989. "Foreign Nurse Recruitment and Authorization for Employment in the United States." In *Managing the Nursing Shortage: A Guide to Recruitment and Retention,* ed. Terence F. Moore and Earl A. Simendinger. Rockville, MD: Aspen Publishers.

Shukla, Sandhya. 1997. "Feminisms of the Diaspora Both Local and Global: The Politics of South Asian Women against Domestic Violence." In *Women Transforming Politics: An Alternative Reader,* ed. Cathy J. Cohen, Kathleen B. Jones, and Joan C. Tronto, pp. 269–83. New York: New York University Press.

Simon, Rita. 1992. "Sociology and Immigrant Women." In *Seeking Common Ground: Multidisciplinary Studies of Immigrant Women in the United States,* ed. Donna Gabaccia. Westport, CT: Greenwood Press, 1992.

Simon, Rita, and Carolyn Brettell, eds. 1986. *International Migration: The Female Experience.* New Jersey: Rowman and Allanheld.

Small, Cathy. 1997. *Voyages: From Tongan Villages to American Suburbs.* Ithaca: Cornell University Press.

Smith, Michael P., and Luis Eduardo Guarnizo, eds. 1998. *Transnationalism from Below: Comparative Urban and Community Research.* Vol. 6. New Brunswick, NJ: Transaction Publishers.

Smith, Timothy. 1978. "Religion and Ethnicity in America." *American Historical Review* 83 (December): 1155–85.

Soja, Edward W. 1996. *Third Space: Journeys to Los Angeles and Other Real-and-Imagined Places.* Cambridge, MA: Blackwell.

Soto, Isa Maria. 1987. "West Indian Child Fostering: Its Role in Migrant Exchanges." In *Caribbean Life in New York City: Sociocultural Dimensions,* ed. C. Sutton and E. Chaney, pp. 131–49. New York: Center for Migration Studies.

Spangler, Zenaida. 1992. "Transcultural Care Values and Nursing Practices of Philippine-American Nurses." *Journal of Transcultural Nursing* 4, no. 2: 28–37.

Stack, Carol B., and Linda M. Burton. 1994. "Kinscripts: Reflections on Family, Generation, and Culture." In *Mothering: Ideology, Experience, and Agency,* ed. Evelyn Nakano Glen, Grace Chang, and Linda Rennie Forcey. New York: Routledge.

Swidler, Ann. 1986. "Culture in Action: Symbols and Strategies. "*American Sociological Review* 51, no. 2: 273–86.

Thomas, Annamma, and T. M. Thomas. 1984. *Kerala Immigrants in America: A Sociological Study of St. Thomas Christians.* Cochin, India: Simon Printers.

Thomas, T. J. 1978. "The Shepherding Perspective of Seward Hiltner on Pastoral Care and Its Application in the Organizing of a Congregation in Dallas of East Indian Immigrants from the Mar Thoma Syrian Church of India." Doctor of Ministry thesis, Perkins School of Theology, Southern Methodist University.

Thorne, Barrie, and Marilyn Yalom, eds. 1982. *Rethinking the Family: Some Feminist Questions.* New York: Longman.

Tienda, Marta, and Karen Booth. 1991. "Gender, Migration, and Social Change." *International Sociology* 6, no. 11: 51–72.

Toro-Morn, Maura I. 1995. "Gender, Class, Family, and Migration: Puerto Rican Women in Chicago." *Gender and Society* 9, no. 6 (December): 712–26.

Vaid, Jyotsana. 1989. "Seeking a Voice: South Asian Women's Groups in North America." In *Making Waves: An Anthology of Writings by and about Asian American Women*, ed. Asian Women of California. Boston: Beacon Press.

Valenzuela, Abel. 1999. "Gender Roles and Settlement Activities among Children and Their Immigrant Families." *American Behavioral Scientist* 42, no. 4: 720–42.

Visvanathan, Susan. 1989. "Marriage, Birth, and Death: Property Rights and Domestic Relationships of the Orthodox/Jacobite Syrian Christians of Kerala." *Economic and Political Weekly* (June 17): 1341–46.

———. 1993. *The Christians of Kerala: History, Belief, and Ritual among the Yakoba*. Delhi: Oxford University Press.

Walby, Sylvia. 1990. *Theorizing Patriarchy*. Cambridge, MA: Basil Blackwell.

Warner, R. Stephen. 1992. "Religious Institutions Emerging among New (Post-1965) Immigrant Groups." Paper presented at the annual meeting of the Midwest Sociological Society, Kansas City, April.

———. 1993. "Work in Progress toward a New Paradigm for the Sociological Study of Religion in the United States." *American Journal of Sociology* 98: 1044–93.

Warner, R. Stephen, and Judith Wittner, eds. 1998. *Gathering in Diaspora: Religious Communities and the New Immigration*. Philadelphia: Temple University Press.

Waters, Mary C. 1999. *West Indian Immigrant Dreams and American Realities*. New York: Russell Sage.

West, Candace, and Don H. Zimmerman. 1987. "Doing Gender." *Gender and Society* 1, no. 2: 125–51.

Wilkinson, A. 1965. *A Brief History of Nursing in India and Pakistan*. Madras: Trained Nurses' Association of India.

Williams, Raymond Brady. 1988. *Religions of Immigrants from India and Pakistan: New Threads in the American Tapestry*. Cambridge: Cambridge University Press.

———. 1996. *Christian Pluralism in the U.S.: The Indian Immigrant Experience*. Cambridge: Cambridge University.

Wilson, Amrit. 1985. *Finding a Voice: Asian Women in Britain*. London: Virago Press.

Wolf, Diane L. 1992. *Factory Daughters: Gender, Household Dynamics, and Rural Industrialization in Java*. Berkeley: University of California Press.

———, ed. 1996. *Feminist Dilemmas in Fieldwork*. Boulder, CO: Westview Press.

Yamanaka, Keiko, and Kent McClelland. 1994. "Earning the Model-Minority Image: Diverse Strategies of Economic Adaptation by Asian American Women." *Ethnic and Racial Studies* 17, no. 1: 79–114.

Zelizer, Viviana. 1989. "The Social Meaning of Money: 'Special Monies.'" *American Journal of Sociology* 95, no. 2 (September): 342–47.

Index

Text:	10/13 Galliard
Display:	Galliard
Indexer:	Kevin Millham
Cartographer:	Bill Nelson
Compositor:	BookMatters, Berkeley
Printer and binder:	Maple-Vail Manufacturing Group